Mapping the Psyche

Volume 2

CPA Seminar Series

Mapping the Psyche

An Introduction to Psychological Astrology

Volume 2: The Planetary Aspects and the Houses of the Horoscope

Clare Martin

CPA

Centre for Psychological Astrology Press
London

First published 2007 by the CPA Press, BCM Box 1815, London WC1N 3XX, United Kingdom, www.cpalondon.com.

MAPPING THE PSYCHE: AN INTRODUCTION TO PSYCHOLOGICAL ASTROLOGY, VOLUME 2

ISBN 978 1 900869 34 8

British Library Cataloguing-in-Publication Data. A catalogue record for this book is available from the British Library.

Printed in the United Kingdom by Antony Rowe Ltd, Chippenham, Wiltshire, SN14 6LH.

Table of Contents

Lesson One: An Introduction to the Houses

It is good to see everyone again for the next stage of our astrological adventure. This term things get really interesting because we are going to add two major new levels to our astrology, both of which explain how the birth chart actually manifests in real life.

Just to recap: last term we explored the meaning of the planets – the characters in the play of our lives – and by putting them in the astrological signs, we explored how each planet seeks to express itself, its motivation, values, desires and goals. We looked at the way the zodiac signs are constructed, by polarity (positive or negative), modality (cardinal, fixed or mutable), and by element (earth, air, fire or water). This term we are going to bring our astrology down to earth – literally. We are going to see how the planets and signs function in the world. It is not until the moment of our birth that the astrological houses and angles are created, and it is at that moment that the universal pattern becomes personalised, setting the scene for the unfolding drama of our lives. In addition to the two axes created by the angles, we will add a third major axis to our charts, that of the Moon's Nodes. With the angles functioning as our personal doorways into the world, we will see how the nodal axis functions as a doorway into other dimensions that appear to hold our pattern and remember our soul's purpose.

When we have identified the houses and the three axes in the chart, we will go on to explore the aspects, the relationships between the planets, and consider whether they support or do battle with each other. The aspects describe the dynamic tension, struggle, talent and potential in every chart. They tell stories that are both intensely personal and yet reflect universal themes which, to a greater or lesser extent, we all recognise. Finally, with all the components in place – planets, signs, house, angles and aspects – we will spend the last evening of this term on the general interpretation of a birth chart, integrating everything we have learned so far.

Audience: There just seem to be so many layers to all this. I think I am beginning to lose my confidence. I used to think I knew a great deal of astrology, and now I increasingly feel as if I know nothing.

Clare: Well, you can now join the club, because you are not alone. When we first come across astrology, we tend to approach it just as we would with any other kind of learning – we seek to master it. We feel that once we have learned the grammar, we should be able to speak the language fluently. But ultimately, astrology is a living and constantly evolving tradition that cannot be mastered in this way; we can only hope to participate in its wonders and mysteries. Astrology teaches us to question, to open our minds to multiple and subtle layers of meaning. It is one of the ancient mystery traditions which leads us into a dialogue with living forces which are sometimes opaque or hidden from us, sometimes capricious, often humorous, and occasionally overwhelmingly astonishing and meaningful. Our best approach is one of enquiry and humility – we can ask astrology questions and wait patiently for the answers. If we attempt to impose our own preconceived notions upon it, then we will not hear it speak to us. So don't despair – I think this is an excellent sign.

Incarnation and the angles

We are going to add a new dimension to our astrology tonight. Up until the moment of our birth, the planets and signs are disembodied – they are of universal, collective significance only. They exist as principles, unable to take any particular, specific shape or form. However, at the exact time and place of our birth, the forever-changing pattern of the heavens becomes fixed, in what is the most powerful, seismic moment of our lives. At the moment of birth our undifferentiated wholeness comes to an end, and we find ourselves quartered, nailed, as it were, to the cross of matter, to the two major axes which are the angles of the chart. From that moment on we are concretised, caught in the drama of opposites, which is also the drama of life itself.

Every birth chart is a reflection of the symbol for the earth, the cross within the circle, describing the precise nature of the specific material, solid, concrete world into which we have been born and through which each of us must manifest ourselves. It is the angles which make time and space comprehensible, which give us our orientation, our east, west, north and south. The horizon, or east-west axis at that moment, forms the Ascendant-Descendant of the chart, and the meridian, or south-north axis, forms the MC (Medium Coeli) and IC (Immum Coeli). Simultaneously, the twelve astrological houses come into being, taking their starting point from the Ascendant. The houses describe every area of life and all the relationships that we will encounter – they describe 'where' or 'in what area of life' we will meet, experience and express the planetary principles. It is the angles and the houses that turn the universal picture into a highly particular and specific map of the individual psyche and into an entirely personal life story.

Whether or not we believe, as the ancients did, that our souls choose the specific time and place of our birth, nevertheless from the moment of birth our lives are circumscribed and defined within the limits of our birth chart. We cannot trade in or exchange any of the positions of the planets, or decide to have another birth sign or a different house placement of Pluto, for example. We are literally stuck with our birth charts, which means that nothing can come to pass which is not already present as potential in our birth charts. In this sense, our birth charts are indeed our fate. But they are also a tiny and unique piece of the great project, the *magnum opus* of collective human evolution. What is of interest from this point of view is not the birth chart itself, but how each of us engages and actively participates with the unique part of the whole which has been allotted to us, knowing that the way we live our own lives will add to the sum total of all human experience and existence.

The astrological birth chart remains exactly the same for our entire lives. There is no guarantee that we will be any more integrated, evolved or conscious at the end of our lives than we were at the beginning. The question is whether our lives are going to make a difference, 'for nature's continued existence depends ultimately on the kind of consciousness we bring to bear on it'.[1] Ultimately, it is up to each one of us to decide what to do with our birth chart and how to live it.

> Once a vision of life as an organic whole is accepted in principle, humanity becomes in one sense a co-creator with nature, in so far as it can foster, ignore or destroy its identity with nature.[2]

If we are working alchemically, then there is work to be done. Our job is to work against the blindness of our natural state in the service of increased consciousness:

> Things are created and given into our hands, but not in the ultimate form that is proper to them ... For alchemy means: to carry to its end something that has not yet been completed; to obtain the lead from the ore and to transform it into what it is made for.[3]

Let's see how a horoscope is created at a particular time and in a particular place. I thought it would be interesting to use today's

---

[1]Baring, Anne and Jules Cashford, *The Myth of the Goddess* (London: Penguin/Arkana, 1991) [hereafter Baring and Cashford], p. 681.

[2] Baring and Cashford, p. 681.

[3] Paracelsus, *Selected Writings*, ed. Jolande Jacobi, trans. Norbert Guterman, Bollingen Series XXVIII (Princeton, NJ: Princeton University Press, 1951).

astrology as an example of how this works. Have a look at the positions of the planets in this chart. On this day, no matter where in the world we happen to be, the Moon, Sun, Neptune, Uranus and Mercury are all in Aquarius. Mars is in Scorpio, Pluto and Chiron are in Sagittarius, Venus is in Pisces, Saturn is in Taurus, and Jupiter is in Gemini.

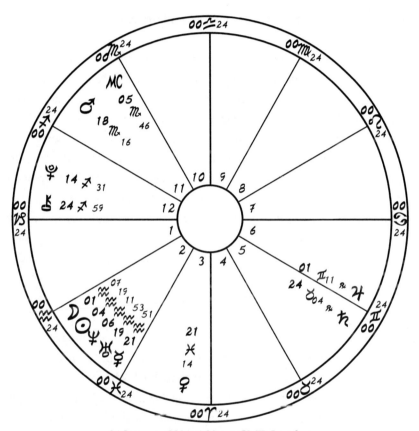

24 January 2001, 6.00 am GMT, London
Equal House system

From what we learned last term, we can already get a good sense of the astrological themes described by the planets in these signs, and the many millions of people born today will carry these themes with them throughout their lives and live them out in a variety of specific, individual ways. However, the houses, or areas of life in which these themes will be expressed, depend upon the exact time and place of each person's birth. I have fixed this horoscope in time and space by setting it for 6.00 am this morning, in London.

The east-west horizon: Ascendant/Descendant axis

Imagine that you are standing right in the centre of this horoscope. The Ascendant is on your left, which tells us that at 6.00 this morning, 0° 24' of the sign of Capricorn was rising over the eastern horizon. The Descendant is on your right, and you can see that 0° 24' of the sign of Cancer was setting over the western horizon. The Sun *ascends* over the eastern horizon every day at dawn and *descends* over the western horizon every day at sunset. You can see from this horoscope that it is still dark because the Sun is under the horizon, which is something we know anyway, because the Sun does not rise in London in January until just before 8.00 am.

From our position at the centre of the chart, the entire zodiac and all the planets and stars appear to rotate around us in a clockwise direction every twenty-four hours at an average rate of approximately 1° every four minutes. The Ascendant is also the starting point of the twelve houses, with the first house beginning at the Ascendant, and all the houses follow anti-clockwise around the chart, until you can see that the 12th house ends at the same point that the 1st house begins: at the Ascendant. Houses 1 to 6 are below the horizon, hidden from view under the earth, and houses 7 to 12 are visible above the horizon.

The south-north meridian: MC/IC axis

The other major axis of orientation is the point where the Sun's path crosses the north-south meridian, the points due north and due south at the moment of birth, known as the MC/IC axis. Once again, if you are standing in the centre of the chart, with the east on your left and the west on your right, then you will be facing south, and the Midheaven or MC (an abbreviation of *Medium Coeli*, the Latin for 'middle of the heavens') will be directly ahead and above you. The IC (an abbreviation of *Immum Coeli*, the Latin for 'lowest part of the heavens') will be directly behind you and under the earth. At 6.00 am this morning in London, the MC was 5° 46′ Scorpio, which means that the IC was exactly opposite, at 5° 46′ Taurus.

Audience: I am having difficulty with this, because in normal maps the west is on the left and the east is on the right, with the north above and the south below. How does a natal chart fit in with the normal way we look at a map?

Clare: That is a good point. Imagine that you are looking at an atlas. Where are you actually looking from?

Audience: Well, I suppose you are looking down at the earth from some place in space?

Clare: Exactly. You are disembodied – looking down at the earth from somewhere outside the earth, and indeed from somewhere outside your body. Astrology is geocentric, so we are looking out at the heavens from our place on the earth and in our bodies. Now, imagine that you are standing in a wide-open place, somewhere like Salisbury Plain. Facing due south, the MC will be directly ahead of you and the IC, or north point, will be directly behind you, invisible, under the earth. All the constellations and planets will appear to rise over the eastern horizon to your left; they will gradually rise higher in the sky until they cross the MC, and then their height will gradually diminish until they set somewhere over the western horizon.. Imagine that the entire zodiac is moving around you in a clockwise direction. At 6.00 am this morning, the five planets in Aquarius were all in the 2nd house, and Chiron had just risen over the Ascendant and entered the 12th house. You can also see very graphically that there is about to be a new Moon, because the Moon is just over 3° behind the Sun and, since it moves very rapidly through the signs, at approximately 1° every two hours, we can immediately see that there was a new Moon today, at about 12.00 noon.

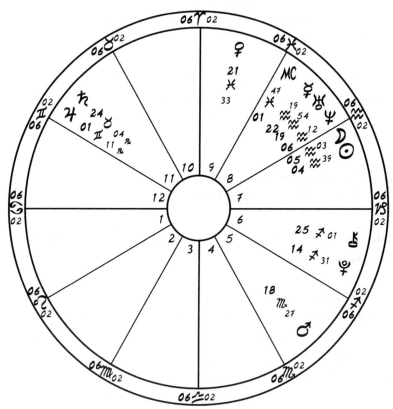

24 January 2001, 2.00 pm GMT, London
Equal House system

We are now going to look at the situation eight hours later, at 2.00 pm this afternoon. All the planets in Aquarius have moved from the 2nd house through the 1st, 12th, 11th, 10th and 9th houses, and across the MC. The Sun and Moon are now in the 7th house, with

Neptune, Uranus, and Mercury still in the 8th house. The new Moon has already occurred, and the Moon is now ahead of the Sun and quickly approaching Neptune. Incidentally, it is most auspicious to begin a new term in a new year at the new Moon. So this is a perfect time for our new beginning.

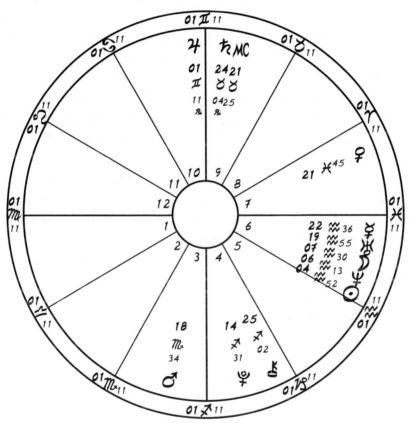

24 January 2001, 7.00 pm GMT, London
Equal House system

By 7.00 pm, which is the moment when our class and the second term of this course began, the picture has changed again. You can see that all the planets in Aquarius have crossed the Descendant and entered the 6th house, which means that it is now dark, as you can see by looking out of the window. Saturn is just about to cross the MC, to be followed by Jupiter. The Moon has already crossed over Neptune and is now more than a degree away, moving rapidly towards Uranus and then Mercury. In actual fact, of course, the signs and planets are not revolving in a clockwise direction around us every twenty-four hours – they just appear to do so from our position in the centre of the chart. Rather, it is the earth itself that is turning on its axis every twenty-four hours. So another way of seeing the same thing is to focus on the fact that the east-west and north-south points are moving anti-clockwise at a rate of approximately 1° every four minutes against the backdrop of the planets and signs. This means that the Ascendant gradually moves anti-clockwise from Sagittarius to Capricorn to Aquarius to Pisces, and so on right around the zodiac, until it returns to the same point in Capricorn once again, roughly twenty-four hours later.

Understanding how all this works in practice is very helpful, because then we can visualise for ourselves exactly what a birth chart is from an astronomical point of view. It is worth visiting the Greenwich Observatory or the London Planetarium, just to experience for yourself how this mechanism actually works. It can be confusing until you understand that the east-west and north-south axes are moving in an anti-clockwise direction around the chart, whereas all the planets and signs appear to be moving in a clockwise direction from your place of observation.

Audience: Looking at a chart in this way helps to see the whole thing visually. Does this mean that people born at night, with the Sun under the horizon, are more comfortable in the dark?

Clare: Well, it is certainly true that people with the majority of their planets under the horizon tend to be more private and to draw their strength and their meaning from within themselves. This is a good example of the way that our astrological interpretations are put into context if we understand the astronomical structure of a birth chart.

Audience: Can you say something about the different house systems? I find this particularly confusing and don't really know where to start.

About house systems

Clare: This is turning into a rather technical lesson but, as you can see from our own chart this evening, that is not really surprising. Saturn is the most elevated planet in the chart at the moment, and it is strongly emphasised because it is on the MC. And since Saturn is in the fixed earth sign of Taurus, we are working to bring the chart down to earth, to understand the structure. Jupiter in Gemini indicates that we all want to learn, and with all the Aquarian planets in the 6th house of work, this also tells us that we are interested in bringing the heavens down to earth and making them work for us.

There are many different house systems in astrology, and no doubt you have already come across this and wondered which is the 'correct' house system to use. However, house systems, like everything else in astrology, are subject to fashion and to personal preference. The only contribution I can make here is to suggest that a horoscope is like a hologram – no matter how it is divided, the overall pattern and structure remain identical, since the meaning of the whole is reflected in each of its parts. Perhaps the major house systems used today are the Placidus, Koch and Equal House systems. Placidus and Koch are quadrant systems, which means that the meridian, or MC-IC axis, is always found on the 10th and 4th house cusps, with three complete houses in each quadrant of the chart.

For the purposes of this course, I am using the Equal House system, in which the zodiac is divided into twelve equal sections of 30°, beginning at the Ascendant. This means, as you can see from the three charts we have already looked at tonight, that the meridian is not anchored to the cusps of the 10th and 4th houses, but 'floats', being found anywhere from the 11th-5th houses to the 10th-4th houses, the 9th-3rd houses, and the 8th-2nd houses. The reason for this is that the angle between the horizon (Ascendant-Descendant axis) and the meridian (MC-IC axis) is constantly changing, depending on the time of day, the time of year, and the latitude for which the horoscope is set.

Have another look at the series of charts above. At 6.00 am this morning, the meridian was in the 11th and 5th houses, because the angle between the meridian and the east point of the horizon was less than 60°. By 2.00 pm this afternoon, the meridian was in the 8th and 2nd houses, because the angle between the meridian and the east point of the horizon was just over 120°. By the beginning of our class at 7.00 pm, the angle had altered again to just over 90°, and it will continue to decrease until 6.00 am tomorrow morning, when it will be around 60° once again. We will look at the interpretation of the MC-IC axis over the next few weeks, but for the time being it is just worth noting that, no matter which house system we use, the meaning of this axis is not identical to the meaning of the 10th-4th house cusps. This is clear when we use the Equal House system, but not necessarily so clear when we use a quadrant system of house division.

Let's have a look at some of the similarities and differences between the Placidus and Equal House systems of house division. Here is the chart for 6.00 am this morning in both house systems. You will see that the positions of planets, the angles of the chart, and the relationship between the planets remains identical. However, some of the planets have changed houses. You can see, for example, that in the Equal House system, the five Aquarian planets are in the 2nd house, with Venus in the 3rd, Saturn in the 4th, Jupiter in the 6th and Mars in the 11th. In the Placidus house system, however, the Moon, Sun and Neptune are in the 1st house, with Uranus, Mercury and Venus in the 2nd, Saturn in the 4th, Jupiter in the 5th, and Mars in the 10th.

Audience: Now I am really confused. Surely these two charts are now completely different and their interpretation will be totally different?

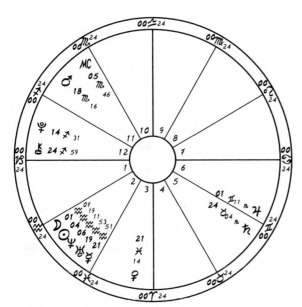

24 January 2001, 6.00 am GMT, London
Equal House system

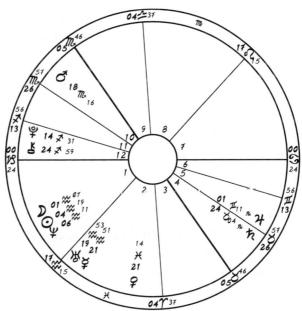

24 January 2001, 6.00 am GMT, London
Placidus system

Clare: I am afraid that the answer to this is both yes and no, because as astrologers we are going to find ourselves inevitably confronted with the whole issue of the nature of objective truth, and of the meaning we impose upon the objective world. Astrology does not respond well to any ideas we might have about there being only one truth. At the end of the day, the art of interpretation will always depend upon each astrologer's individual perceptions and preconceptions, and on the particular nature of each astrologer's relationship to factual, symbolic and mythic thinking. Perhaps the best thing you can do is to experiment with several house systems, and no doubt you will gradually find the one you prefer – the one that works for you. It is not uncommon for astrologers to use different house systems for different astrological techniques. So try and hang on in there and see what emerges for you over time.

Let's look at some of the other differences between these two house systems. With the Placidus chart, the houses can be very different sizes, and this difference in size tends gets more and more extreme as the latitude of the place of birth increases. In fact, the Placidus system breaks down altogether at high latitudes, which was never a problem traditionally, since astrological lore was developed around the temperate zones of the Mediterranean. Large houses can contain whole signs, which are referred to as *intercepted signs*. These signs are considered to be 'buried' in the particular houses they fall into, and the planetary ruler/s of that sign are generally considered to have more difficulty functioning 'in the world' because they are not anchored to a house cusp and do not rule any of the houses. You will see from the Placidus chart that the signs of Pisces and Virgo are intercepted, being 'buried' in the 2nd and 8th houses respectively. When signs are fully contained within a house, the planetary rulers of those signs may not be anchored in time or space – may not have a home, which means that they may not be able to function particularly strongly in the world.

Audience: Can you confirm what you mean by planets ruling houses?

Clare: Each house has a 'cusp' which marks the place where the house begins. In this chart, the 1st house cusp is 0° 24' Capricorn, so Saturn, which rules Capricorn, will rule the 1st house. The 2nd house cusp is 17° 15' Aquarius, so Saturn is the personal ruler of the 2nd house and Uranus is the collective, transpersonal ruler. This is important because we will all have 'empty' or 'untenanted' houses with no planets in them, but this does not mean that nothing is happening there. It simply means that we will look to the ruler of the house for information about the way that house is functioning.

Audience: Can you say how this might actually work out in this chart?

Clare: Let's go back to the first chart I showed you tonight, and imagine that we are studying the chart of somebody born in London at 6.00 am this morning. The signs of Pisces and Virgo are intercepted, and the rulers of these two signs are Jupiter (traditional ruler of Pisces), Neptune (transpersonal ruler of Pisces), and Mercury (ruler of Virgo). As the co-ruler of Aquarius, Saturn rules the 2nd house, so it is grounded in the chart. Taking the intercepted signs of Pisces and Virgo, the rulers are Jupiter, Neptune and Mercury. Jupiter and Mercury are grounded in the chart because they also rule Sagittarius and Gemini, the signs on the 12th and 6th house cusps. But Neptune has no home. And it may be difficult for Venus to find tangible expression, since it is in the intercepted sign of Pisces. So it looks as if this person may be rather disembodied and diffuse and imaginative. This is supported by the fact that there is very little earth in the chart apart from the Capricorn Ascendant – only Saturn in Taurus.

On the other hand, whenever there are intercepted signs in the large houses in the Placidus system, it will also be the case that the same pair of planets will rule two of the smaller houses, and those planets function strongly in the world because they are anchored to more than one house cusp. For example, you will see that Mars and Pluto rule both the 10th and 11th houses, because the cusp of both houses is Scorpio, and Venus rules both the 4th and 5th houses, because the cusp of both houses is Taurus. This information tells us about the relative strength of the planets. and where to put the emphasis in our interpretation. Mars, Pluto, and Venus will be strongly emphasised in the chart. But as we have already seen, Venus is in the intercepted sign of Pisces, so we can assume that the person born at 6.00 this morning will be particularly imaginative and sensitive but may have difficulty finding an outlet for this.

Finally, because the Placidus system is a quadrant house system, three complete houses are found in each of the four quadrants. Starting from the angles, these are known as angular, succedent and cadent houses, and the meaning of these terms is not dissimilar to the meaning of the cardinal, fixed and mutable modes. In an Equal House chart, on the other hand, each planet has equal weight 'in the world' because each sign (and therefore the planetary ruler of each sign) is 'anchored' to a house cusp.

The twelve houses

Now that we have looked at how the twelve houses are constructed in the first place, we can consider how each house describes different ways in which we engage with the world. Every area of experience and every relationship we will ever have are right there in our own birth charts, with each house describing a particular kind of relationship, as you can see from this table. The planets in each house and the condition of the planets ruling each of these houses will describe the *quality* of these kinds of relationships in our lives. Now have a look at this overview of the types of activities we will be engaged in, and the people we are likely to meet in each of the twelve houses.

1st house	Relationship to our immediate environment
2nd house	Relationship to our body, our money and our possessions
3rd house	Relationship to siblings, neighbours, cars, and teachers
4th house	Relationship to father, family and early environment
5th house	Relationship to our children, pleasures, and risk-taking
6th house	Relationship to work, co-workers, daily ritual and routine, health, pets.
7th house	Relationship to partners and spouses
8th house	Relationship to sex, death, and shared resources
9th house	Relationship to travel, foreigners, higher education, meaning, and to our god.
10th house	Relationship to mother, public world, profession, boss
11th house	Relationship to friends, colleagues, politics, and society
12th house	Relationship to dreams, images, and hidden worlds

Nature and nurture

Before we look at each of the houses individually, it is worth saying a bit more about the relationship between individual perception and external reality. It is clear from our birth charts that we are not blank slates when we are born. Rather, we are born with our pattern already complete, which means that we are inherently attuned to perceive and process our experiences and our relationships according to the inbuilt frequency and resonance of our birth charts. Imagine, for example, that you are discussing your mother with your brother. Logically, we would expect you to have similar or even identical impressions of her since, objectively speaking, she is the same person. But it is our own perceptions and experiences, rather than her 'objective reality', which are found in our birth charts, so it is likely that each of you sees her rather differently.

As you can see from the tables above, it is the 10th house that describes our relationship to our mother and our contribution to the world. Say, for example, that you have Jupiter in the 10th house and your brother has Saturn in the 10th house. This would indicate that your perception of your mother is that she is philosophical, gregarious, and popular, that she encourages you to believe in your potential for success, that she opens up the world for you and broadens your horizons. Your brother, on the other hand, is more likely to perceive her as a figure of authority, a woman who carries responsibility at work, someone who is strict and demands that he work hard in order to achieve success and respect in the world, leaving nothing to chance.

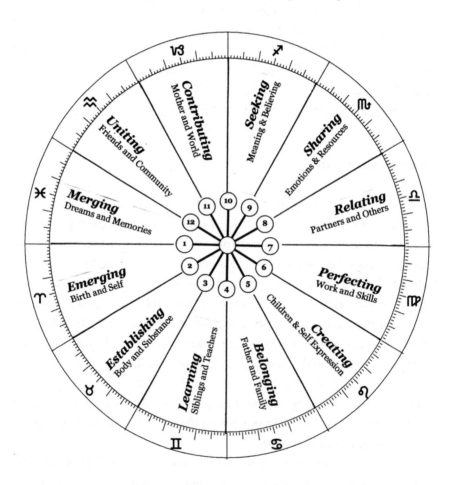

The interesting question here is, which of you is right? From an astrological viewpoint, the people in our lives are a reflection of who we are. 'They are our mirrors, reflecting back to us not only what we consider positive about ourselves, but also what we are unconscious of, or reject in ourselves.'[4] This means that no relationship is possible which is not already indicated somewhere in our birth chart. According to the law of resonance, we can only perceive something if we have a corresponding vibration. 'Anything which lies outside our capacity to resonate cannot be perceived by us and therefore does not exist for us.'[5] Resonance can either be sympathetic, an affinity with another person or thing, or it can be antipathetic, an aversion to another person or thing. This is why the external world and other people are the most reliable source of information about ourselves.

Going back to this particular example, you are more likely to elicit a warm, positive, and enthusiastic response from your mother, whereas your brother is more likely to elicit from your mother a strict and rather more demanding response. And it is highly likely that your mother will have both these themes in her own chart, although your experience of her will be determined by your own charts.

Time and space

No doubt you can see straight away that there is a natural affinity between the twelve signs of the zodiac, starting with Aries, and the twelve houses of the horoscope, starting with the 1st house. They are not the same thing but, since the signs describe a temporal cycle and the houses describe a spatial cycle, the two systems can be superimposed upon each other because, in astrology, every cycle has the same intrinsic

---

[4] Idemon, Richard, 'Part One: The Basics of Relating', in *Through the Looking Glass: A Search for Self in the Mirror of Relationships* (York Beach, ME: Samuel Weiser, Inc., 1992).

[5] Dethlefsen, Thorwald, *The Challenge of Fate* (London: Coventure Ltd., 1984).

meaning.

Audience: So we have two systems which are similar but not the same. Can you say a bit more about that?

Clare: Yes, that was a fairly broad statement. The cycle of the zodiac is *temporal*, because the signs are an expression of the annual, seasonal cycle of the Sun's changing relationship with the earth – so it is a cycle defined by time. Just as the Sun always moves in one direction – through time, from Aries all the way through to Pisces before beginning again a year later – we also develop temporally, but our sphere of consciousness also develops *spatially*, from our totally subjective awareness in the 1st house, through our developing awareness of our family, of others and of the world, right through to the point where we become totally merged with all of human experience in the 12th house. So there is a natural progression in both signs and houses that reflects our development through time *and* space. In practice, we are working with both these dimensions simultaneously. This means, for example, that no matter which planets are in our 5th house or which planet rules our 5th house of creative self expression, this house will always be naturally associated with the sign of Leo and its 'natural ruler' will always be the Sun. Hopefully you are still with me at this stage?

Audience: Yes, that does make sense. It is like doing a three-dimensional sudoko puzzle.

Clare: Exactly right. With the introduction of houses, we are in fact adding a third dimension to our astrology. We are moving beyond the simple 'what' and 'how' of the planets and signs, and adding the 'where' of the houses, so we have to hold three different factors in our minds all the time.

Chart shapes

Before we consider the meanings of the individual houses, it is useful to stand back and look at the general shape of each birth chart, according to the distribution of the planets in the houses. At this stage we are looking for any kind of special emphasis – crowded areas of the chart will immediately tell us where the emphasis will lie. I would recommend Howard Sasportas' book, *The Twelve Houses*, in which he divides the houses into two, three, and four general *realms of experience.*[6]

North-south hemispheres

Every chart is divided by the angles into two sets of hemispheres. The first six houses describe our personal development, and the following six houses describe our relationship to others, to society, and to the world in general.

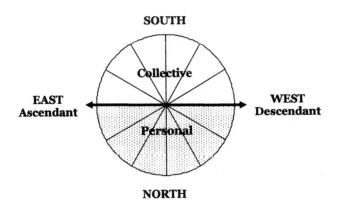

The horizon (Ascendant-Descendant axis) divides the chart into a northern hemisphere below the horizon and a southern hemisphere

---

[6] Sasportas, Howard, *The Twelve Houses: An Introduction to the Houses in Astrological Interpretation* (Wellingborough: Aquarian Press, 1985), 'Chapter 15: Grouping the Houses'.

above the horizon. Houses 1 to 6 lie under the horizon, under the earth, and are therefore hidden from view. They are houses of self-development, describing our subjective, internal worlds. Houses 7 to 12 lie above the horizon, in full view, and describe how we relate to others and to the world around us.

As with all opposites, these two hemispheres oppose, challenge, depend upon and complement each other. If we have an emphasis of planets below the horizon, no matter how active and successful we are in the outer world and however involved we are with other people, we will ultimately draw meaning and fulfilment from within ourselves, from our personal, private lives. Every house has a planetary ruler, which means that the houses above the horizon will be ruled by planets below the horizon. Experiences gained in the outside world need to be internalised, taken back into the inner world for processing. This means that the outer, public world always remains, to some extent, unfamiliar and rather uncomfortable territory.

Conversely, if we have a marked emphasis of planets above the horizon, then no matter how stable and secure we are on a personal level, we will ultimately draw meaning and purpose and find fulfilment through our relationships with others and with the outer world – it is these areas of life which will energise us. The personal, subjective, introverted approach is not for us, since the houses below the horizon will be ruled by planets which are above the horizon, so that our inner resources and values will be externalised, taken into the world and shared. This means that the inner, private world will remain, to some extent, unfamiliar and uncomfortable territory.

Does anyone have a marked emphasis of planets in one of these hemispheres?

Audience: Yes, I have. Almost all my planets are below the horizon, in the first six houses.

Clare: So we can presume that you are, fundamentally, a private person with a rich inner life. However demanding and active and successful your outer life is, nevertheless it appears that you will draw your strength and your energy from within yourself, and that it is there that you are most at home and most fulfilled, at the end of the day. We can also say that your outer life, your involvement with others and with the world, does not really fulfil you on a fundamental level. Does this ring true at all?

Audience: Yes, that is very interesting. Given the choice, I would much rather do my own thing than get involved with group activities, but I have always thought of this as a weakness and criticised myself for being anti-social.

Clare: Once again, this is a good example of how astrology can give us the confidence to accept ourselves just as we are, rather than feeling obliged to become what we think we ought to be.

East-west hemispheres

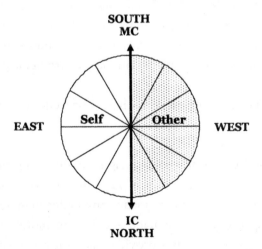

The other major division of the houses is defined by the MC-IC axis which divides the chart into eastern and western hemispheres, with the eastern hemisphere being on the left, or 'oriental' side of the chart, and the western hemisphere being on the right, or 'occidental' side of the chart. Broadly speaking, if we have a marked emphasis of planets in the eastern hemisphere houses, we are likely to be self-defining – our orientation and perspective will be fundamentally subjective. With such a chart, we tend to create our own reality, and to rely primarily on ourselves and on our own resources. Ultimately, relationships, however significant, will tend to be measured against our own subjective needs and wishes, since the houses in the western hemisphere will be ruled by planets in the eastern hemisphere. This means that relationships are always going to be rather uncomfortable territory, although it is also easier, with an eastern hemisphere emphasis, to break off from negative or destructive relationships which do not serve our personal needs.

Conversely, a marked emphasis of planets in the western hemisphere tends to indicate that we will define ourselves primarily in terms of our relationships, whether to family, children, work colleagues, partners, or to the philosophical or religious beliefs to which we adhere. Ultimately, it is through these kinds of relationships and connections that we define ourselves, and our subjective or individual identity outside these kinds of relationships is likely to remain unexplored, unfamiliar and rather awkward, since the houses in the eastern hemisphere will be ruled by planets in the western hemisphere.

Audience: The chart for our class has a marked western hemisphere emphasis.

Clare: Yes, and that is an excellent sign, because it means that we are likely to want to learn from each other and to listen to each other. Naturally, none of these orientations is any better than any other, since astrology is a descriptive language and has no moral agendas. But a marked hemisphere emphasis provides us with a valuable clue about the general orientation of our clients. I have almost always found that people with a strong eastern hemisphere emphasis take their autonomy for granted, and are much more likely to consult an astrologer about relationship issues, which are far more puzzling to them. Likewise, the big question for those with a strong western hemisphere emphasis tends to be how to define and identify themselves as individuals, outside the area of relationship. Perhaps that is our real motivation in this class.

Audience: Well, that is certainly true from my point of view.

Three phases of relationship

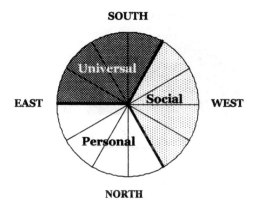

The houses can also usefully be divided into three areas of relationship: personal, social and universal. The first four houses describe our personal orientation and our relationship to our immediate environment. Howard Sasportas called this the experience of 'Me-in-Here'. For people with a strong emphasis in the personal houses, a major focus of their lives will be on personal development and security. Houses 5 to 8 are socially oriented, describing how 'Me-in-Here-meets-You-out-There'. For people with a strong emphasis in the social houses, relationships will be particularly important. Houses 9 to 12 are universal houses, describing our involvement with the world at large. The emphasis is on *'Us-in-Here'*, and on our contribution to the greater picture which involves us all. In each of these phases, we begin with the enthusiasm and optimism of the natural fire houses (1st, 5th, and 9th), consolidate and establish ourselves in the earth houses which follow (2nd, 6th, and 10th), develop new understanding as a result of these experiences in the air houses (3rd, 7th, and 11th), and withdraw to absorb and emotionally process what has been learned in the water houses (4th, 8th, and 12th) before moving on to the next phase, which will begin with the fire houses once again.

Quadrants

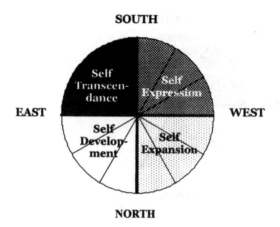

We can go one step further and divide the houses into four quadrants, which have been described by Howard Sasportas as the quadrants of self development, self expansion, self expression and self transcendence. I would also recommend Alexander von Schlieffen's book in the CPA seminar series, which is devoted to this subject and provides an excellent exploration of the meaning and interpretation of the quadrants in the horoscope.[7]

---

[7] Von Schlieffen, Alexander, *When Chimpanzees Dream Astrology: An Introduction to the Quadrants of the Horoscope* (London: CPA Press, 2004).

Lesson Two: Houses 1 to 6

The houses can be interpreted environmentally and psychologically, operating simultaneously on both levels. They usually reflect aspects of the objective truth as well as of our subjective perception. As we go through each of the houses in turn, I hope to illustrate how this works in practice.

1st house: emerging (Aries house – natural ruler Mars)

There are two major factors to consider with the 1st house, since the cusp of the 1st house is also the Ascendant. The east-west horizon, or Ascendant-Descendant axis, is so significant that it deserves separate exploration, and we will spend some time looking at the angles in more depth next week.

For the time being, I want to focus on the Ascendant as the cusp of the 1st house, which is possibly the most important house cusp in the birth chart, since it describes the threshold between our existence in the womb and our physical birth into the world. It describes, often with extraordinary accuracy and detail, the process of birth itself. Amongst other things, the 12th house describes our pre-natal experiences. In the 12th house we are in a totally symbiotic relationship with our mother, dependent and vulnerable, experiencing everything that she experiences without any way of protecting ourselves or screening anything out. In the 12th house we also seem to be at one with all of human experience and with the whole universe, picking up mysterious influences and emotions that cannot be reduced to personal content only. There is so much going on that it is difficult not to be overwhelmed by the pervasive atmosphere of the 12th house, which continues to affect us throughout our lives. The 1st house describes our subjective experience of the world into which we are born, and the Ascendant or 1st house cusp describes the actual birth moment itself, our struggle to be born and to achieve our independent existence. This is such a powerful event that it continues to operate strongly throughout our lives, being re-constellated every time we approach a new beginning, however great or small, whether this is a new meeting, a new opportunity, a new job, a new relationship, or even the beginning of a new day.

Let's look at some examples of Ascendants in different signs, and planets conjunct the Ascendant, so we can begin to see how this actually works in practice. The 1st house is entirely subjective, describing our personal approach, response and reaction to the world around us. The entire Ascendant complex describes our instinctive outlook on life and the way we navigate through and engage with the world around us. I want to approach this on two different levels, one profound and one trivial, but both of which, in my experience, tend to be relevant.

Audience: Can you explain what you mean by the Ascendant complex?

Clare: Yes, the Ascendant complex is a combination of different factors which include the sign on the Ascendant, the condition of the planet or planets which rule that sign, any planets within 8° of the Ascendant, and any planets which make aspects to the Ascendant. When all these factors are combined, it is possible to make a particularly accurate and specific interpretation about the way an individual engages with the world and with all new beginnings. For this reason, the general descriptions I am about to give you are really just caricatures, because every Ascendant is much more complex and personal and accurate, when analysed properly.

Aries Ascendant

Keeping it simple for the time being, how would you imagine that someone with Aries rising, or Mars in the 1st house, will perceive, and therefore relate to, the world?

Audience: Will they approach the world competitively and forcefully, and see everything as a personal challenge to be conquered?

Clare: That's right. They are likely to be instinctively independent, and approach life with considerable energy, determination and courage. Aries rising people are often initiators, looking for the next new project, goal or challenge to launch themselves into. And this approach will be reflected in the circumstances of their physical birth. Perhaps they were born very quickly, charging into life, a pattern that will continue to repeat itself every time they embark on new beginnings. Perhaps they were the first-born in the family, or are destined to lead the way, leaving their siblings to follow in their path. And since Mars rules knives and other sharp instruments, the birth process may have involved surgical instruments, some kind of cutting or tearing, or injections. In this case, there will be a deep memory, often on an unconscious level, that the world is a violent place, and that our personal survival demands the use of 'weapons' and courage in the face of obstacles and pain. This can be expressed positively by embarking on heroic missions to rescue and defend, or negatively with a particularly aggressive, combative approach to life.

Audience: So the planet that rules the Ascendant and the 1st house in this case is Mars. Does that give extra emphasis to Mars in the chart?

Clare: Yes, it certainly does, and the sign and house in which Mars is placed will significantly modify the interpretation of the Ascendant and the way we relate to the world around us. If, for example, you have

Aries on the Ascendant, then that sounds very spontaneous, courageous and instinctive, but if your Mars is in the 4th house in Cancer, then that will modify the Ascendant, and you will be more cautious and sensitive and self-protective about the way you approach the world. Alternatively, if your Mars is in the 2nd house in Taurus, then that will lend more patience and perseverance. In fact, the planet which rules the 1st house and the Ascendant is so important that it is the ruler of the entire chart.

Audience: But I always thought that the ruling planet was the planet which rules your Sun. So if you are a Gemini, for example, then your ruling planet would be Mercury.

Clare: This is a logical assumption, but in fact the ruling planet is the ruler of the sign on the Ascendant. This reflects the importance of the moment of birth and the significance of the angles in the birth chart. It also explains why it is so important to have an accurate time of birth.

Audience: You were going to mention the 'ridiculous' level.

Clare: Oh yes, that's right. The point about the Ascendant and 1st house is that it represents not only our personal approach to the world, but it can also describe the personal vehicle in which we navigate through life. And our vehicle is our body, but it can also be our car – which is a way of making a personal statement about ourselves and our approach to life. So, for example, what kind of car would someone with Aries rising drive?

Audience: A red sports car?

Clare: Exactly. This makes a strong statement about personal potency, speed and drive, as well as independence, aggression and freedom. A red sports car is a message that everyone else should get out of the way and let us through. With Mars ruling or in the 1st house, we are unlikely to make good passengers, insisting that we are at the wheel ourselves – in the 'driving seat'. I have also noticed that many Aries rising or Mars ruled or Aries Sun people actually ride motorbikes – which represent freedom, speed, potency, and a refusal to be held back by the traffic. Although this may seem rather absurd at first glance, it can actually be psychologically revealing, since the car we choose often does say something about the way we approach life.

Taurus Ascendant

With Taurus on the 1st house cusp or Venus in the 1st house, our approach to life will be more passive, practical, gentle and graceful. With Venus ruling the chart, our personal security and comfort will be of primary concern, and we will want to take our time before embarking on any new ventures. It is also likely that we will resist change, since Taurus is perhaps the most fixed of all the fixed signs. The placement of Venus in our birth charts and of any planets in the 1st house will provide additional information, although it is likely that our personal appearance and, for that matter, our choice of car will be strongly influenced by practical concerns and by our personal values. Taurus is an earth sign, so we may, for example, be very conscious of ecological issues, dress ourselves in natural fabrics in soft earthy colours, and drive a car that uses very little fuel. Alternatively, we might want to show our substance and wealth to the world by wearing expensive jewellery and driving an expensive car. Speed will be less important than comfort and our main priorities may be the music system, heated seats, and make-up mirror. If we are engaging with the world in a particularly practical, earthy way, we may well drive a work vehicle, such as a catering van, flower delivery van, transporting musical instruments for our band or orchestra, or even drive a mud-splattered farm tractor. All of these options are ways of approaching the world in a Taurean or Venusian manner. The birth process itself is likely to have been a well-planned and gentle experience, and with Venus ruling the chart, the child may well have felt welcomed into the world.

Gemini Ascendant

With Gemini on the 1st house cusp and Mercury ruling the chart, or Mercury in the 1st house, it is likely that we have entered the world with great curiosity, looking around us at our new environment and taking everything in. Our approach to life will be inquisitive and curious, and we will engage with our immediate environment as an opportunity to gather information, to play, to have fun and to learn. There always seems to be a particularly light and youthful quality to Gemini rising or Mercury in the 1st house. Life is an opportunity to learn and to make connections, and should not be taken too seriously. People with Gemini rising or Mercury in the 1st house are often great walkers, since this gets them out into the open air, stimulates the lungs, and exercises the legs. Gemini rising or Mercurial people may not like the feeling of being inside a vehicle, which can make them feel trapped or restricted. So if they are not walking, then it is likely that they will travel around by bicycle, an archetypally Geminian mode of transport. Alternatively, a pair of roller skates or a skateboard might serve just as well.

Cancer Ascendant

With Cancer rising, and the Moon ruling the chart, or with the Moon in the 1st house, we are likely to have experienced an intense emotional symbiosis with our mother during the process of birth, an overwhelming experience of the power of nature, and feelings of being expelled from the womb, which is translated during our lives into a strong need for personal protection and care. With Cancer rising, there will be a marked emotional sensitivity to our surroundings, and a cautious, self-protective approach to life. As you can imagine, people with this placement tend to carry their shells around with them, both for their own protection and for the protection of their children and family members. It is therefore not unusual for those with Cancer rising or Moon in the 1st house to drive 'people carriers', or vehicles which are particularly safe, rounded and crab-like. Towing a caravan or driving a mobile home would also be appropriate for Cancer rising. Equally likely is the possibility that they don't drive at all, which might be one way of asking to be cared for.

Leo Ascendant

With Leo on the 1st house cusp or the Sun in the 1st house, there will be an innate feeling of being special, a sense that we have been born to be noticed and recognised, to be in the limelight and to be the subject of praise and adoration. It may well be, for example, that our arrival into the family was of particular significance, for example in the case of a pregnancy after many years of difficulty conceiving. An individual with Leo rising may have a deep memory of being a much-wanted child, whose birth was a cause for joyful celebration. Leo rising or Sun in the 1st house people will naturally expect the world to reflect back to them how special and unique they are, and they will often demand special treatment, attention and recognition. They approach the world with warmth and generosity. The particular way they go about seeking recognition will depend on the position of the Sun in the chart.

In an ideal world, we could imagine that someone with Leo rising or the Sun in the 1st house would prefer to be chauffeured or, better still, carried around in a sedan chair. Their car of choice would be grand and eye-catching. Certainly, they would prefer not to have to travel with the masses, although other people also represent a potential audience, providing the Leo rising or Sun in the 1st house individual with an opportunity to take centre stage, drawing everyone's attention towards them. There is often something particularly dramatic about the way that Leo rising people approach the world and make their entrances.

Virgo Ascendant

With Virgo on the 1st house cusp, Mercury rules the chart once again, although this Mercury-ruled sign is concerned with practical efficiency rather than curiosity, as in the case of Gemini. Virgo is an earth sign and is particularly associated with health and the body. Virgo rising people are specialists and perfectionists and cannot take too much on board at once, since they are easily overwhelmed and, because of a strong psychosomatic or body-mind connection, they tend to be prone to intestinal or digestive problems. Virgo rising people are naturally modest and self-effacing, and they need to analyse, assimilate, restrict and carefully digest their experiences of the world. They want to get it right and they need to feel in control.

Audience: What kind of car do you think someone with Virgo rising would drive?

Clare: Well, first of all, they are unlikely to want to take up too much space, so a small white car would be ideal, since white is the colour of purity. However, because Pisces is always present where Virgo is concerned, there could be plenty of chaos in the boot or in the glove box. And because of the strong psychosomatic link, there may well be a sense of personal physical violation if the car gets scratched or damaged in any way. Virgo rising tends to drive slowly and carefully, paying great attention to detail. There may also be an element of anxiety about driving, because they are likely to be particularly concerned about following the rules of the road, obeying the speed limits, parking restrictions, and so on.

Libra Ascendant

The person with Libra on the 1st house cusp, and Venus once again ruling the chart, is likely to present a pleasant and attractive face to the world, and to wish to make everything in their environment beautiful, peaceful, and harmonious. There is often a noticeable style, grace and balance about the way Libra rising relates to the world. It is almost as if both mother and child wanted to behave well and look their best during the birth process. And I have noticed that those with Libra rising generally prefer to be driven, rather than drive themselves, which is not surprising, since Libra is opposite Aries.

Scorpio Ascendant

With Scorpio on the Ascendant or Pluto rising, the world is experienced as a dangerous place, full of hidden threats that may strike at any time. There is nothing superficial about this placement, and it is not unusual for the birth process itself to have involved a struggle for survival for either the child or the mother, or both. People with Scorpio rising are extremely private, but seem destined to experience many personal crises during their lives. As always with this sign, which is either black or white and very rarely anything in between, they tend to engage with the world either as ice or fire. For example, an individual with Scorpio rising can be impossible to read – inscrutable and silent, with a powerful magnetic presence that can be felt as soon as they walk into a room. If the element of fear is particularly strong, this can result in a kind of paranoia and a desire to manipulate the world in order to remain in control. The intense, burning side of Scorpio comes to life during crises, with the result that those with a Scorpio Ascendant or with Pluto rising often seem to live many lives during their one life, being impelled, like the phoenix, to walk into the fire again and again in order to renew and regenerate themselves. Every new beginning, for Scorpio rising, will evoke the original struggle for survival, a theme which will remain throughout life. As you can imagine, transport is a difficult issue for Scorpio rising because it is never safe to travel in the world. They may well choose a car that is as invisible as possible – just like every other car – in order to avoid attention. Alternatively, they may drive a black or maroon car with darkened windows so that nobody can see inside.

Sagittarius Ascendant

The individual with Sagittarius rising or Jupiter on the 1st house cusp is likely to approach life with enthusiasm, optimism and faith, seeing all new beginnings as opportunities for exciting new adventures. Life is a continuous journey into new territory and, because Sagittarius is a mutable sign, the adventures along the way are likely to be even more important than the eventual destination. Sagittarius rising people tend to make a big entrance into the world, and their birth is often dramatic or theatrical or larger-than-life in some way. They may, for example, be born in the middle of a thunderstorm or other kind of dramatic weather (since Jupiter, the god of storms, rules the chart), or on the move – for example, in the car on the way to the hospital, or on an aeroplane or ship. Whether or not these events are literally true, from a psychological point of view all Sagittarius rising people seem to be born on a wagon heading west, through new and unexplored territory and towards new adventures. Physically, those with Sagittarius or Jupiter rising are in some sense 'larger than life' – they often have the kind of presence which seems to extend beyond their physical bodies.

Audience: That's interesting, because I have Sagittarius rising and I am always covered in bruises, because I am clumsy and find myself crashing into things and other people. I think that is because I don't really know my limits.

Clare: I think that is often the case, and this is something you can try out for yourself next time you meet someone with Sagittarius rising. Ask them to show you their most recent bruises, and no doubt they will oblige, responding with the typical generosity of this sign. As for the mode of transport, Sagittarius and Jupiter rising people tend to catch planes as often as other people catch colds. Alternatively, they might drive long-distance coaches, taking groups of people on pilgrimages or other kinds of adventures. A gipsy caravan would be equally acceptable.

Capricorn Ascendant

With Capricorn on the Ascendant or Saturn in the 1st house, life will be approached carefully, cautiously, responsibly and even fearfully. There is often a strong feeling of isolation, a sense of being alone in the world, as if one had been put straight into an incubator at birth, or a feeling that the birth process has been an experience of abandonment, of being expelled from the womb, cold and alone and isolated. Capricorn or Saturn rising people may feel that there is something particularly unsafe about the world and that they are unlikely to get their needs met. The actual birth process may well have been slow and painful, with a long labour involving extremely hard work for both the mother and baby, and all new beginnings will be coloured by this experience. They might drive an old black car, which can only go very slowly.

Aquarius Ascendant

There is usually something cool, detached, charismatic and magnetic about Aquarius rising or Uranus in the 1st house. Aquarius rising people often engage with the world from something of a distance, and there is likely to be something unusual about their appearance or the way they dress.

Audience: I have Mars in Aquarius in the 1st house. Does that mean that I will engage with the world by competing? I can see the Mars in the 1st house part of this, but how do I make sense of the fact that Mars is in Aquarius?

Clare: The sign tells us how the planets will function, so Mars in Aquarius tells us how you will compete. I would imagine that you assert yourself in a detached, rational, idealistic, perhaps unusual or eccentric, manner. You are likely to have high expectations of yourself, and of other people, and will seek to make your mark on the world (Mars in the 1st house) by imposing (Mars) your personal ideals and particular vision (Aquarius) on your environment (1st house), making sure first of all that you have all the intellectual ammunition (Mars in Aquarius) you need. There is a great deal of forceful intellectual precision in this placement, and it could even describe the circumstances of your birth, which in this case may have been assisted by the latest scientific advances (Aquarius) or the use of a sharp instrument (Mars) of some kind.

Audience: This is amazingly accurate, although not in the way you have suggested. My mother is a Christian Scientist, and she was determined to give birth to me naturally, using the power of the mind to get through it, but in the end she had acupuncture for the pain, so there are the sharp instruments!

Clare: This is an excellent example of the multi-levelled meanings we find everywhere in astrology. The houses can be interpreted on many levels, from symbolic to intellectual to psychological to physical, and often we can find meaning on all these levels simultaneously. I don't think people with Uranus in the 1st house or Aquarius rising are particularly interested in transport, since they tend to find it difficult to accept their physicality, and often don't seem to live in their bodies at all, but rather in their minds. The Saturn co-ruler of Aquarius adds caution and reserve and hesitation to the way in which they meet the world.

Audience: Yes, I think that's true, because I have always felt rather disembodied.

Pisces Ascendant

Clare: With Pisces rising or Neptune in the 1st house, there are unlikely to be clear boundaries between life in the womb and life in the world. The birth process may well have involved the use of drugs or anaesthetics, so that the child was born, as it were, without consciously crossing the threshold. This might be the case with an induced or Caesarean birth. This is an immensely sensitive Ascendant, and the individual is likely to absorb their environment like a sponge, taking on the colour of their surroundings like a chameleon, without any clear sense of personal definition. People with Pisces rising or Neptune in the 1st house can be particularly hard to get hold of, since they tend to change shape all the time.

Audience: I have Pisces rising, and journeys are never simple for me. I never seem to be able to get anywhere on time, and I have no sense of direction at all. And I can certainly relate to the sensitivity you mention – I can be completely overwhelmed by what is going on around me, to the extent that I seem to lose myself altogether. I have had to learn to keep life as simple as possible.

Clare: I have spent quite a bit of time looking at the different

Ascendants because people often consult an astrologer when they find themselves at a crossroads in their lives, perhaps contemplating a change of direction or a new beginning of some sort. At these times, it is worth remembering that the birth chart is exactly that – a chart of the birth moment itself – and an astrologer's role can often be that of a midwife, helping their client through and across this threshold of new beginnings. So it is important that we examine the Ascendant complex very carefully whenever we are consulted about new ventures or new directions, since our client's approach to new beginnings is very likely to be different from our own.

Let's assume, for example, that we have Sagittarius rising, but that our client has Capricorn rising. Unless we are sufficiently self-aware, we could find ourselves reassuring our client, trying to convince them that all they need to do is to trust and have faith and that everything will turn out just fine. This may not be true at all in our client's experience, and they may well feel even more fearful or inadequate and alone by the time they leave your consulting room than they did when they arrived. But if we pay particular attention to the Ascendant complex of our clients, then we can more accurately reflect their experience of the world and provide the support and mirroring which will help them to navigate any changes in their lives.

2nd house: establishing (Taurus house – natural ruler Venus)

We have spent a great deal of time looking at the 1st house and at the Ascendant, and we need to move on now to the 2nd house. The 2nd house is the house of physical and material substance, of incorporation, our first experience of which is our relationship to our body. The 2nd house describes what we feel about our body, whether we can trust it, whether we value it or not, and how safe and secure it feels. This will often be a reflection of the way our bodies were – or were not – valued, respected, nourished, affirmed, and protected by our primary carers. This extends to our relationship to our possessions, our personal resources, and to what we feel we are worth. This also relates to money which, in our culture, is such a powerful symbol of personal substance and worth. So in a very material sense, the 2nd house describes how we earn our money, and from a psychological point of view it describes how we value ourselves and our attitude to the money we earn.

Audience: I have Neptune in the 2nd house, and I have read that this is a terrible placement, since money just slips through your fingers, like water.

Clare: Certainly, you may not have a particularly strong sense of your own physical boundaries or limitations, but this can also be an immensely creative placement. It could indicate that you earn your money in a Neptunian profession, such as advertising, charity work, film, fashion, dance, or as an artist. Ultimately Neptune in the 2nd house tells us about your values, which may well be more idealistic and altruistic than materialistic. Unless we actually value money, it is unlikely that we will bother to accumulate it. The 2nd house tells us so much about our values and attitude to substance of all kinds. Saturn in the 2nd house, for example, can describe a psychology of poverty which remains with us all our lives, no matter how much money we have in the bank.

Audience: What does Pluto in the 2nd house mean?

Clare: Pluto is about intense control, so it can describe someone who needs to have total control over their body, as in the case of athletes or ballet dancers, for example. Pluto is the planet of crisis, repeated purging, purification and ultimate survival, and I have seen it in the charts of people who amass huge wealth and then lose it all, as if there was a repeating compulsion to radically purge any substance or matter which has accumulated in order to be stripped down before once again emerging and building again from scratch. Sometimes people with Pluto in the 2nd house have been strictly controlled or manipulated, perhaps exploited, in their early years, and the personal battle which ensues can be an obsessive need for personal control, in order to avoid being controlled by others.

Audience: I have to be in total control of my body. Every day I do hours of exercise, and I am always putting myself on strict diets and purges. I wish I could find a way not to be so extreme or obsessive, but I suppose there is no hope for me.

Clare: Well, it may be that on some level you experience your body as dark or corrupt or unacceptable in some way. In Freudian terms, the 2nd house relates to the anal stage of development, when the child seeks for the first time to have control over its body and the products of its body, and a battle of the wills develops between the child and the parent. A psychological interpretation might be that you have 'introjected' this battle, which means that you may well be treating your own body in the way it was treated when you were much younger. If this is the case, then you have choices as an adult that were not available to you when you were a child, when the balance of power was inevitably unequal. It may be possible for you to listen to your body more, and to question whether it is really necessary to keep on punishing and purging it.

3rd house: learning (Gemini house – natural ruler Mercury)

The 3rd house describes our early environment, our exploration of and interaction with our immediate surroundings, the development of thinking, learning, language and communication. This house indicates how we absorb and process information, which in turn defines what and how we perceive, and for each of us this will be different. It also describes our relationships with our brothers and sisters, our experience of early schooling and of schoolteachers and neighbours. True to its natural Gemini association, the 3rd house also describes short journeys and local travel.

Audience: I have Saturn in the 3rd house and I don't like to travel – I always try to find reasons why I don't need to go somewhere.

Clare: I wonder if there is any connection here with your journey to school when you were much younger. With Saturn in the 3rd, it may well be that this was a fearful event for you.

Audience: That's right. Now I think about it, I used to be picked up every day by the mother of two children at my school, a brother and sister, and I always felt awkward and alone because they would ignore me, or talk about things which I didn't know anything about. And the reason I was taken to school in the first place was because my mother was a single parent and had to leave for work even before I left for school, so I always felt alone and abandoned. I remember pleading with my mother to take me with her and to drop me off at school on her way to work, but she wouldn't do that because it would mean I would arrive before the school gates were opened and it would be unsafe.

Clare: That story describes very graphically what it feels like to have Saturn in the 3rd house. It can also mean that you are an only child, that you feel you have been denied brothers and sisters, or, alternatively, it could mean that you are the oldest child, with early responsibility for your younger brothers and sisters. This can be tough, because it means that you have not had an opportunity to learn how to play or spat or fight with your siblings.

Audience: In my case, it describes the fact that I was an only child, but I have always wanted brothers and sisters.

Clare: Saturn normally describes what we crave and what we feel we have been denied, so this is a good example.

Audience: I have Neptune in the 3rd house, and I never had a clue what was going on at school.

Clare: Neptune in the 3rd would indicate that you have a poetic and imaginative mind, and you may have spent your school years staring out of the classroom window and dreaming. With Neptune in the 3rd house, you are likely to absorb information like blotting paper and you probably need to feel things before they make sense to you. I suspect that you have a visual and holistic way of processing information. Logical analysis or rote learning would no doubt have been meaningless to you and you are more likely to respond to the way something is said rather than to the actual meaning of the words themselves.

4th house: belonging (Cancer house - natural ruler Moon)

The 4th and 10th houses are the parental houses, describing the home environment we grew up in (4th house) and the family's relationship to, or status in, the world (10th house). Generally speaking, the 4th and 10th houses tend to describe our perception of our father and mother respectively, although to some extent that is interchangeable, since our parents play different roles at different times in our lives, and our perception of them can change. Nevertheless, we usually learn about the world from our mother, who is generally the more visible parent (10th house), and we take our name, our basic identity and our connection to the family line from our father, who is generally the more hidden parent (4th house).

The 4th house describes our early home environment, the atmosphere we absorbed there, and the nature of our early physical and emotional container: our biological and social roots and origins. This is the watery Cancerian house, with the Moon as the natural ruler, describing the quality of the nurturing we experienced in our early lives, and how safe we feel about belonging to our family, clan or tribe. The level of acceptance, love and encouragement we receive from our family stays with us throughout our lives and describes how safe we feel on an emotional level. Our family can provide a firm and nurturing foundation upon which we can build, or, alternatively, at the other end of the spectrum, an unsafe, neglectful, critical, or leaky container, in which case we may never feel safe on a fundamental level. The primal matrix of the 4th house is eventually internalised, describing how we create our own home and family and where we come home to ourselves, which will include the sign on the cusp of the 4th house and the condition of ruling planet or planets, as well as any planets in the 4th house. In the equal house system, the IC – which is a much more personal point describing our own deepest inner foundation and root system – is not necessarily found in the 4th house. In other words, it is not necessarily tied up so closely with our parents. We will look at this in more depth next week, when we explore the angles of the chart.

Audience: I have Jupiter in the 4th house and was born into a very large extended family, with lots of uncles and aunts and cousins coming and going all the time.

Clare: That is a great example of Jupiter in the 4th. With this placement there is an inherent sense of the meaning and value of belonging to a family, which is often both very sociable and gregarious. It can sometimes mean a strongly religious background that supports family structures and values, so that the family itself is supported by a larger matrix in which it is embedded.

Audience: Well, I come from a large Italian family, so there is a strong Catholic background.

Audience: I have Saturn in the 4th house, and absolutely none of this Jupiter stuff applies to me. I remember reading that Saturn in the 4th is like 'Bleak House', which feels much more appropriate.

Clare: Yes, this is a very graphic image of Saturn in the 4th. I always think of the 4th house as being like a flowerbed. Some of us are planted in fertile soil and tenderly nurtured and watered so that we can grow tall and strong without too much difficulty. Some of us are planted too close together or too far apart, some of us are uprooted before we have had time to establish ourselves properly, and some of us are water plants or plants which grow in the air, like orchids. With Saturn in the 4th, the experience is often one of being sown in hard, dry ground from which it is difficult to draw nourishment, and in which it is hard to put down any kind of root system – we are like desert plants, having to survive on the very barest minimum of nutrients. And this eventually makes us very strong and self-sufficient.

5th house: creating (Leo house – natural ruler Sun)

The 5th house is the house of recreation – self-expression, enjoyment and pleasure. It describes what we do for fun, how we play, what makes us feel alive and glad to be alive. The 5th house describes our experience of being a child, and our attitude towards our own children. It also describes our attitude to romance, speculation and risk-taking: all those activities which make us feel as if we are at the centre of the universe, uniquely blessed, special, and favoured by the gods. The 5th house describes what we enjoy and do for fun rather than for any particular goal or result. We all have different ideas about what is fun. With Venus in the 5th house, for example, this might be love affairs, whereas with Saturn in the 5th house our pleasures are likely to be solitary and serious. With Mercury in Virgo in the 5th house we might be a stamp collector or train spotter, with Mars in Aries we might be a sportsman or woman, and with Jupiter in Pisces we might love to dance. 5th house pursuits are any activities which give us joy and make us feel really alive.

Audience: But I have Pluto in the 5th house.

Clare: That is a good example, because we have to make sense of what this powerful god of the underworld is doing in the 5th house of creative self-expression. The first thing we can say is that your pleasures are likely to be intense and you may be rather obsessive about your hobbies. I suspect that you won't really be enjoying yourself unless you are doing something with total focus and intensity. I also suspect that you should keep away from superficial party or board games, since Pluto is about survival and the 5th house is about competition, so the experience of being beaten is not trivial – it can feel like a personal threat, and you may find yourself wanting to annihilate your opponent.

Audience: Yes, I don't seem to be able to play on a light-hearted level like most other people. If I compete, then I must win, so I have ended up not competing at all, because it is too painful and difficult.

Audience: I have nothing in the 5th house. Does that mean I am not creative or that I won't have any children?

Clare: Absolutely not. In this case you will need to look for the planet which rules the 5th house, and the story will be found there.

Audience: I have Chiron in the 5th house in Cancer, with Cancer ruling the 5th house. The Moon is in the 4th house in Gemini.

Clare: Well, there is something of the wounded child in this placement, and it may well be that you have always felt as if you were an outsider, perhaps that you didn't belong to your family in some way. And with the ruler of the 5th in Gemini in the 4th house, I wonder if you had two homes when you were a child.

Audience: Well, that is amazing, because I was fostered at a very young age, but I did spend periods of time with my birth family. So I never really felt that I belonged anywhere, and you are right that I have always felt like an outsider.

Clare: And this could mean that your gift is your sensitivity to children's feelings. Do you work with children at all?

Audience: Yes, I work in an adoption agency, but the part I like best about that is going into the families of people who want to adopt and checking that the children will be safe and properly cared for there. I also run an animal refuge, where I look after animals that have been abandoned.

Clare: That is a wonderful expression of your Chiron placement in the 5th house. No doubt it gives you great pleasure to be able to find homes for the children and to look after the animals.

Audience: Yes, it does.

6th house: perfecting (Virgo house – natural ruler Mercury)

Clare: Let's move on to the 6th house, which completes the personal hemisphere and is the final house of self-development, in which we perfect ourselves and develop particular skills that can be put into useful service. The 6th house is the workhouse, describing how and where we earn our daily bread. It also describes how we approach, cope and deal with the demands and details of everyday life at home and at work. The 6th house says a great deal about our contribution and attitude to work, and the kind of work situations we find ourselves in. It also describes our relationship to work colleagues and to those who serve us.

The 6th house describes how we serve and service our bodies, whether we feed them properly and give them enough rest and exercise. In this context, we can see our body as our servant. How do we treat it? Is it overworked, driven to exhaustion, starved, overfed or overindulged? The 6th house can also indicate the kinds of health issues that might arise if we neglect or abuse our body. With Jupiter in the 6th house, for example, we might have a tendency to over-work or to over-indulge generally, which could eventually lead to liver problems, since Jupiter rules the liver. With Mars, which rules the head, in the 6th house, we might be prone to headaches. The 6th house also describes how we treat and care for our pets. These two things are not so far apart, because we can easily appreciate that small animals that are in our care need to be looked after, loved, and fed at regular intervals, but it is sometimes much harder to appreciate that we need to care for our own bodies in the same way, to ensure that they are properly cared for and get the right diet and exercise and enough rest, for example.

The 6th house, therefore, describes how we navigate unequal relationships: those who work for us – it is traditionally the house of servants – and those for whom we work. Let's look at some examples. What do you think would happen, for example, if you had Uranus in the 6th house and went to work for the Civil Service?

Audience: You wouldn't last long.

Audience: You wouldn't go there in the first place.

Clare: Not if you knew your chart. Uranus in the 6th will fight against being hemmed in by red tape or bureaucracy. It can't bear these kinds of restrictions and will no doubt rebel against the system. Uranus describes where in the chart we refuse to engage, so we may well refuse to submit to the demands of duty, work and service

Audience: I have Uranus in the 6th house, and it is also the ruler of my chart.

Clare: So presumably this applies to you? It could also mean, of course, that you work in the area of invention or science, or that you are involved with new technology of some sort. Or that it is important for you to be in a work environment where everyone is equal and works side by side. The ideal solution for Uranus in the 6th house would be to go freelance, so that you can work on your own terms, in which case you might sometimes be free and sometimes very busy. Or you might work in a co-operative serving a shared ideological vision. What sort of 6th house work do you do?

Audience: Well I am not working now. I also have Pluto in the 6th house.

Clare: Do you find that you are drawn into any kind of power struggles at work? It could well be that you have a well-developed nose for hidden issues or any kind of corruption which might be going on under the surface in your working environment. Alternatively, you might even work as a private detective, or in some kind of healing area where people go through intense transformation.

Audience: Well, I used to work in a small company doing office stuff, managing the library and the accounts and taking my turn at the reception desk. But I found it very hard, actually, and I did get into power struggles with a woman there, so I left. I am now unemployed, but I am thinking of training in some kind of healing work, and maybe working as an astrologer.

Clare: With Uranus and Pluto in the 6th house, I suspect you will want some kind of work that brings about powerful change and transformation, because this combination is very high voltage, so working with healing on an energetic level might suit you well. It would also give you the opportunity to work for yourself, and I suspect that you would prefer work that is non-routine. Eventually, since you belong to the Uranus-Pluto in Virgo generation, you are likely to want to radically rethink and change the way things are done, and this will no doubt apply to any area of work you find yourself doing. I doubt that office work or sitting behind a desk is right for you.

Lesson Three: Houses 7 to 12

Last week we explored the meaning of the first six houses, and it is worth pausing for a moment to consider the relationship between the first six houses and the remaining six houses. Every chart is divided by the angles into two sets of hemispheres. The first six houses lie under the horizon, which means that they are under the earth when we are born, hidden from view. They are the houses of self-exploration, describing our subjective, internal worlds. The natural rulers of the first six houses are personal planets, with Mars ruling the 1st, to Venus ruling the 2nd, and so on to Mercury (3rd), Moon (4th), Sun (5th) and finally back to Mercury again, which is the natural ruler of the 6th house. The point about this is that, in order to engage successfully and creatively with houses 7 to 12, the collective houses which describe how we relate to others and to the world around us, we need to be able to build on and draw from the personal resources, self-development and self-knowledge we have achieved in the personal houses.

For example, successful adult-to-adult relationships (7th house) depend upon our having a good sense of our own identity, on our ability to decide what is right for us personally (1st house). Nor can we safely surrender to the emotional depths of intense encounter with another (8th house) until we have a sense of our own personal stability, self-worth, security, and enough personal 'ballast' to support us (2nd house). Nor can we make any sense of or gain any benefit from higher education, philosophy travel, teachers or experiences outside our ken (9th house) until we have learned to process information and order our thoughts (3rd house). Nor can we take our place effectively in the world (10th house) until we have a stable enough base from which to operate (4th house). Nor can we make a meaningful or creative contribution to the society in which we live (11th house) until we have something of personal value to offer (5th house). Nor is it appropriate to retire from the world (12th house) until we have mastered its demands (6th house).

Otherwise we would be turning our back on the world and trying to get straight back into the womb.

In this sense, the houses tell the story of our gradual sequential development and maturation, and it is worth taking this into consideration when we are interpreting charts. There is always a temptation to live our lives backwards, and on some level I think we all try to do this, to some extent, until the world teaches us otherwise. For example, we tend to start out from a narcissistic position in which we assume that the world owes us a living and expect it to accommodate our every wish (12th house), paying no attention to the actual practical realities or to the way in which we might serve or contribute to the world (6th house). Or we might expect the community or society to which we belong (11th house) to recognise and accept and include us immediately, without us having to go to the trouble of developing our own particular talents, or discovering the unique and special contributions we can make to the group (5th house). Or we might expect the world to provide us with a job, or a public platform, or respect and influence in world (10th house) before we have built an inner sense of security and stability for ourselves (4th house). Or we might expect exciting opportunities and adventures to open up for us (9th house) without bothering to prepare or learn anything about them beforehand (3rd house), or we might give our power to others (8th house) and end up feeling used and abused because we haven't established a sense of personal security and self-worth (2nd house). Finally, we might seek to find ourselves solely through our partner (7th house) without getting to know ourselves first. These descriptions may sound rather harsh, but hopefully you can see what I am getting at. Can you see how these opposite areas of activity are intimately connected and, in fact, dependent upon each other?

Audience: Actually, this sounds fairly realistic to me. I suspect we all instinctively take the second route around the chart but, as you say, life teaches us otherwise. It seems that life is meant to be difficult.

7th house: relating (Libra house – natural ruler Venus)

The cusp of the 7th house is also the Descendant, and we will be looking in more detail at the Ascendant-Descendant axis next week. The 7th house describes all one-to-one relationships of a contractual nature, such as business partnerships and marriage. It is the house of equal, negotiated relationships, and describes what we meet through others and how we find ourselves through such relationships. Traditionally, this is also the house of open enemies, so it is the battlefield on which we meet our equal opposites.

Although we usually recognise that the first six houses belong to us, the 7th and 8th houses almost invariably seem to describe the qualities belonging to those with whom we are in relationship. It is very difficult indeed to recognise ourselves in these two houses. In the 7th and 8th houses it is no longer us, it is 'them'. The 7th and 8th houses describe the qualities we draw towards us, and we find these particularly hard to identify with. Ultimately, however, they do tell us more about ourselves than about others, although it seems that we can only learn these things about ourselves through our relationships. Ultimately, our task is to recognise that these two houses tell us more about ourselves than about those with whom we are in relationship. With Saturn in the 7th house, for example, we may find that our partner is boring, withholding, critical and heavy. However, if we move on to another relationship, then before long our new partner will start to become boring, withholding, critical and heavy. Eventually we may realise that there is a pattern and that this may have something to do with us. This is often a very difficult realisation, because with Saturn in the 7th it is possible that we are afraid of relationships, and that we have made our choice based on our need for safety and security. It may be that we can only enter into relationships cautiously or formally, wearing our protective armour, which eventually becomes rigid and prevents our continued growth and development – something for which we then blame our partner.

Audience: I have Venus and Uranus conjunct in Gemini in the 7th house, and I would say that I recognise that as belonging to me, and always have. I have always been the disruptive one in relationships.

Clare: So what would you say that you value about relationships, with Venus conjunct Uranus?

Audience: Freedom and space.

Clare: I wonder if this is something of a two-edged sword, because it may hark back to early experiences of being abandoned by loved ones. It is possible that you may expect your partners to leave you in the end, so you break off the relationships before they can do so, and take the blame yourself. Where the 7th house is concerned, there is always the question of 'who is doing what to whom'. But with this placement, relationships don't necessarily need to end in separation. It may be possible to negotiate enough space and freedom within a relationship, or a real friendship in which each of you respects the other as individuals and adults, so that neither of you feels trapped.

Audience: Well, I have certainly always taken the blame for breaking off from relationships in the past. And I do see that it would be nice to find this kind of space within a relationship.

Audience: I have Jupiter in the 7th.

Clare: With Jupiter in the 7th house, we are often attracted to people from different cultures or religions, or to people we feel we can learn from, because they expand our horizons.

Audience: I have Mars and Neptune and Saturn there. Saturn and Neptune are in Libra, and Mars is in Scorpio.

Clare: Well, what we could say first of all is that relationships are a big area for you.

Audience: Yes.

Clare: Saturn in the 7th indicates that relationships are a serious issue for you, and you are unlikely to enter into them lightly. Many of your most important lessons will be learned through relationships. With Neptune in the 7th, you are likely to idealise your partner. There can be a fantasy about finding a perfect partner, someone who will redeem and rescue you, or someone you can rescue. The same thing happens when Pisces is on the Descendant. On the one hand we can accept our partner uncritically, exactly as they are, but on the other hand we can be deluded, and end up feeling disappointed or betrayed or let down. And Neptune is where we are always thirsty, where we always want more, so we will long for the perfect, ideal other who exists in our dreams, and feel dissatisfied with the ordinary mortal we end up with. On some level it is we ourselves who are unavailable for relationship. The dilemma with Saturn and Neptune in the 7th house is that they are opposites, in the sense that Saturn has strong boundaries and Neptune has no boundaries. So do you stick with the reality or hold out for your dream?

Audience: Does this also mean that we sacrifice ourselves for our partner?

Clare: Yes, that can be one interpretation, although we are unlikely to realise that this is what we are doing, as long as we are tied up in the fantasy of perfect love. With Mars in Scorpio in the 7th house, we are likely to attract intense relationships and power struggles. So there is a combination of the romance and idealisation of the Neptune in Libra generation, the hard work indicated by Saturn, and the sexual intensity and passion of Mars in Scorpio.

Audience: Well, I did say it was complicated. I certainly find it very hard.

8th house: sharing (Scorpio house – personal ruler Mars, collective ruler Pluto)

The 8th house is where we meet with intense emotional experiences and encounters which change us forever. The natural Scorpio house, the 8th house is where we are confronted by inherited issues and secrets which lie deep beneath the surface and which are often taboo, or which most of us would prefer not to look at all. Our 8th house inheritance is not just about hidden personal or family issues, but extends to our inheritance of unresolved issues and old poisons which exist in our society and in the collective generally. If we have planets in the 8th house, then at some point in our lives we will be impelled – forced – to engage with and to purge whatever has become corrupt or poisonous about them. Our task appears to be to bring the issues associated with these planets to the light, so that they can be cleansed and healed. I often advise students to knock carefully before entering the 8th house. The reason for this is that 8th house issues can be so deeply buried in the unconscious that our clients may have no idea they are there, so I think the astrologer therefore needs to tread very carefully.

The 8th house describes the most primitive, archaic emotions which lie quietly under the surface until they are activated. When planets in the 8th house are active, they are volcanic, unstoppable forces that take us over and possess us. This is the house of sex, death, taxes and joint finances, where hidden emotions come to the surface, often shocking us with their intensity.

Audience: I have Mercury, Uranus, and Sun in Leo, and Venus and Pluto in Virgo, and they are all in the 8th house. And Leo is the sign on the 8th house cusp.

Clare: Right. So the ruler of the 8th house is in the 8th house. Now I am assuming that, because you have offered your own 8th house as an example, you have opened the door for us and we are allowed to enter?

Audience: Yes, you can enter. Uranus and the Sun are together, and Pluto and Venus are together, but Mercury is by itself.

Clare: With five planets in the 8th house, no doubt the underworld is familiar territory to you. It is your home. Let's start by looking just at Mercury in the 8th house. It is like having a Pluto-Mercury contact, which means very deep, penetrating, intense, and secretive or private ideas and thoughts. This is the investigative mind – you need to get to the root of things, to understand what is not being said or communicated, to read the signs. The 8th house is very deep but non-verbal, so it works on the level of intuition and emotion. It could even say something about your siblings, because Mercury is also the natural significator for brothers and sisters, so it might be a particularly intense relationship with a brother or sister. With the Sun and Uranus in Leo in the 8th house, you will feel compelled to plumb the depths of understanding. and use your insight to bring new knowledge to the surface. This configuration is about bringing things from the dark, where they are hidden, into the light, into the open air. This is the seat of your creativity and your unique gift.

Audience: In fact I am bringing things from the dark into the light all the time, because I am a midwife.

Clare: Well, it seems that you are in exactly the right profession, because you are dealing with life and death issues, and Leo is the sign of the child, of new life and potential. You have the ability to be both detached and scientific, with the Sun-Uranus connection, but I suspect that you are also strongly guided by your intuition and by your instinctive understanding of medicine and healing, which is also an 8th house matter. The Venus-Pluto connection describes your love of intensity and your function as a powerful woman working with women who are going through profound and often terrifying and painful experiences. With so many planets in the 8th house, you will be wonderful in a crisis. That is when you come into your own and into your power.

Your work is a wonderful expression of these 8th house planets, and no doubt there are more personal issues here as well, which will concern your relationship with your father. Sun-Uranus can describe a distant father, and you may have feelings of abandonment around him, although there will be a strong psychic connection between you because it is in the 8th house. And the Venus-Pluto connection in the 8th house can describe your sexual power as a woman, and issues about power and powerlessness in relationships, so there are many other personal levels of meaning here which are probably best explored in a private setting.

9th house: seeking (Sagittarius House – natural ruler Jupiter)

The 9th house is the house of god, and describes what we believe in, what is meaningful to us, and how and where we draw meaning from life. It is a Sagittarius house, ruled by Jupiter, so the 9th house describes how we broaden our horizons, either physically through travelling and having contact with different cultures, or mentally and intellectually through higher education and our philosophy of life – seeking the bigger picture – or spiritually, by finding a god we can serve and who serves us. On a mundane level, it can describe our experiences of higher learning, or of groups devoted to spiritual or philosophical exploration. Whatever specific shape this takes, what we are really doing in the 9th house is searching for wisdom and meaning in order to find out what we believe in. It is about what makes life worth living, not just in the personal sense, from a 5th house point of view, but in the context of the bigger picture.

Saturn in the 9th house can, like every planet, be interpreted on a variety of different levels. It might mean, for example, that we were denied the opportunity to go to university, or that we studied structural engineering at university. It may mean that we have never been abroad because we are afraid of travelling outside our immediate environment, or that our work is a 9th house matter, so we might be a travel agent or a tour rep. And it is likely that, if we have one at all, our god is rather strict and demanding. It will be hard work to build our 9th house and it may take a long time, but we will build on rock. So we might end up going to university in our fifties, or eventually finding our own faith based on real experience of the world.

Audience: I have Saturn in the 9th house, and I find it very difficult to have faith.

Clare: In my experience, with Saturn in the 9th we often feel as if our god lays down the law and demands strict obedience if we are to avoid being punished. This can lead to a kind of cynicism and to periods in the wilderness, where we may feel utterly unsupported and alone on a spiritual level. With Uranus in the 9th house, on the other hand, we might have studied science or politics at university, and we could have unexpected experiences and encounters, or sudden insights when we are travelling abroad. We may be seeking enlightenment, or our god may be rational, highly intellectual, or egalitarian, so we may be a Quaker or belong to a non-denominational church.

Audience: I have Neptune in my 9th house.

Clare: With Neptune here, you are likely to have a longing to merge with god, seeking a mystical union in which you are in god and god is in you. And you may have studied music or dance at university, or spent periods of time abroad in ashrams or on retreats. But, unless you are travelling by boat or ship, there may be problems when you are travelling.

Audience: Why do you say that?

Clare: Because it is possible that you will encounter confusion and chaos. Or your luggage might get lost, or your reservations turn out not to have been made, or your passport and money might get stolen – that sort of thing.

Audience: I have travelled around the world without any problems. The only thing is that other people always let you down – they can't be trusted.

Clare: Perhaps you have projected your Neptune, in which case it will be evoked in the shape of other people when you are travelling.

10th house: contributing (Capricorn House – natural ruler Saturn)

The 10th house describes our 'public face' – our public or professional image and position in the world, our career or job, and our relationship to authority figures such as our boss. It is the house of status, responsibility, authority, and mother, to the extent that she was the authority in our lives, the rule-maker, when we were children. The 10th house is the house of worldly ambition, describing the kinds of achievements we seek recognition for.

Because it is also the house of the mother, it can also describe very accurately the ambitions our mother or our family have for us, their vision of what we can be in the world. More often than not, we find ourselves trying to fulfil our mother's ambitions and try to become what she wants us to become, at least to start with. For example, if your mother was a frustrated ballet dancer and you happened to have Venus in Leo in the 10th, you might find yourself becoming a ballet dancer because since, from the moment you could walk, you may have been taken to ballet classes. With Venus in Leo in the 10th house, this would be a way of gaining praise and recognition, not just in your mother's eyes, but in the eyes of the world as well. With Mars in the 10th house we may be ambitious and forceful, and seek to lead. With Saturn in the 10th we are likely to work hard to achieve the authority and respect we crave.

Audience: Is the sign important?

Clare: Yes, and it is always important to check on the positions of the planet or planets which rule the 10th house. This will give us more accurate and detailed information about the specifically individual expression of 10th house matters. The 10th house describes our attitude to authority and to worldly success and failure. It is also what we project onto the outside world. So, for example, we might see the world as demanding and critical, if we have Saturn in the 10th house or Capricorn on the cusp of the 10th. Or we might find the world scary and oppressive if we have Pluto in the 10th or Scorpio on the cusp of the 10th. Or the world may seem full of exciting possibilities and opportunities, if we have Jupiter in the 10th or Sagittarius on the cusp.

11th house: uniting (Aquarius house – personal ruler Saturn, collective ruler Uranus)

The 11th house is traditionally the house of hopes and wishes, describing the ideals and aims we have for the group, community or society to which we belong. It is the house of political and social beliefs and of the causes with which we are likely to become involved. The 11th house describes how we function as part of a group or community, amongst our friends and colleagues. The natural house of Aquarius, the most mature of the air signs, the 11th house is where we engage with the world and others according to our ideals and principles and hopes for humanity as a whole, respecting the rights of others, treating them as equals, and allowing them the space and freedom to be who they are. The 11th house is a good place to look if you want to understand more about how you respond to group situations.

With Jupiter in the 11th house, for example, we are likely to find it easy to make friends because we expect everyone to be basically benevolent and gregarious. With Saturn in the 11th house, we are likely to be more cautious and take longer to make friends. Planets in the 11th house describe the sort of friends and colleagues we tend to attract.

Audience: I have Uranus and Pluto in the 11th house, and I try to avoid group situations whenever possible.

Clare: As a member of the Uranus-Pluto generation born in the mid-1960s, this indicates that you will have new ideas about society, and that you will want to break down the old structures and build again from scratch. You are likely to be very political, and even subversive, finding yourself impelled to challenge the way communities or collectives or groups are run, seeing them as corrupt and in need of revisioning.

Audience: That sounds much better, and it also explains why my best friends always seem to be involved in some sort of political activism.

12th house: merging (Pisces House – personal ruler Jupiter, collective ruler Neptune)

Now we have reached the 12th house, we are almost back where we began. We have already considered the 12th house as our experience of being in the womb and, as with all water houses, this house describes our psychic inheritance and any unfinished business we have inherited from our parents and ancestors. The 12th house does not belong to time-space 'reality', because it has no boundaries. It is the house where everything happens all the time, and where everything is connected. There is no place here for the ego, which can only function in time, and so it describes that part of ourselves which never fully incarnates or engages with the world – the place where our dreams and fantasies hold sway, where visions, hopes and fears inspire, support or paralyse our lives. It is our bolt-hole, the place we escape to, whether psychically, emotionally or physically, just to be alone and to heal ourselves. In the 12th house we can experience a feeling of universal support, guidance and inspiration, which can in turn help us to inspire and support others. Alternatively, this can be where we are our own worst enemies, refusing to engage with the world, overwhelmed by the 'going home project', seeking oblivion, dissolving ourselves in addictive or other kinds of self-destructive behaviour.

People with a 12th house emphasis need time by themselves because they are like psychic sponges, absorbing everything which is going on in the environment around them, which can be overwhelming. The 12th house is where we merge, escape from our separateness and identify with that which is greater than ourselves – it describes our memories of life before birth and our feelings about life after death. It is the desire to retreat or to escape from the hard edges of the world; it is the pull of the monastic life, a life of contemplation and communion with the divine. It is the house where we replenish and heal ourselves in order to gain enough strength for our next venture into the real world. The 12th house is also the house of institutions, hospitals, prisons, monasteries, nunneries and retreats, all of which are containers which protect us from the world. It describes our relationship to such institutions.

Audience: I have the Sun in the 12th house, and this all sounds rather daunting.

Clare: Well, you are no doubt immensely sensitive to the environment around you, and I would imagine that you need plenty of privacy and solitude, to retreat from the world and be alone on a regular basis. When you do this, you will no doubt feel as if you are deeply supported in some way that is quite hard to define. It is worth remembering that the natural rulers of this house are both Neptune and Jupiter, so the 12th, like the 9th, is also the house of god, in the sense of being deeply connected on a mystical level. Your life will be embedded in the big picture, and you may well find yourself through working in any of the

12th house institutions I mentioned earlier. You are at home when you can flow and merge and dream, living in an imaginal world where everything changes all the time. I would also imagine that your father was somehow rather hard to get hold of – nebulous or absent, either physically or psychologically.

Audience: I have Uranus in Cancer in the 12th house, and I always want to be at home.

Clare: With Uranus in the 12th house, I think there is always a part of us which refuses to believe that the 'real' world is all that there is, and in Cancer it is likely that the home you are speaking of actually has more to do with a memory of your spiritual home than any kind of home which can be found here on earth. I also think that Uranus in the 12th house represents access to spiritual guidance that provides us with a welcome sense of perspective and detachment.

Lesson Four: Polarity and the Angles

This evening I want to spend some time looking at the six pairs of polarities present in every chart. We will then go on to look at the meaning of the angles. The birth chart tells us that, from the moment of our birth, we are confronted with a series of polarities. It is these polarities which cause us to become strangers to ourselves, divided, split, separated and fragmented, with the result that we keep meeting the split-off parts of ourselves in other people or in the world 'out there', not realising that they belong to us.

> For the individual, the struggle to deal with irreconcilable opposites generates the development of psyche. Individuation, in other words, is made possible through the tensions caused by the neurotic aspects of the personality.[8]

I want to spend some time considering the signs and the houses as six pairs of complementary opposites because, as Dane Rudhyar wrote, 'It simply does not make any sense to try and define the meaning of one end of an axis without including in the definition the meaning of the other end'.[9] This approach helps us to work with the mechanism of projection, which is one of the most important ideas in psychology and in psychological astrology. It is also much easier to understand what something actually *is*, if we study at the same time what it is *not*. So we are going to spend this evening caught up in the drama of opposites, which is, of course, what makes life so interesting.

Like a pendulum, the more extreme one pole becomes, the more extreme the opposite pole becomes. Whenever we identify consciously with one end of a polarity, the opposite end is constellated in the

---

[8] Guggenbuhl-Craig, Adolf, *From the Wrong Side: A Paradoxical Approach to Psychology* (Dallas, TX: Spring Publications, 1995), p. 143.
[9] Dane Rudhyar, *The Astrological Houses*, p.154

unconscious, compensating for and balancing the consciously held position. Have a look at this table of opposites. In the last column are words describing the extreme opposites of the same spectrum. We already know from last term that opposites are inseparable; they repel and attract each other in equal measure. The interesting question, which is not necessarily clear from the birth chart itself, is where do we stand on each of these axes – where are we consciously identified?

Natural zodiac and house axes

Houses	Signs (natural zodiac)	Planets (natural rulers)	Psychological dynamic
1st/7th	Aries/Libra Fire/Air CARDINAL	Mars/Venus	Axis of relationship Self/not-self Me/you Autonomy/compromise Self-assertion/ cooperation Desire/acceptance Personal goal/context
2nd/8th	Taurus/Scorpio Earth/Water FIXED	Venus/Mars (Pluto)	Axis of exchange Mine/yours Valuing self/other Dependency on self/other Retention/release Incorporation/ elimination
3rd/9th	Gemini/ Sagittarius Air/Fire MUTABLE	Mercury/ Jupiter	Axis of exploration Learning/teaching Information/meaning Intellect/beliefs Student/teacher Near/far

4th/10th	Cancer/ Capricorn Water/Earth CARDINAL	Moon/Saturn	Axis of structure Child/parent Home/world Private life/public life Belonging/ self-sufficiency The clan/the hermit
5th/11th	Leo/Aquarius Fire/Air FIXED	Sun/Saturn (Uranus)	Axis of identity Self/society Individual/collective The heart/the head Personal good/ common good Autocracy/democracy Egocentric/altruistic
6th/12th	Virgo/Pisces Earth/Water MUTABLE	Mercury/ Jupiter (Neptune)	Axis of devotion Order/chaos Control/trust Duty/compassion Form/content

In fact, it is not uncommon for people to consult an astrologer precisely because a situation in their lives, or a relationship, has become polarised. In such cases, they may find themselves veering dramatically from one extreme end of a polarity to the other, not realising that the two poles are fundamentally connected. One of our major tasks as astrologers is to 'hold the opposites' for both ourselves and our clients. This is always an uncomfortable and difficult thing to do, but it can protect us from colluding with our clients, on the one hand, or from taking an unhelpful 'problem-solving' approach on the other hand.

Aries/Libra axis

Planetary rulers: Mars and Venus
Natural houses: 1st/7th

The Aries/Libra axis concerns the struggle to find the balance between autonomy and compromise, self-assertion and cooperation, respect for the self and respect for the other. Naturally associated with the 1st/7th houses, this is a cardinal, fire-air axis ruled by Mars and Venus, mythic lovers and antagonists in equal measure. It describes the inherent tension that exists in all relationships: the struggle to find a balance between personal freedom and autonomy on the one hand, and the support, approval and appreciation we all need from others on the other hand.

The question is, how can we be independent and focused on the achievement of our own goals, and at the same time find completion and fulfilment in our relationships? Like all apparent contradictions, this conflict can be so uncomfortable that we usually identify with one side or with the other. If this axis becomes particularly polarised, the split-off side can become so powerful that it can start to dominate our lives. For example, if we choose total independence and autonomy, we can end up feeling lonely and isolated, having nobody special in our lives to fight or strive for, and nobody with whom to share our triumphs and disappointments. Ultimately, there is no inherent meaning in being strong and independent and focused in isolation. It is much easier to gain a sense of personal fulfilment and achievement if we are fighting for a principle, such as justice, or on behalf of another person.

On the other end of the spectrum, if we choose to live solely for and through our relationships, we can end up feeling angry and resentful that we have sacrificed our self-development and independence. Say, for example, we are identified with the civilised, cultured Libran end of this axis, with its strong sense of fairness, its love of peace and harmony, and its diplomatic talents. Then, no doubt, we will constantly find ourselves surrounded by extremely selfish people who show no consideration for others. This could well make us extremely angry, and anger, of course, belongs to Aries, not to Libra.

Audience: So we end up acting out the negative aspects of the other side of the spectrum?

Clare: Exactly. And of course, neither extreme works at the end of the day. Both sides need each other, so ideally we will find some kind of relationship between them. For example, we know that heroes in mythology are always dependent on the help of others.

John William Waterhouse, 'Jason and Medea' (1907)

Theseus could never have killed the Minotaur in the Labyrinth without the help of Ariadne and her golden thread. Jason could never have stolen the Golden Fleece without Medea's magic, and Perseus could never have rescued Andromeda without the sword and mirrored shield given to him by Athena. It is therefore the support of our partners which not only enables us to achieve our goals, but also gives our achievements real meaning, because they can be shared.

Audience: Are you referring to the Aries/Libra axis in general?

Clare: Yes. We all have this axis somewhere in our charts, so these themes are archetypal, although they will find personal expression in the houses across which these signs fall. But the Aries/Libra axis is also naturally associated with the 1st and 7th houses of relationship, so these themes will also be present to some extent across the 1st and 7th houses in every horoscope.

Taurus/Scorpio axis

Rulers: Mars (Pluto) and Venus
Natural houses: 2nd/8th

On the Taurus/Scorpio axis we meet Mars and Venus again, although this time in their fixed, earth-water manifestations. As a fixed axis, the confrontation between Taurus and Scorpio can be particularly entrenched and unyielding. Naturally associated with the 2nd/8th house axis, the inherent conflict on this axis revolves around issues of resources and ownership, values and possessions, both personal and shared. Taurus is a gentle, peace-loving and practical sign, which prefers to stay within its own sphere of comfort. However, if this axis becomes particularly polarised on the Taurus end of the spectrum, then the simple, biological drive towards stability can become inert and stagnant. This inevitably evokes and stimulates the kind of intense crises that are associated with the sign of Scorpio, which breaks down fixed structures in the interests of growth and new life.

Audience: I have often wondered why Taureans seem to have such battles in relationships. I suppose this is what happens when they are identified with the Scorpio end of the spectrum?

Clare: That's right. When we start to think in terms of axes, then we will start thinking of a Taurus person as being somewhere on the Taurus-Scorpio axis, although we don't know exactly where until we have explored this with them first. But this means that we will no longer be surprised if we have a Taurus client who is consumed by intense and complex emotional or relationship problems, sexual issues, power struggles, battles over money and shared resources, and the like. None of these things belongs to the sign of Taurus, which is very simple, stable and grounded, but they are not uncommon themes with Taurean clients. I am using the term 'Taurean' to describe a person who may not have the Sun in Taurus but could have several planets in Taurus or in the 2nd house, or Taurus on the Ascendant. In such cases, the Taurean can gradually restore their equilibrium by developing a sound sense of self-worth, providing materially for themselves, cultivating a fixity of purpose, a pride in their own accomplishments, and the courage to defend themselves, rather than engaging in power struggles which appear to be caused by the emotional demands of others.

A useful Taurus-Scorpio myth is that of King Midas, who was extremely wealthy. He was, we could say, identified entirely with the Taurus end of this axis. When he was granted a wish by the god Dionysus, he wished that everything he touched would turn to gold, and so it did. However, when he touched the flowers in his garden they turned to gold, and everything he tried to eat turned to gold, so he became increasingly hungry. Worst of all, his beloved daughter turned into gold when he accidentally touched her. Fortunately, and because King Midas was so full of remorse when he realised the consequences of his greed, Dionysus agreed to reverse the spell, and everything came to life again.

Walter Crane, 'King Midas and his daughter who has turned to gold', in Nathanial Hawthorn, *A Wonder Book for Girls and Boys* (1892), British Library

We could say that he realised that, without the destructive aspect of the life-force that belongs to Scorpio, everything would become static, incapable of change or growth. The point is that Taurus begets Scorpio, retention leads to release, incorporation to elimination, to ensure that nature remains in balance and that the life force is constantly regenerated.

Audience: What happens if this axis is reversed and the identification is on the Scorpio end? Can you give us an example of a Scorpio that needs to find its Taurus?

Clare: In this case the individual may seek to find their security and self-worth through other people or other people's resources, rather than their own. If we depend completely on others for our security and sense of self-worth, then we have given our power to them, and we naturally feel that they owe us something in return. If we have no sense of our own inner intrinsic value or worth, we have nothing to contribute to the relationship. The Scorpio client can therefore be extremely possessive, feeling that other people are their possessions and that they belong to them, body and soul. With such a great investment in the other, it is not surprising that, before long, intense feelings of jealousy, suspicion and insecurity emerge. The interesting thing about this is that possessiveness belongs to Taurus and is not a Scorpio trait at all. In essence Scorpio is where we are forced to surrender and let go. Scorpio does not hold onto things – it purges and eliminates, because everything which no longer serves life has to die to make way for new life.

The myth of Pluto and Persephone is relevant here because it harks back to the ancient seasonal rituals celebrating the relationship between life and death in nature. Taurus is springtime, celebrated in the fertility festival of Beltane at the beginning of May, when Persephone is said to make her annual return to the earth from the underworld and all of nature begins to thrive and grow. But at the opposite end of the year, in Scorpio time, marked by Samhain, the festival of death, Persephone returns to the underworld, her earth-mother Demeter goes into mourning, and everything in nature dies. Scorpio and Pluto signify the great organic processes of death and renewal. The life force ebbs and flows on a seasonal basis, since growth cannot continue indefinitely – nature has to be stripped bare in order to ensure renewed life. So the

Taurus/Scorpio axis is one entire process, and we cannot really understand one without understanding the other.

Frederick Lord Leighton, 'The Return of Persephone' (1891)

Gemini/Sagittarius axis

Rulers: Mercury and Jupiter
Natural houses: 3rd/9th

On the mutable air/fire, Gemini/Sagittarius axis we meet the planetary rulers Mercury and Jupiter, which describe learning and the gathering of information on the one hand, and its dissemination on the other hand. This axis of exploration concerns the relationship between information and meaning, facts and knowledge, the student and the teacher, the primary school and the university. The poles of this axis complete and complement each other. If the Gemini end loses touch with the bigger picture, with the value or purpose of the information it is gathering, then everything can become trivial, superficial and meaningless, even to the point of nihilism. If, on the other hand, Sagittarius loses touch with Gemini, the sense of having privileged access to the one truth can lead to arrogance and fundamentalism, cut off from the detachment and relative truths of Gemini.

Charts in which this theme will come to life are those with several planets in Gemini or Sagittarius, in the 3rd or 9th houses, or with this axis on one of the angles. If we are identified only with the Gemini end of this axis, then we may become caught in a kind of perpetual childhood or as a perennial student, living a provisional existence which allows us to remain uncommitted and unaccountable, refusing to be pinned down in any way. In the end, this can become the very kind of trap we have always been so determined to avoid, since it is a refusal to mature or to contribute anything meaningful to the society to which we belong. If, on the other hand, we identify only with the Sagittarius end of this axis, then our quest for wisdom, meaning and for the philosophical fire will expand unchecked until it begins to overwhelm us. If we lose our objectivity, and ignore the actual facts, then we will find ourselves increasingly out of touch with, and alienated from, the very sense of vision and meaning which was so important to us, because we will not have any perspective or have learned to put our vision into words, or developed the ability to discuss it objectively with others, to compare it to other schools of thought or to teach it. We may well start to demand acolytes and disciples who will follow us unquestioningly and, paradoxically, become increasingly dependent upon them for our sense of authority, status and meaning. When this axis becomes particularly polarised, either end can become a trap, which is inappropriate to the mutable nature of these two signs.

Audience: So if you are on the Gemini end of this axis, then you are going to be identified as a student and start attracting teachers?

Plato teaching Aristotle in Raphael's 'The School of Athens' (1509-10)

Clare: Yes, but in fact this would mean that you have projected your own inner teacher, your own wisdom and knowledge, onto others.

Audience: So you need to develop your own wisdom and meaning? But if you did this, then you wouldn't need to learn anything from anyone else in your life again.

Clare: With a mutable axis such as this, there is no point at which we will stop learning or exploring. But hopefully, we will be able to absorb what we are learning, so that it increasingly becomes a part of who we are, before we move on to the next chapter. If these axes are strongly polarised and projected, however, then we may well be unable to incorporate what we know or what we believe, choosing instead simply to teach or preach what we know and believe, without making any use of it in our own lives. In other words, we will not 'walk our talk' – our words may be hollow and our gods made of tin.

Cancer/Capricorn axis

Rulers: Moon and Saturn
Natural houses: 4th/10th

Ruled by the Moon and Saturn, the Cancer-Capricorn axis, naturally associated with the 4th/10th house axis, describes the child and the parent, the one who needs nurturing and the nurturer, our need to belong and our need to stand on our own feet in the world. This is the parent-child axis, and of course there is no child without a parent and there is no parent without a child. Taken to extremes, the signs of Cancer and Capricorn can describe the twin core fears of engulfment and abandonment, which seem to be universal themes deeply lodged in all of our psyches. The sphere of Cancer and the Moon concerns nourishment and nurturing, early experiences of safety and care, and our need for protection. The Moon is the child in all of us, and the child the part of us that doesn't grow up. The sphere of Saturn, on the other end of the spectrum, is the sphere of the parent, the carer and provider, the one who is responsible for establishing safe boundaries. The entire axis is concerned with issues of security, safety and protection. This axis polarises very easily in relationships, with one partner becoming needy and dependent, demanding to be cared for and looked after, and the other partner becoming the provider and competent parent. In fact, relationships are often the arena in which we seek to resolve uncompleted primal nurturing issues, and this will be particularly so if we have Cancer and Capricorn on the Ascendant-Descendant axis, or several planets in Cancer and Capricorn or in the 4th and 10th houses. When this axis polarises, the Cancer end becomes increasingly needy and the Capricorn end becomes increasingly withholding and withdrawn.

Opposites becoming each other: Francisco de Goya y Lucientes,
'Saturn Devouring One of His Sons' (1815)

I once had a client for whom this was a particularly painful theme in her life, and I learned a great deal from her. She had Cancer on the Ascendant, which of course indicates that issues of self-protection were very important. However, as is generally the case with this axis, she had projected the Saturn-ruled Capricorn parent-figure onto her husband, whom she experienced as judgemental, cold and distant. As the axis became further and further polarised, she became more and more needy as she felt increasingly rejected and judged by her husband, and very alone. What made this theme even stronger was the fact that Saturn, the ruler of the Descendant, was right on her Ascendant in Cancer. The first thing I noticed when I met this client is that she was extremely overweight, which is not something you would expect with Saturn on the Ascendant. But I realised that this was a physical manifestation of her feeling of emotional starvation. The whole Cancer-Capricorn axis concerns our ability to give and to receive nourishment – what is enough and what is not enough. My client felt so emotionally starved in her marriage and by her husband that food had become her only comfort.

Audience: And I suppose her size was also a suit of armour – a way of protecting herself, if she had Saturn rising. Were you able to help her?

Clare: No, I don't think so, because this axis had become so polarised that I was unable to reach her. I did spend quite a bit of time suggesting that she could learn to parent herself, and to take care of her own needs. I was trying to encourage her to start taking responsibility for herself as an adult. After all, we all start off being spoon-fed, but there comes a time when we take the spoon and learn to feed ourselves. In other words, I was trying to help her to find a more conscious relationship between the Cancer and Capricorn poles of this spectrum.

Audience: But she didn't get it?

Clare: No, because she was just so needy. And the last thing you want to hear, when you are craving some kind of support, some kind of emotional food, is that you will not get the emotional support you are looking for from your partner, and that you will eventually need to learn to protect, nurture and nourish yourself. Hopefully she was able to hear this later, when she listened to the recording of the session. But in this case, I heard that she did eventually leave her husband and went into a relationship with another man who – guess what? – turned out to be cold, judgemental and withholding. She repeated the pattern because nothing had changed within, and this axis remained polarised.

Audience: What happens if you are identified with the Capricorn end of this spectrum?

Clare: Then it is likely that you will be more self-contained, and may well end up playing the role of parent in relationships.

Audience: This has always bothered me, but I can see how it works now. I have Capricorn rising, but I always have men in my life who behave like a wife.

Clare: Or a mother?

Audience: Exactly. They cook for me and look after me. I don't know why this always happens, because I am not really needy. I work really hard, much harder than they do, so they end up doing things for me. I always wonder why I end up going out with these passive, 'house-husband' types who look after me. It's very easy to live with, but my problem is I am bored to death. On the one hand it is really good, but I feel stifled. I also have a lot of fire and air in my chart, so I suppose I want to break away and rebel against it.

Clare: But perhaps this is saying that, instead of feeling stifled by the man who is there in your home, who looks after you and runs about and cooks for you, that you have projected – by delegating onto your partner – your need to be cared for and protected and fed, rather than doing this for yourself.

Audience: I know I have that side, but it is due to a lack of time that I delegate that to him.

Clare: And so he does it for you. With Capricorn rising, you are adult, responsible and self sufficient, so naturally you attract all those Cancerian qualities in partners, and so the relationship axis polarises, with one of you doing the caring and looking after the domestic side of things, and the other doing the career and the work and bringing home the bacon.

Audience: The problem is that, because I don't like this situation, I find myself living a double life. That is my great dilemma – that I end up having a secret life on the side.

Clare: So we can see clearly how the Cancer-Capricorn story is working out, but of course every chart has more than one story, and there is obviously something else here as well.

Audience: I don't look for it.

Clare: You may not be consciously looking, but no doubt you are unconsciously looking.

Audience: I keep on searching for partners who are Capricorns or Aquarians, but when they are with me, they seem to transform almost immediately into Cancerians.

Clare: In your case it seems that you have embodied the qualities of

Saturn and the Capricorn Ascendant so successfully that it is difficult to recognise your neediness and dependency, which is why you meet it 'out there' in your partners. This is really the opposite situation to the client I was talking about, who was just feeling desperately lonely and needy.

Leo/Aquarius axis

Rulers: Sun and Saturn (Uranus)
Natural houses: 5th/11th

Ruled by the Sun and Saturn, the Leo/Aquarius axis is another aspect of the parent-child relationship, although this time it is a positive, fire-air axis. The Sun-ruled Leo pole describes our unique creativity and individual potential, and the Saturn-ruled Aquarius pole describes the collective rules and laws to which we are all subject. Uranus, the transpersonal ruler of Aquarius, also has its part to play on this axis, and often operates as a refusal to obey any rules other than its own or to function as part of a group. The Uranian urge is to challenge and disrupt the status quo. It is led from the head rather than the heart although, ultimately, there is nothing more powerful or effective than the harnessing of 'hearts *and* minds'.

The Leo/Aquarius axis describes the relationship between the individual and the group, between what is right for me, as an individual, and what is right for everyone else. These two things are not so easy to integrate, because we find ourselves once again entrenched on a fixed axis, in which neither pole is prepared to adapt, adjust or negotiate. It is all too human to behave as if the rules that govern society do not apply to us personally. On the other hand, if we are particularly law-abiding citizens, then we will no doubt find ourselves repeatedly outraged by the selfish, thoughtless behaviour of those who refuse to become responsible members of society or conform to its rules. Nevertheless, the heart and the head do co-exist, since most of us have the conviction, or the proof, that amongst all the millions of people in the world, there will be one unique and special person who is absolutely perfect for me.

Arthur Hacker, 'The Temptation of Sir Percival' (1894)

The famous Grail legend of the Fisher King can also help us understand the Leo/Aquarius polarity. The story begins at the point where the Aquarius pole has become cut off from the Leo pole. The King is wounded, the land is barren, and the entire kingdom has become frozen and paralysed. And along comes Percival, who plays the Leo role: an innocent soul with a pure heart, who has never learned the rules. Eventually, after many adventures and mishaps, Percival manages to free the king of his suffering and the land of its desolation. He learns that the Fisher King is his grandfather, which makes him the rightful heir to the throne of the Grail King. Ultimately, the collective is dependent on the individual, and the individual is dependent on the collective. The question here is: Where does the individual stand in relation to society, and where does society stand in relation to the individual?

Audience: How does this axis work in one-to-one relationships?

Clare: Well, once again, it is very common for this axis to polarise in relationships. In this case, one partner may well play the role of the special child, creative, warm, and full of potential and spontaneous heart energy. So the individual with the Sun or several planets in Leo or in the 5th house, or with this axis on the Ascendant/Descendant, will tend to be strongly attracted to the cool intellectual detachment or social respectability and status of someone who is living out the Aquarius pole. On the other hand, the individual who has strong Aquarian themes in their chart, who is concerned with intellectual respectability and with being an accepted member of society, is often attracted to – and repelled by – the creativity and childish enthusiasm and capacity for joy of someone who is living out the Leo pole.

Virgo/Pisces axis

Rulers: Mercury and Jupiter (Neptune)
Natural houses: 6th/12th

The Virgo-Pisces Axis is ruled by Mercury and Jupiter in their earth and water manifestations, and is naturally associated with the 6th and 12th houses. The themes on this axis are order and chaos, control and trust, form and content, the practical and imaginal worlds, realities and dreams, service and devotion. I often equate this axis to the Grail legend, with the Pisces question being, 'Whom does the Grail serve?' and the Virgo answer being, 'He who serves the Grail".

If this spectrum polarises on the Virgo side, then there will be a strong need for control over the daily routines of life, in an effort to keep chaos at bay. And yet, if the qualities of Pisces are not integrated, they will emerge from the unconscious and the Virgo individual will feel increasingly overwhelmed, and will tend to attract more and more disruption into their lives and feel more and more out of control. Virgo is analytical, self-critical and perfectionist, brilliant at spotting errors and at focusing on the details but prone to missing the whole picture, which belongs to Pisces. If we identify only with the Virgo end of the axis, then we may become consumed by duty and drudgery, and we will long to escape. But until we can see the whole picture, we will always feel that anything we try to achieve is spoiled or imperfect in the making. On the Pisces side of this axis, we prefer to remain merged, undifferentiated and unformed in order to avoid having to grapple with the details and practicalities of life. In this case we are likely to find ourselves forced to engage with the world in practical ways, something we may bitterly resent.

One approach to this axis which I have found helpful is to remember the mantra: 'Trust in Allah but tie up your camel'. Both are necessary. This axis describes the way we attend to the daily necessities of life, not just for their own sake, or to earn a crust, but in the service of something which we find meaningful.

Audience: So are you saying that if we have the Sun in Virgo, then there is always a Piscean aspect to that, which needs to be explored and made conscious?

Clare: Yes, and if we are working in this way as astrologers, when we encounter a person with the Sun in Virgo, we will automatically start placing them on the Virgo-Pisces axis. Our job will be to find out where on that axis they are identified, and hopefully it will not have become too polarised, because that is very hard to work with. For example, if someone has polarised on the Pisces end of the axis, or in the 12th house to the exclusion of 6th house matters, then it may be very hard to reach them, because they will be so diffuse. It can be like trying to grasp a piece of soap. The danger is that the astrologer who doesn't spot what is happening can easily fall into acting out the unconsciously projected Virgo end of the axis, and find themselves taking a particularly analytical, problem-solving or critical viewpoint, or alternatively, start overemphasising the importance of work, diet and routine, all of which are likely to be meaningless to the client.

Divine drudgery: Diego Rodriguez de Silva y Velázquez,
'Christ in the House of Mary and Martha' (1620)

Equally, if someone is polarised on the Virgo end of the axis, or in the 6th house to the exclusion of the Pisces or 12th house end, then we can find that we have been 'Pisced'. We may become confused and muddled and lost, unable to communicate satisfactorily to our client. This will be equally meaningless to our Virgo-identified client. Our only hope is to place ourselves firmly at the centre of the axis, which gives us a chance to navigate the whole spectrum.

Audience: So how do you know where someone is on the spectrum – can you see this from the birth chart?

Clare: Not always, although as a general rule we normally identify with the planets and signs in the 1st and 2nd houses and project the 7th and 8th houses onto others because it is notoriously difficult to see that the qualities of the 7th and 8th houses belong to us. And because it takes a lifetime to develop the full potential of our Sun-signs, then it is not unusual to encounter people with the Sun in Virgo who are chaotic and diffuse, prone to giving themselves away, taking on too much and becoming overwhelmed. There seems to be a gradual process of increasingly refining and defining their personal boundaries. And this is also true of people with the Sun in Pisces, who often present as Virgos, being very dutiful and efficient, practical and down-to-earth.

Audience: I have met that a lot. Perhaps they are just embarrassed to be Pisceans, especially if they are teachers or parents. It doesn't seem to be very acceptable to be a Pisces if you have to work hard and hold it all together.

The angles in the birth chart

The angles in a birth chart are of great importance, since it is through the angles that we meet and relate to and connect with the outside world. The angles function as doorways into the world – they provide us with our basic physical and spatial orientation and pin us down into our incarnation. They are like our personal cross of matter or tree of life, with the Ascendant/Descendant axis reaching out horizontally to connect with the world around us, and the vertical MC/IC axis providing our central stability, our root system from which we draw the strength to grow tall in the world.

Using the natural zodiac, you can see that the parental axis is vertical and hierarchical. The natural signs on this axis are Capricorn and Cancer, and the planetary rulers are Saturn and the Moon, symbolising parent and child. The natural elements are earth and water, indicating that this axis concerns our basic need for safety, support and containment. The MC/IC axis also describes our biological origins, the relationship between our parents, and therefore our primal experience of the masculine and feminine. This remains a powerful influence for our entire lives, and one that is repeated in our adult relationships to the extent that our relationships are driven by a need for security, safety and a sense of belonging, or by the need to resolve parental issues or childhood insecurities and fears. We all have valid dependency needs, because we have all been children and we all have, or become, parents.

The Cross of Matter (natural zodiac)

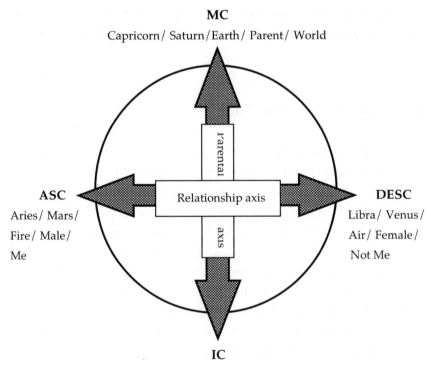

MC

Capricorn/ Saturn/Earth/ Parent/ World

ASC

Aries/ Mars/
Fire/ Male/
Me

Relationship axis

Parental axis

DESC

Libra/ Venus/
Air/ Female/
Not Me

IC

Cancer/ Moon/ Water/ Child/ Roots and Origins

The horizontal relationship axis, on the other hand, represents our potential for equal, adult-to-adult relationships. The natural signs on this axis are Aries and Libra, and the planetary rulers are Mars and Venus, the adult manifestations of the masculine and feminine principles. The natural elements are fire and air, signifying the desire for self-expression and communication in relationships. There is, of course, an inherent tension between these two sets of opposites, between the parental axis, which is yin in character, and the relationship axis, which is yang in character. Jung wrote: 'In the square the elements are separate and hostile to one another and must therefore be united in the circle.'[10] In the birth chart, the opposites are already potentially united in the circle, and our task is to bring these axes into a conscious, creative and dynamic relationship with each other.

> Four is the minimal number by which order can be created and represents the pluralistic state of the man who has not yet attained inner unity, hence the state of bondage and disunion, of disintegration, and of being torn in different directions – an agonizing, unredeemed state which longs for union, reconciliation, redemption, healing and wholeness.[11]

Ascendant/Descendant axis

The horizontal axis describes the drama of adult relationships between two people who are potentially equals. No matter which pair of opposite signs are found on the Ascendant/Descendant axis, this is the battleground on which we build a sense of ourselves as individuals, not in isolation, but through our relationship to our partners and significant others.

---

[10]Jung, C. G., 'The Psychology of the Transference', *in The Practice of Psychotherapy*, CW16, trans. R. F. C. Hull (London: Routledge & Kegan Paul, 1954) [hereafter Jung, CW16], p. 42.
[11] Jung, CW16, p. 46.

Audience: What if your ruling planet is in the 7th house?

Clare: Well, that would mean that you will find yourself, your identity, through your relationship with others. This also means that the whole area of relationships is going to be a major theme in your life. For example, both Freud and Jung had their Sun in the 7th house, and both worked extensively throughout their lives with their clients in significant and committed one-to-one relationships, out of which each developed his own particular ideas and schools of psychological thought.

If the Ascendant describes our personal interface with the world around us, the Descendant, which lies directly opposite the Ascendant and marks the western horizon, describes how we meet 'the other'. The Descendant describes the quality of our one-to-one relationships, and it is here that we are challenged to engage in the balancing act of compromise and adjustment. The 7th house almost always describes what we *project*, and all relationships inevitably catalyse some form of projection, which can be both positive and negative.

Audience: Does that mean that both Freud and Jung met themselves through all their clients and patients?

Clare: Yes, that's a good point and certainly true. Freud's Ascendant/Descendant axis was Scorpio/Taurus, with his Sun in Taurus in the 7th house. Jung's axis was Aquarius/Leo, with his Sun in Leo in the 7th house. It is no accident, therefore, that, broadly speaking, Freud's work centred around sexuality and the buried emotions which can have such a powerful effect on the body, and Jung's work centred around the discovery of the Self, and the relationship of the individual to the collective.

In fact, we can never tell from the chart itself exactly where, on any particular spectrum, an individual will be identified. It is equally possible that we may identify with the Descendant, particularly in our childhoods, when our personal survival (Ascendant) is literally dependent on others (Descendant). So we tend to develop an early and heightened sensitivity to the reactions and attitudes of others towards us. Our sense of identity is often derived from the way we are 'mirrored' by others, an empirical discovery which led to the development of the field of 'object relations' in psychology. What this means astrologically is that we often perceive ourselves, not through our own lens (the Ascendant), but through the mirroring we receive from others (the Descendant).

Take the example of a child with Aries rising, born into an environment where good behaviour, good manners and consideration for others are given the highest priority. This child will receive positive reinforcement for being 'good', 'considerate' and 'accomplished', and negative reinforcement for being 'selfish' or 'self-willed'. It can take many years for that individual to develop the courage to develop their Aries Ascendant, even though it is strongly imprinted from the moment of birth. It is therefore important not to assume that the Ascendant is fully developed and fully functioning. In fact, I think it is normal to identify more readily with the Descendant complex in our youth. Perhaps this is why our adult relationships are so valuable and necessary in helping us to find ourselves, since they activate this axis. Conversely, people with a Libra Ascendant are natural arbitrators and mediators, concerned with avoiding confrontation or disputes. This approach can be the result of having been born into an environment which was at war, or in which the parents were in deep conflict. The Libra rising individual often has a real fear of discord, anger or violence, since in their childhoods this would have been experienced as deeply threatening to their survival.

The price which has to be paid for identifying with the Libra end of the axis is that Mars will be projected, which means that the individual's sense of personal potency, agency and focus is also projected onto partners. This can become an uncomfortable double bind, if they are dependent on their partners for energy, decision-making and direction.

Audience: Sorry, Clare, but you are referring to the Descendant as the parental relationship. Surely the parental relationship is described by the 4th/10th house axis? How can the 7th house describe the parents?

Clare: It is true that the 4th and 10th houses describe the parental relationship, but it is also true that the Ascendant/Descendant axis describes the way we locate ourselves, as children, in relation to the parental relationship. This is the classic Oedipal triangle, with the child on one side and the parents on the other, and the role we played in this triangular relationship will inevitably affect our adult relationships.

Audience: But we are also talking about the Aries/Libra axis in general, aren't we?

Clare: That's right. We all have the Aries/Libra axis somewhere in our charts, so these themes are archetypal, although they will find personal expression in the houses across which these signs fall. Would anyone like to have a look at their own Ascendant/Descendant axis?

Jane: Can we have a look at my Ascendant/Descendant axis, which is Leo-Aquarius, although I don't know whether I have any planets in either the 1st or 7th houses?

Clare: Let's start by considering the general nature of the Leo/Aquarius axis, which we know is going to be constellated in your relationships. This is the axis of identity, of 'finding ourselves in the crowd', of discovering how we can make our own unique contribution to the group or collective to which we belong. And your relationships will no doubt provide you with the kinds of circumstances and experiences that enable you to define and understand yourself more clearly in this context.

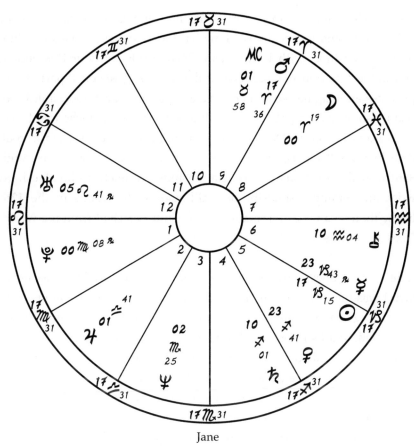

Jane

Chart data omitted for reasons of confidentiality

Let's have a look first of all at the Aquarius Descendant to see how you are likely to have been 'mirrored' by others at an early age. Aquarius is a cool, detached, intellectual sign concerned with conforming to, or rebelling against, the expectations of parents, authority figures in general, and social rules and norms. I would therefore imagine that you were particularly sensitive to the expectations of others from a very young age, and adapted and adjusted your behaviour accordingly in order to gain their acceptance and approval. The personal ruler of the Descendant is Saturn in the 4th house, which indicates early responsibility and a desire to gain your father's love and respect by working hard and being sensible and adult. At the same time, with Uranus as collective ruler of your Descendant and in the 12th house, it seems as if the rebel or 'free spirit' part of you provides an imaginative and creative escape from the responsibilities of relationships, as if a part of you will always remain detached and free. With Aquarius on the Descendant, you are likely to be attracted to cool, detached, intellectuals, or people who are unusual in some way. With Saturn in the 4th house, your relationships are likely to involve hard work and family responsibilities, although with Uranus in the 12th house there is a need to remain separate and detached from the world. Does any of this ring true?

Jane: Yes it does, particularly the Saturn ruler of my Descendant. In fact, I was literally rejected and had to live with my grandparents from an early age because my parents couldn't cope. So I felt very alone in my childhood, and I suspect that I did have to adapt and adjust to the rules and learn to stand on my own feet at an early age. But I can also relate to the Uranus ruler, because there is a part of me that refuses to conform or obey the rules, so I had many fantasies of escape and freedom, and in fact I still do! And my husband was exactly as you describe – cool, detached and intellectual, leaving me to look after all the practicalities, but at the same time he did not support me at all.

Audience: And although Jane has a Leo Ascendant, the Sun, which is her chart ruler, is in Capricorn, which is a similar kind of Saturn story, isn't it?

Clare: That's exactly right, so a strong Sun-Saturn, fire-earth theme is already emerging from this relationship axis. The personal ruler of the Descendant is Saturn in the fire sign of Sagittarius, and the ruler of the Ascendant in fire is the Sun – but it is in the Saturn-ruled earth sign of Capricorn. With Leo rising and the Sun in Capricorn, I suspect that your marriage has been the catalyst that has taught you to value and stand up for yourself in order to gain the recognition your Leo Ascendant needs, and to develop the self-sufficiency and personal authority of the Capricorn Sun.

Jane: That's right, although it has been a long and difficult journey. But I have grown up a great deal as a result of my marriage. I am sure that the 12th house Uranus was also an important factor, because it helped me to eventually separate from my husband when I felt just too trapped. And now I am developing my own writing, which I could never have done before, so my Sun-Mercury conjunction in Capricorn has come to life, and it feels really good.

Audience: How does this work if you have Virgo and Pisces on the Ascendant/Descendant axis?

Clare: With Virgo on the Ascendant, we are usually extremely self-critical, expecting nothing less than perfection from ourselves. So much attention goes into the details of the world, and into getting it right, that our partners can get away with murder. Virgo Ascendant people will have an immense attraction to and admiration of Piscean types, those who are fluid, artistic and inspired in some way, or alternatively, those who are vulnerable or sick, because then they can use all their practical talents and capabilities to care for their partner.

Audience: What about someone born with Pisces on the Ascendant and Virgo on the Descendant? Are they likely to attract Virgoans?

Clare: Yes, Virgo-*type* people. That could be someone who has their Sun in Virgo or Gemini, or someone who is Mercury-ruled or with a strongly tenanted 3rd or 6th house. With Pisces on the Ascendant, we tend to instinctively absorb and merge with our surroundings. This is a very chameleon-like Ascendant, and people with Pisces rising are normally so well camouflaged that they tend to attract partners who take on the role analysing and defining and structuring all this fluidity. This can easily feel like criticism, if you have Virgo on the Descendant, but it is of course one's own projected ability to develop the analytical skills which give shape to, and complement, the Piscean sensitivity and imagination.

Audience: So presumably you will also be aware of the Virgo side of the axis as well?

Clare: It is usually the case that, with Pisces rising, we are born into an environment where practical skills and an orderly, precise and businesslike approach to the world were highly valued. For many years we may try to define ourselves according to the way we have been mirrored. But as we mature and enter into adult partnerships, we will want to let ourselves off the hook and allow ourselves to merge and float, leaving the precision, order and control to our partner. I think that our Ascendant/Descendant axis often works like this – we are subconsciously looking for someone else to inhabit the Descendant for us, so that we can develop the qualities of our Ascendant.

Audience: But Clare, if you have Pisces rising, would you not be subconsciously critical of others, but just not recognise that you are?

Clare: Although we tend to assume that the qualities of the sign on the Descendant will be projected, it is not always immediately obvious 'who is doing what to whom'. However, if we think of the opposites signs on this relationship axis as belonging to one complete spectrum, then we can immediately understand the general quality and the nature of the themes which will emerge in our relationships. We know that the Virgo/Pisces axis will involve themes of merging and separating, accepting and judging, order and chaos, control and trust, sickness and health, and with this axis on the Ascendant/Descendant, we are going to end up doing a Virgo/Pisces dance with our partner.

Incidentally, our discussion seems to have turned into a Virgo/Pisces dance as we speak. I sense from your questions that you are trying to get precision, to analyse this axis so that it can be clearly understood, but remember that we are also talking about Pisces here, so we will also have to allow it to remain mysterious to some extent, and beyond our analytical grasp.

MC/IC axis

As we have already seen, the 4th and 10th houses are the parental houses, with the 4th house describing the family background and the environment within which we grew up, and the 10th house describing our family's social status and relationship to the world. These houses also describe our perception of the parental relationship itself, and it is likely that, to some extent, the roles played by our parents were or are interchangeable. Biologically, of course, we are the product of the union between our parents, so the 4th and 10th houses reflect the tension and the creativity of the meeting of opposites which resulted in our conception. The conflicting demands of our private life and public life, our home and our work, our inner and outer worlds, create the kind of tension and stress that I suspect we have all felt from time to time.

No matter which house system we are using, it is worth pointing out that the meaning of the MC/IC axis is not identical to the meaning of the 4th and 10th houses, which describe the qualities and attitudes of our parents and what we learned on our mother's or father's knee. At the end of the day, the MC/IC meridian is a uniquely personal axis. It is our vertical axis, our central pillar, describing in the deepest sense where we are coming from and where we are going. And although this may very well be an extension of our parents' goals, ambitions and achievements, eventually our task appears to be to extract ourselves from the parental matrix, put down our own roots, and find our own place in the world.

The MC describes our true vocation or 'calling', that 'something' we need to achieve in the world in order to fulfil our unique potential. Unlike the 10th house, it is driven from within, rather than from without. And the IC describes the roots of our being, which support and sustain and nourish us on an inner level, and which are the source of our potency and power in the world. As the midnight point in the birth chart, it is the point where the Sun dies and is reborn, and in traditional astrology it signifies 'the end of the matter', which also makes way for new beginnings. The vertical axis of the MC/IC can be compared to the chakra system, our central pillar, with the IC functioning as the base chakra. As with all axes, the MC and IC depend upon each other, because our capacity to grow upwards will always depend on the strength of our roots.

In the Equal House system, the MC/IC axis will normally be found in the 10th and 4th houses, in which case our own direction in life may well be an extension of that of our family and parents. But if it falls outside the 10th and 4th houses, then our direction in life may be very different from that of our parents. If, for example, the MC/IC axis falls across the 9th/3rd houses, then our vocation may involve education, teaching, law, philosophy, travel, or any of the themes associated with these two houses. We might be the one person in the family, for example, who has gone to university, or who lives in another country or culture, or who adopts a different religion or philosophy from the rest of the family. With the MC-IC axis across the 8th/2nd houses, we are unlikely to feel particularly comfortable with the traditions and values of the culture we grew up in. We will want to plunge deep into the buried issues which that culture or society is not looking at and, with the IC in the 2nd house, to live according to our own inner values, which will be described by the sign on the 2nd house cusp, the planetary ruler of the 2nd house, and any planets in the 2nd house. If the MC/IC axis is in the 11th and 5th houses, then we are likely to have a more political, socially conscious or creative vocation and path in life than that of our parents and family. No doubt we will find ourselves kicking against the old traditions, assumptions, and perceived complacency of the 10th/4th house culture into which we were born, and seek to make our own unique contribution (IC in the 5th house) to the development of political or social awareness (MC in the 11th house).

The curious thing about the MC/IC axis is that it seems to describe talents, goals and potentials which our parents have denied or suppressed; what they would have liked to have been or done if they had only had the opportunity. And so this axis can put us directly in touch with particular gifts and challenges we have inherited from our parents but which have not been lived out by them. There is a poem by Rainer Maria Rilke called *Separate Lives*, which expresses this beautifully:

> Sometimes a man stands up during supper
> and walks outdoors, and keeps on walking,
> because of a church that stands somewhere in the East.
> And his children say blessings on him as if he were dead.
>
> And another man, who remains inside his own house,
> dies there, inside the dishes and in the glasses,
> so that his children have to go far out into the world
> toward that same church, which he forgot.

There is always a powerful ancestral 'charge' around this axis, and it is on this axis that we seem to inherit the as yet unfulfilled, incomplete, still to be manifested or resolved, destiny and calling of our family line. In this sense the MC/IC axis connects us to the archetypal parents which always stand behind or beyond our ordinary human, mortal parents. The parental archetypes, the male and female principles, are symbolised in astrology by the Sun and Moon, which leads us back to questions about the spirit and soul. It would be symbolically valid to suppose that the spirit and soul might be made manifest through the MC/IC axis.

Diagram of the seven chakras in the human body,
from Titus Burckhardt, *Alchemy*[12]

For example, if we relate the MC/IC axis to the ancient system of chakras, there is a correlation between the MC, spirit, and the crown chakra, which relates to consciousness as pure awareness. When fully developed, this chakra brings us knowledge, wisdom, understanding, spiritual connection and bliss. 'It is our place of mergence with God, the Oneness, the All.'[13] By the same token, there is a correlation between the IC, soul, and the base chakra, which, in the body, is located at the base of our spine. As such, it is related to our survival instincts, to our sense of grounding and connection to our bodies, our ability to be present in the here and now. It also relates to our ability to draw nourishment and strength from within, through our physical bodies, and describes how we feel about being incarnate, about being on the earth. Tension here often points to a fundamental sense of insecurity, fear, or threat to our

[12] Diagram of the Seven Chakras in Burckhardt, Titus, *Alchemy* (1986), tr. William Stoddart (London: Element Books Ltd., 1986).
[13] Bruyere, Rosalyn L., *Wheels of Light: A Study of the Chakras*, Volume 1 (Sierra Madre, CA: Bon Productions, 1989), p. 44.

survival.

Audience: But it is difficult to think of the MC/IC axis as our central pillar because in charts it is always veering around, changing its relationship to the Ascendant/Descendant all the time.

Clare: That is certainly how it seems, and this is simply because, in modern birth charts, it is the convention to keep the Ascendant/Descendant axis horizontal. However, from a geographical point of view, it is the north-south meridian, the MC/IC axis which stays the same, while the Ascendant/Descendant axis veers around this meridian, with the Ascendant being anywhere from south-east right through to north-east, as we stand in the centre of our charts looking south.

Audience: But what if you have nothing on the IC? Does that mean you have no root system or that you have to wait for a transit to get that going?

Clare: We all have important stories around the IC, whether or not there is a planet there. The IC will be in a sign, and that sign will have its planetary ruler or rulers, which will be in certain signs and houses and make certain aspects, so that is where we would look for the IC story. Let's have a look at some planets on the MC/IC axis.

Tom: I have two planets on the IC: Saturn and Uranus. Can we have a look at one of those?

Clare: Yes, let's have a look at them both and see how they function. This is a good example, because your MC/IC axis is in Sagittarius/Gemini and falls in your 11th and 5th houses. This indicates that your own personal vocation in life has been very different from that of your parents and from the themes described by the 10th/4th houses.

No doubt your personal journey has led you to discover your own ideas and your own particular talents and capabilities (IC in the 5th house), and to develop and explore them across a wide spectrum of society, or even of the world (MC in Sagittarius in the 11th house). I would imagine that your life has been lived on a much larger scale, and with more political or social involvement than your parents.

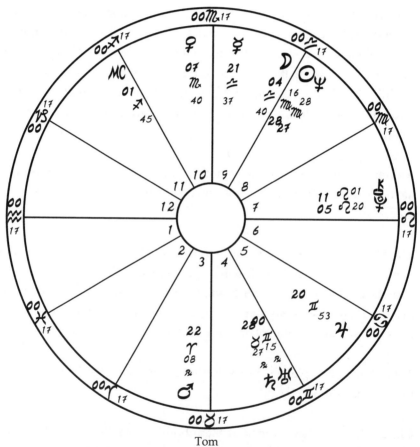

Tom

Chart data omitted for reasons of confidentiality

Tom: That's right and very interesting. Can you say some more about this?

Clare: Let's have a look at the parental background first, to try to understand something about your family background and the role of your parents in your life. Your 10th/4th houses are ruled by the fixed signs of Scorpio and Taurus, the axis of exchange. Taurus on the 4th house cusp indicates stability in the family, and Venus, which rules your 4th house, is in Scorpio in the 10th house, which indicates that your father may have had a powerful role in the world – perhaps dealing with other people's money or resources. Scorpio on the 10th house cusp, ruled by Mars and Pluto, indicates that you saw your mother as a powerful, determined, ambitious and opinionated woman, since the Mars ruler is in Aries in the 3rd house, and the Pluto ruler is conjunct your Descendant in the 7th house. Perhaps you experienced her as rather controlling and invasive?

Tom: Yes, that is certainly true. I do come from a large landowning family who have been farmers for generations, although my father was a merchant banker in the City. He was certainly a very powerful man, and he was determined that I would also become a banker and follow in his footsteps. My mother was an intelligent woman who ruled the roost at home, devoting all her energies to her family and children. Had she been born in another era I suspect she would have been a successful career woman.

Clare: From the point of view of your MC/IC axis, I imagine that you may have found your family background and your parents' expectations rather oppressive. The Gemini/Sagittarius axis is one of space, expansion and exploration, and with Saturn and Uranus conjunct your IC, it looks at if, in order to forge your own way in the world, you have had to sever your family connections and learn to stand on your own feet. This cannot have been easy, with Saturn on your IC, but no doubt you have felt compelled to break away from family ties.

Tom: I think this all started when I was sent to a Jesuit boarding school at a young age. That was a huge shock to me at the time, but it also opened up my mind, and I will always be grateful for the education I received. I learned to think and to question and to challenge ideas, and that has stood me in good stead throughout my life. And I did cut off entirely from my family for a while, because I refused to go into banking and there was a huge row. In fact, my father did literally 'cut me off' and out of my inheritance.

Clare: This is a very graphic description of Saturn in Taurus and Uranus in Gemini on the IC. Saturn in Taurus in the 4th house describes your duty to your family, the importance of tradition and the heavy sense of responsibility imposed upon you by your father as well as the denial of your inheritance. But Uranus in Gemini is even closer to your IC, and that describes the rebel and the free thinker, and the fact that you had your own ideas. I think we can see why you had to break free and follow your own path, which is very flexible and expansive and autonomous. It is particularly interesting that both Saturn and Uranus are your chart rulers, since you have Aquarius rising, so no doubt this has been a major theme in your life.

Tom: And as it happens, I went into marketing, and ended up being the managing director of a multinational company. I have been travelling extensively my entire career, negotiating and dealing with people from all over the world until recently, when I was suddenly and unexpectedly asked to take early retirement. But at least it has given me the time to study astrology.

Clare: Well, that is a perfect description of your Sagittarius MC, with its ruler in Gemini in the 5th house. It is also another example of being suddenly cut off at your roots and from your income. But Uranus is often associated with astrology, so perhaps this is also about finding your vocation in life, or a way of making sense of it all. But the MC/IC axis can also indicate where we have inherited the unlived lives of our parents, or particular gifts and talents from our ancestors, so I am wondering whether your father may have been a free spirit himself, who was unable to escape his family responsibilities and duties, and whether your mother, who was such a powerful force in your life, was unable to fulfil her intellectual or educational potential. If so, then on a deeper level, by breaking away from the expected family pattern, you may even have been fulfilling and living out the unlived lives of your parents.

Tom: Well, certainly it is true that my father was obliged to follow in his father's footsteps, and my mother met and married my father when she was very young, and at that time married women did not pursue their own careers. This has given me a great deal of food for thought.

Clare: That is a wonderful example, Tom. Thank you.

Lesson Five: The Nodes of the Moon

There is more to human life than our theories of it allow. Sooner or later something seems to call us onto a particular path.[14]

Looking back over the course of one's own days and noticing how encounters and events that appeared at the time to be accidental became the crucial structuring features of an unintended life story through which the potentialities of one's character were fostered to fulfilment, one may find it difficult to resist the notion of the course of one's biography as comparable to that of a cleverly constructed novel, wondering who the author of the surprising plot can have been.[15]

While we are on the whole subject of axes, I want to spend time this week exploring the Moon's nodal axis, which is the third axis of particular significance (in addition to the angles – the Ascendant/Descendant and MC/IC axes) in our charts. We need to begin, as always, by understanding what the Moon's Nodes actually are from an astronomical viewpoint, since this provides the basis and foundation of our astrological understanding and interpretation. Have a look at your birth charts, and you will no doubt see the north Node symbol.

   ☊   **North Node**   ☋   **South Node**

But the symbol for the south Node is not always shown on horoscope print outs, which explains why this important axis may not be immediately obvious. As with all axes, the south Node is exactly 180°

---

[14] Hillman, James, *The Soul's Code: In Search of Character and Calling* (London: Bantam Books, 1996), p. 3.

[15] Campbell, Joseph, *The Inner Reaches of Outer Space: Metaphor as Myth and as Religion* (Novato, CA: New World Library, 1986).

from, or opposite, the north Node.

You can see from this diagram that the plane of the Moon's orbit is at an oblique angle of approximately 5° to the plane of the Sun's orbit (the ecliptic). The nodal points mark the position where these two planes cross, and every month the Moon crosses the ecliptic twice, once travelling north (at the north Node) and once travelling south (at the south Node).

THE NODAL AXIS

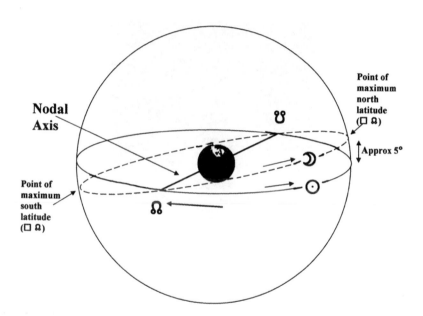

When the Moon crosses the ecliptic, then, from the point of view of the earth, the Sun and Moon are in alignment. This means that, when a new or full Moon coincides, or nearly coincides, with one of the Nodes, then there will be an eclipse, and, of course, eclipses are powerful celestial events which have always had immense significance throughout the history of astronomy and astrology.

The Nodes have been known from ancient times as the head and tail of the celestial dragon – a monstrous creature that devours the

Sun or the Moon at eclipses. The Nodes have played a particularly important role in Indian, Vedic astrology, where the north Node ('Rahu') is the dragon's head and the south Node ('Ketu') is the dragon's tail. I am sure you can understand why both Nodes were considered to be dangerous, or malefic. We will look at eclipses in much more detail next term, but perhaps the main point I want to make now is that, when they do occur, we look upwards, away from the earth and all our day-to-day concerns, and stand in awe as we watch these great events take place.

The 'Serpent in the Sky'[16]

Audience: They sound like rather scarey points.

Clare: That's right, particularly since they have always been associated with fate and with fated events, in both Vedic and Western astrology. Traditionally, eclipses are associated with tragedies, catastrophes and deaths, particularly the death of kings. As psychological astrologers, I think we still have to find another way to understand them.

Now that we have identified where everyone's nodal axis

---

[16] Image reproduced from West, John Anthony, *Serpent in the Sky: The High Wisdom of Ancient Egypt* (New York, NY: Julian Press/Crown Publishing Group, 1987), p. 70.

actually is, the next question is how we interpret it – and this is actually rather more complicated to answer.

Audience: Do you interpret the Node like the Moon?

Clare: Well, the Nodes are in fact empty places in space, except during eclipses, so we have to resist the temptation to interpret them as if they were 'simply' planets. They seem to have a profoundly metaphysical meaning, since it is on these points that the Sun, Moon and Earth are in alignment, so they are the meeting place, symbolically, of spirit, soul and matter, both collectively and individually. Another important point about the nodal axis is that it is moving in the opposite direction to the Sun and all the other planets. As the angles and all the planets move forward or *anti-clockwise* around our charts, they describe how we engage with and relate to the world around us. The Ascendant/Descendant axis and the MC/IC axis are doors into the world, describing our struggle to extract ourselves from the parental matrix, to put down our own roots and find our own place in the world, and to define ourselves through partnerships. In contrast, the nodal axis moves backward or *clockwise* around our charts. It is not so tied up with the dramas of life. Rather, it seems to function as a doorway into other dimensions, where we can sometimes glimpse or sense our soul's purpose and pattern, our *entelechy*, the deeper purpose and function of our existence. And this can be very different from the more conscious or worldly goals we set for ourselves.

There is no doubt that the nodal axis is of immense significance in our lives. It is an axis of tension and compulsion, around which ideas of 'fate' and 'destiny' always seem to hover. As Richard Idemon writes: 'It's as if life constantly returns you to this axis to work something out'.[17] What do those of you who are already familiar with the Nodes think of

---

[17] Idemon, Richard, *The Magic Thread: Astrological Chart Interpretation Using Depth Psychology* (York Beach, ME: Samuel Weiser, Inc., 1996) [hereafter Idemon, *The Magic Thread*], p. 105.

when you see them in a birth chart?

Audience: Lessons to be learned.

Audience: Past and present. They are about time, with the south Node having to do with the past, and the north Node having to do with the future.

Audience: The north Node is what we are striving to become.

Audience: Is it something to do with reincarnation?

Audience: It's about special people coming into your life.

Clare: Just for a moment, take the nodal axis out of your chart. What does it feel like?

Audience: Directionless.

Audience: We lose our soul.

Clare: That's very interesting. So without the nodal axis, we lose our direction and we lose our soul. Let's have a look at some of the other ideas you have mentioned. Although both the Nodes were originally considered to be malefic, at some point in the development of Western astrology their interpretation began to polarise. In traditional horary astrology, for example, a planet conjunct the north Node is said to be helped, strengthened or increased. Conversely, a planet conjunct the south Node is said to be harmed, weakened or decreased. In addition, the north Node began to be interpreted as the 'evolutionary path', the direction in which we are 'meant' to be going in our lives, and the south Node started to be interpreted as the 'regressive path', the direction from which we have come, or our past.

In Western astrology, it seems that Alan Leo is responsible for making the specific connection between the nodal axis and karma. The Theosophical movement, out of which astrology was reborn at the end of the 19th and beginning of the 20th centuries, was strongly influenced by Indian culture and religions. As an astrologer, Alan Leo did much to breathe new life into Western astrology, and as a Theosophist he was convinced that the natal chart could only be properly understood in the context of karma, past lives and reincarnation. It is important to recognise straightaway that the horoscope itself has nothing to say on this subject. A horoscope is just a horoscope. The meaning we impose on it depends upon our specific cultural and historical background, as well as upon the individual philosophies and world-views of astrologers themselves.

And so we have inherited an interesting conundrum, because Western astrology has developed enormously since Alan Leo's day, and we no longer see astrology in terms of cause and effect, so it seems that our interpretation of the Nodes has become rather stuck. For example, we don't tend to look at the whole chart in terms of karma, do we? We wouldn't look at someone's Saturn-Mars conjunction and start wondering if they might have been a murderer in their past lives – we simply don't work like that any more.

Audience: I hope not, because I have a Saturn-Mars conjunction in my own chart.

Clare: Let's go back and look at the diagram again. You can see that the north Node is the point where the Moon moves 'upward' into the northern hemisphere, and the south Node is the point where the Moon moves 'downward' into the southern hemisphere. Perhaps this explains why the north Node came to be associated with the spiritual path, because our astrological symbolism tells us that spirit is fundamentally solar – associated with height, light and transcendence. Spirit is abstract, linear and vertical, calling us upward, forward and outward.

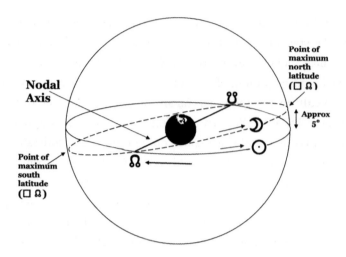

As such, the north Node has become associated with our individual heroic quest, requiring the development of our personal will, so that we may fulfil our spiritual destiny. And because of this, there is often an assumption that our south Node is regressive and tends to pull us backward and downward, away from our spiritual path. And so a good/bad split and a future/past split has crept into our interpretations, along with a kind of moral imperative. For example, it is not uncommon for astrologers, who are otherwise working very psychologically, to start using words like 'should' and 'ought' when they are interpreting the nodal axis.

Going back to the actual astronomy of the Nodes, however, we can see that they are in fact the meeting point of the Sun, Moon and earth, and that they are therefore the symbolic meeting point of the spirit, soul and body – *liminal* places where opposites come together and merge. From an alchemical perspective, the Nodes represent the *sacred marriage* of the Sun and Moon, of the masculine and feminine principles, the *mysterium coniunctionis* which is the goal of the alchemical opus. Throughout our lives there is an equal emphasis on both Nodes – they are equally active, since eclipses, whether solar or lunar, occur on both Nodes. Perhaps the best way to demonstrate this is to show you an illustration of the DNA double helix represented in complete symmetry as a pair of serpents.[18]

Naturally, because of the way our minds are wired, we are likely to find ourselves falling into our habitual either/or kind of thinking, but all the same, although we know that the Sun and Moon are opposites, it is important to try not to polarise, since we also know that opposites cause and depend upon and complete each other. Have a look at this table, which lists some of the words associated with the Sun and the Moon.

SUN	MOON
Spirit	Soul
Linear	Circular
Vertical	Horizontal
Focussed	Diffuse
Time	Space
The One	The Many
Transcendence	Immanence
Will	Destiny
Individual	Collective
Light	Dark
Mind	Body

Let's consider the lunar side of this table. The Moon is symbolically

---

[18] Wills, Christopher, 'Exons, introns and talking genes', in Narby, Jeremy, *The Cosmic Serpent: DNA and the Origins of Knowledge* (Phoenix, AR: Orion Publishing Group, 1998).

associated with the soul, being diffuse, immanent and collective. It is circular, dark, and has to do with the body and with matter. It calls us downward into our birth charts, into nature and into our incarnation. Because the Nodes are the points where the Sun and Moon come together – places where the opposites merge – both sides of the table need to be taken into equal account in our interpretations.

Audience: Yes, I can see what you are saying now. We seem to be using mainly solar words or coming from a solar perspective when we look at the Nodes.

The collective nature of the nodal axis

Clare: Marking the two points where the Sun and Moon cross each other's paths, meet, and come together, where the spirit and soul unite from the point of view of the earth, we can see that the nodal axis is equally solar and lunar – and it is therefore of both personal and collective significance. From a collective point of view, everyone born within a particular eighteen-month period will have the nodal axis across the same signs. We studied the six axes last week and, if we are working alchemically in the interests of the development of individual and collective consciousness, it appears that our task is to work with, and endeavour to integrate, the opposite poles of the particular axis we were born on. We could say that we have been born into a particular polarity – into an unresolved imbalance in the collective – and that our personal efforts to recognise the equal validity of both poles of any archetypal spectrum will make a difference to the entire human endeavour, 'for nature's continued existence depends ultimately on the kind of consciousness we bring to bear on it'.[19]

Developing the collective, lunar aspect of the nodal axis further, we know that in the Western mystery traditions within which astrology

---

[19] Baring and Cashford, p. 681.

developed, the collective aspect of the soul is known as the *anima mundi*, the 'soul of the world', a living, breathing dimension of reality which is teeming with life. I have come to think of the nodal axis as a threshold or doorway between the manifest, physical world and the soul of the world, the *anima mundi*. The 'world soul' is itself liminal, mediating between the divine and human realms, between the gods and mankind, and it is not only 'full of gods', as Proclus wrote, but, astonishingly, it also appears to be interested in us.[20] We may not be as alone as we think. The existence of this permeable, intermediary realm, and of the beings that reside there was, once upon a time, taken for granted. The more mystically inclined ancient Greek philosophers believed in the existence of a whole range of intermediaries and messengers – archons and daemons – which inhabited the liminal realms between this and other worlds and which were of both personal and impersonal significance.

Audience: This sounds a bit like the 'otherworld' in the Celtic tradition.

Clare: Yes, and in fact these intermediary or otherworlds are found in all traditions and cultures. To mention just a few, in Tibetan Buddhism they are known as the *bardos*, the place between life and death. In Australian aboriginal culture they are known as the *dream time*; in Hindu culture it is the *akasha* – a vast memory store which belongs to all of human kind and within which we can move anywhere in human history instantly. In the Western tradition, this realm is known as the *anima mundi*. The otherworlds are accessed through the imagination, in myths, stories, dreams, and in altered states of consciousness. They are particularly perceptible when we find ourselves at liminal times and places in our lives, at crossroads or on thresholds or in the moments

---

[20] Raine, Kathleen and George Harper (eds), *Thomas Taylor the Platonist: Selected Writings*, quoted in Harpur, Patrick, *Daimonic Reality, A Field Guide to the Otherworld* (Enumclaw, WA: Pine Winds Press, 1992) [hereafter Harpur, *Daimonic Reality*], p. 49.

between sleeping and waking. If you are familiar with rebirthing, regression therapy, or shamanic practices, then no doubt you are already familiar with these realms, in which neither time nor space conform to our normal expectations. The past, present and future exist simultaneously, always and everywhere, *behind* and *beneath* the surface of our everyday perception. This is unknown and yet strangely familiar territory. When we visit the otherworlds, we have access to a vast store of experience which is both personal and collective, which is both individual and belongs to all of humanity. In this sense, we could see the Nodes as the meeting place of temporal or time-based dimensions with the spatial dimensions where all of human experience is occurring all the time.

The personal nature of the nodal axis

Although the signs describe our collective, inherited nodal axis imbalance, it is the houses in which the Nodes are found, and the planetary rulers of the Nodes, which describe our personal relationship to this axis and our personal experience of the liminal realms. This will, of course, be different for each of us. In addition to the collective dimension of the otherworlds, there is also a long tradition that each one of us is attached at birth to an individual daemon which is uniquely interested in our personal destiny. In our own charts, we could even imagine that the nodal axis is our individual threshold between this and other worlds, presided over by our own personal guides, mentors, teachers, ancestors, messengers, guardian angels, and daemons.

Audience: This reminds me of the Philip Pullman trilogy, *His Dark Materials*, in which everyone is attached to their own personal daemon.

Clare: Exactly, and this is by no means a new idea. You can find this in the Myth of Er in Plato's *Republic*. In this myth, Plato describes how the soul of each of us is given a unique daemon before we are born, which selects the image and pattern which we are to live on the earth. This sounds exactly like the birth chart, doesn't it? Our soul's companion guides us toward birth, but in the process of our arrival we forget all that, and believe instead that we are alone in the world. It is said that our daemon remembers our image and our pattern and is therefore the carrier of our destiny.

I am approaching the nodal axis as a threshold between the worlds, populated by a host of intermediaries from the *anima mundi* which remember, when we forget, what on earth we are doing here. This explains why the nodal axis is so strongly associated with significant meetings with people who may challenge us, appear to thwart us, or who function as messengers, guides or teachers, helping us, and sometimes forcing us, to cross thresholds which would otherwise never occur to us, or which we are afraid to cross without some kind of help, guidance or encouragement. Reinhold Ebertin also found that there are often strong nodal links between partners and in families.[21] It is perhaps not surprising that people with whom we are in close relationship are also the agents of our personal destiny.

> Why is it so difficult to imagine that I am cared about, that something takes an interest in what I do, that I am perhaps protected, maybe even kept alive not altogether by my own will and doing? Once upon a time what took such good care of me was a guardian spirit and I knew how to pay it appropriate attention... Why not keep within psychology proper what once was called providence – being invisibly watched and watched over?[22]

The influences from the otherworlds remain shadowy, but they are experienced in our intuitions, in our imagination, and in fleeting

---

[21] Ebertin, Reinhold, *The Combination of Stellar Influences*, trans. Alfred G. Roosedale (Aalen: Ebertin Verlag, 1940 [1960]).
[22] Hillman, *The Soul's Code*.

glimpses. No doubt we have all had the feeling, at different times in our lives, that we are being blocked from taking a particular decision or line of action. We wonder, for example, why we can't get that job or sell our house. No matter how hard we try to make things happen in a particular way, they just refuse to oblige. At times like this, it seems that 'life is what happens while we are busy making other plans', as John Lennon so accurately said. Conversely, we will all have had experiences when everything just seems to fall into place quite naturally. A series of events will occur which don't apparently need much effort from us, and we will find ourselves, often in spite of ourselves, on a new path. At these times it is likely that our nodal axis is particularly active, either because it is receiving transits or because the transiting node is making significant aspects with our natal chart. The interesting thing about this is that, whether or not we have other ideas for ourselves, and whether or not we know anything about astrology, it seems that we are invariably forced into our pattern and our birth chart comes to life.

Audience: Is there an inevitability about the Nodes, like Chiron? It sounds as if there is not much choice involved.

Clare: Yes, that certainly seems to be the case, and it may well be that our task, as far as the nodal axis is concerned, is to keep our eyes and ears open for clues, listening for messages and for messengers whose function may well be to help us across thresholds or to give us a kick when we refuse to wake up. In my experience, the application of heroic efforts and the use of our willpower are neither relevant nor appropriate where the nodal axis is concerned, because we don't necessarily get what we think we want, do we?

Audience: No way!

Clare: The nodal axis seems to describe the threshold between different realities or perceptions, between the literal and the imaginative, and ultimately it is possible to develop the ability to stand on this threshold, identifying with neither side exclusively, but holding the opposites. Ultimately, this is exactly our function and role as astrologers and it is, of course, a very delicate and difficult place to stand. Let's see if we can make all this a bit more real by getting down to the natal chart and looking at some examples. Both Nodes appear to personify in the form of people who have significant influences in our lives. These people are often teachers, guides or mentors who inspire us and give us the confidence and support to do things that we wouldn't otherwise do.

Audience: Would you say that our ancestors are there on the Nodes?

Clare: Yes I would, because we know that in indigenous cultures which have not lost their roots, the ancestors, as well as the descendents who have yet to be born, are considered to be living forces, actively involved in the continuing life of the clan or tribe, functioning as teachers, guides and mentors. So they would certainly be included in these realms.

In our natal charts, it is the houses across which the nodal axis falls that describe particularly highly charged areas of our lives and particularly significant relationships. The planetary rulers of the Nodes should be taken into account, since they will provide more specific and detailed information. But tonight I want to focus on the relationship of the planets to the nodal axis, particularly those planets which are conjunct or square to the nodal axis, by which I mean any planets within 8° or 90° of the nodal axis, on the Moon's 'bendings'. These planets seem to demand expression in our lives, regardless of our conscious intentions. There is something ruthless and compulsive about them – they appear to function with absolute certainty and conviction, driving us to fulfil our destiny.

Audience: I can understand that a planet on the nodal axis will be significant, but can you explain what the Moon's 'bendings' are?

Clare: Have another look at the diagram of the nodal axis. You can see that the Moon crosses the ecliptic twice every month, once moving upwards at the north Node and once moving downwards at the south Node. But there is a point between the nodal crossings when the Moon has reached its maximum latitude north or south, and at this point, which is 90° from the nodal axis, the Moon changes direction. When a planet is on this 'bending' point, then it seems to make a particularly challenging connection to the nodal axis itself.

The angles and the nodal axis

If the nodal axis is conjunct or square to either of the angles (the MC/IC or Ascendant/Descendant axis), then it seems that we find ourselves compelled to make some kind of personal contribution to the world. However, our motivation in these cases has nothing to do with ego-gratification or our drive for recognition or fame. It is usually quite the opposite. We tend to find ourselves acting as agents of forces that drive us to engage with the world, no matter what the personal cost may be.

One example is that of Nelson Mandela, who has his north Node conjunct the Ascendant in Sagittarius and his south Node conjunct the Descendant in Gemini. The collective challenge of the Gemini-Sagittarius axis is to speak out and act on our beliefs, something Mandela did with great effectiveness, eventually changing the face of African politics. Mandela qualified as a lawyer and joined the African National Congress, leading the resistance to the ruling National Party's apartheid policies. After the banning of the ANC in 1960, he advocated the use of violent tactics, and in 1963 he was tried for plotting to overthrow the government and sentenced to life imprisonment. Mandela's nodal axis is in the 12th and 6th houses, on the axis of service, personal sacrifice, and devotion to a cause. The 12th house is associated with incarceration and imprisonment, and the 6th house is associated with hard labour. During Mandela's twenty-nine years of imprisonment, his reputation grew steadily, and he became a potent symbol of resistance as the anti-apartheid movement gathered strength, consistently refusing to compromise his political position in order to obtain his release. His autobiography, published in 1994, is very appropriately named *The Long Walk to Freedom*, a perfect Gemini/Sagittarius title.

The Sun and the nodal axis

The Sun aspecting the nodal axis, particularly by conjunction or square, is often found in the charts of those who have a strong inner sense of their unique destiny and purpose, often from a very young age, which they feel compelled to achieve in the world. This is not necessarily something which can be explained rationally, since it is just a fierce inner conviction.

Audience: My father had his north Node conjunct the Sun on the MC. He was born in a small town in Spain, but when he was fifteen years old he wanted to go to America. His mother said he was too young, he could not go alone, and anyway he was needed to work on the family farm. But he cried for three months until eventually he got permission, and then he went to live with some distant relatives in Argentina. He became very successful. One day I asked him why he had done that, and he said, very simply: 'Because it was my destiny'.

The Moon and the nodal axis

Clare: When the Moon aspects the Nodes, we are connected on a very deep instinctual level to the feelings, to memories, and to the past. There is also a strong connection to the earth, to nature, and also to the feminine.

Audience: I have the Moon conjunct the south Node, and when I discovered Gaia theory, I thought, 'That's me!' And from that moment on, I have tried to find out everything about Gaia.

Clare: I would imagine that this discovery would have felt like a revelation – something which gripped you strongly, like a door opening.

Audience: Absolutely, just like a door opening. I knew at once that I had found my connection. And I am still there – I am always connected with Gaia, and trying to respect the Gaia equilibrium.

Audience: Well I have that same connection, the Moon conjunct my south Node. And I have written a book, actually, which is all about women.

Clare: It is clear from what you are saying that this connection between the nodal axis and the Moon is very meaningful to both of you, and you are drawing great support from this lunar connection. If we were working from the perspective of leaving the south Node behind, then you would be cutting off your living connection to the support which the Moon gives you. Rather, it seems as if this configuration provides an important clue about what you are here to do. Incidentally, it is interesting that Bob Geldof has Moon square his nodal axis, and his life long mission has been to 'feed the world'.

Mercury and the nodal axis

As the messenger of the gods, Mercury's function is to carry messages from one world to another. Hermes was the only god in Greek mythology who could visit all the worlds, and if you have Mercury conjunct or square to the nodal axis, then you may be challenged to mediate and navigate between different dimensions, perceptions, realities and languages. This placement also indicates that our ideas can change radically during our lives. Carl Jung, for example, had both Mercury and Venus square his nodal axis, and in his personal life and work with patients, he was constantly listening for messages from the otherworlds, communicated in the form of symbols or as actual events occurring in nature. His personal daemon, Philemon, was a living reality to him. He lived within its grip, as it drove him ruthlessly to complete his life's work.

Audience: My partner has his Mercury square my Nodes, and I think that without him I wouldn't have got in touch with astrology.

Clare: So he is like a teacher and a guide?

Audience: Yes, he has taught me a different way of thinking and seeing.

Venus and the nodal axis

When Venus is involved with the nodal axis, there can be a strong appreciation of beauty and form, and an intense desire to give shape to some kind of poetic or artistic expression. The writer, Marcel Proust, had Venus and Mercury in Virgo in a tight square to the nodal axis, and his writing is carefully shaped and crafted. Not only did his life change dramatically from that of a social dilettante to that of a recluse by the end of his life, but his monumental work, *In Search of Lost Time* (*A la recherché du temps perdu*), consisting of seven volumes which he worked on almost continuously for over fourteen years, gradually became substantially different from his original conception, as he drew increasingly upon his inner world, his imagination, and personal memories.

Mars and the nodal axis

With Mars aspecting the nodal axis, there is a powerful compulsion to act. We feel forced to take action. It seems to be our destiny to fight for something, to find an effective channel for the use of our energy and determination. Princess Diana, who publicly challenged the general ignorance and prejudice toward people with AIDS, and took up the cause to eliminate land mines, had Mars, Uranus and Pluto on her north Node in Leo, and Moon and Chiron on her south Node in Aquarius, so there is a very significant nodal story here.

Jupiter and the nodal axis

Jupiter can describe someone who has access to deep faith and a feeling of being protected, of being specially favoured by the gods, or of having a guardian angel who protects them throughout their lives. This may drive them to achieve more than they ever thought possible, and which they would certainly not have attempted unless they felt they were acting as agents of divine providence. Although this contact brings faith, it is not necessarily easy to live with, particularly if Jupiter is conjunct or square the axis, because then it will have us in its grip – driving us to fulfil our destiny, however hard this may be on a personal level. Martin Luther, whose passionate conviction that human beings have direct access to God, led directly to the Reformation, had Jupiter and Mars on his south Node. On a personal level, Luther's journey caused him immense suffering and hardship, but eventually he felt he had no choice but to act and challenge the established Catholic Church with his doctrine of 'justification by faith alone'.

Saturn and the nodal axis

When Saturn is connected to the Nodes, there can be very

strong barriers and boundaries between the worlds, and a fear of trusting or opening up these thresholds. Saturn is a hard taskmaster, throwing obstacles in our way, teaching us lessons, and insisting that we learn to stand on our own feet and develop self-discipline, responsibility and mastery. We may well turn back from this threshold because it is so hard, and decide, because it is safer, to confine our activities solely to this world. Alternatively, we may continue to meet teachers who force us to undertake long and difficult periods of apprenticeship, hard work and discipline, which eventually lead us to becoming 'gatekeepers' ourselves, guarding the thresholds between the worlds on behalf of others. One example is Tina Turner, who has Saturn conjunct the south Node in Aries. Her task has been to learn to stand up for and defend herself and to become her own authority, and it has been an extraordinary journey, although extremely difficult, with the kind of life-and-death struggle which is indicated by the fact Pluto is also square to her nodal axis.

W.B. Yeats is also an interesting example, with Saturn conjunct the north Node and the nodal axis square to his Ascendant/Descendant axis. Yeats and his wife consciously collaborated with the daemonic realms via the medium of automatic writing. However, it is not surprising that, with Saturn aspecting the nodal axis, this work was disrupted by beings which Yeats called the 'Frustrators', who communicated meaningless information until the 'real' daemons returned.

> When I think of life as a struggle with the Daemon who would ever set us to the hardest work among those not impossible, I understand why there is a deep enmity between a man and his destiny…I am persuaded that the Daemon delivers and deceives us, and that he wove the netting from the stars and threw the net from his shoulder.[23]

---

[23] Yeats, W. B., *Mythologies*, quoted in Harpur, *Daimonic Reality*, p. 40.

Chiron and the nodal axis

In relation to the nodal axis, Chiron appears to have a doubly daemonic function, as teacher and healer. If Chiron is connected to our nodal axis, that can indicate shamanic illnesses, crises, suffering, and unwilling initiation into our true vocation or calling – which is never chosen by the ego, but which is both our gift and our curse, since it leaves us with the unmistakable stamp of the outsider. It is interesting that Princess Diana had a strong Chiron-Node connection. Healers, teachers and astrologers often have such a strong Chiron emphasis in their charts. When Chiron is connected to the nodal axis, our function and purpose is to be guides, helping people to understand and accept their own inner wisdom and truth, which they are never likely to find reflected or supported or even recognised by the outside world at large.

The outer planets and the nodal axis

When the outer planets are connected to the nodal axis, we are subject to, and in the grip of, powerful collective forces. With Uranus here, for example, there can be a brilliance and a blinding clarity and absolute conviction which enables the individual to break through the normal patterns and see the whole picture, all at once. It is an evolutionary and Promethean force that can feel like a revelation. Those with Uranus connected to the nodal axis can, like Charles Darwin, be at the forefront of scientific innovation and breakthrough. The definition of the word revelation is 'the act of revealing or disclosing, a dramatic disclosure of something not previously known or realised'. In the theological sense, revelation is the manifestation of divine will or truth, and this is what it can feel like with a nodal connection to Uranus.

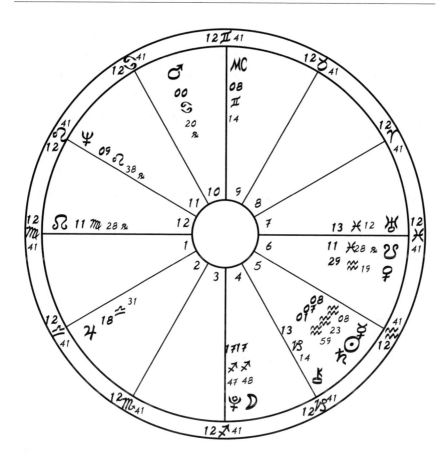

Wolfgang Amadeus Mozart
27 January, 1756, 20.00 LMT, Salzburg, Austria
Source: Astrotheme

In Mozart's chart, the nodal axis is in Virgo and Pisces across
the 12th and 6th houses, picking up his Ascendant/Descendant axis,
which indicates that his sense of personal destiny was clear to him and
to all who came in contact with him. His nodal task is to find a container
or a vessel (6th house) for the expression of the divine (12th house), and
his music is a clear expression of this. But Uranus is also there, and he
was writing full concertos by the age of three. It is also said that he
could hold entire symphonies in his head and write them down without

any errors or hesitation. It is as if they were given to him whole, and his music was astonishing, new and unexpected. Although his genius is unquestioned, Pluto and the Moon are also square to his nodal axis, and it was out of his emotional pain and loss in his family (4th house) that the intense depth of feeling present in his greatest music emerged. It is very difficult to be born with such a powerful destiny, because it is a driving force which has us in its grip and it is never easy or comfortable. James Hillman explores this subject in *The Soul's Code*, which I would highly recommend if you are interested in finding out more about the subject of destiny, and the role of daemons, guides and mentors in our lives.

One way of working in more detail is to consider the positions of Jupiter and Mercury, which rule Mozart's nodal axis. This will give us more information about the specific expression that this particular nodal axis might take. Jupiter in Libra in the 2nd house indicates that he will seek to find a physical expression for balance and harmony and the creation of beauty. Mercury is closely conjunct Saturn and the Sun in the 5th house in Aquarius, which indicates that Mozart's creativity will be expressed in a clear and structured way, and it also describes his father's role as a stern mentor and teacher. I think you can see how helpful the planetary rulers can be when we are working to make the nodal story more precise and personal.

Audience: Would you use Neptune as well, since it is the transpersonal ruler of Pisces, or would you just stay with Jupiter?

Clare: I would certainly include Neptune, and in this case it is in the 11th house in Leo, opposite the Saturn-Mercury-Sun conjunction. Once again, we can read this opposition as the personal creative struggle to give structured shape and form to the magical, mythical and beautiful realms which opened up to Mozart from the collective. And because he was also only human, we can see how this opposition polarised at difficult times in his life. When his work became too much, or his sense of duty and responsibility to his father or his sensitivity to criticism were particularly strong, he would escape to the Neptune end of the spectrum, and go drinking with his friends. On the other hand, when he was open to the Neptunian realms of the imagination, he would work hard to give this structure by writing them down in the form of music. Neptune is such a sensitive planet, and so in touch with other dimensions of reality, that it tends to go one of two ways when it picks up the nodal axis. The individual may surrender completely and give over their own will, such as, for example, in the case of mediums or healers. Alternatively, the individual may feel that the demands of the other realms are so overwhelming that they seek to push them away and turn their back on them.

Audience: That is interesting, because I have Neptune squaring my Nodes, and in fact I used to work as a medium.

Clare: With Neptune aspecting the nodal axis, the veil between the worlds is particularly thin and permeable, and it is likely that if we ignore them, the daemons will continue to knock on the door or start to create chaos. Dante Gabriel Rossetti had Neptune on the MC square the nodal axis, and Chiron and the Moon on the south Node. His destiny was to create a more beautiful and romantic world, and his life was consumed by his imagination and by the dreams, fantasies and visions which informed his paintings and the paintings of the other artists who joined his Pre-Raphaelite Brotherhood. He was immensely sensitive and attracted to beautiful, wounded, and unobtainable women, and succumbed to a drug addiction which eventually killed him. So we could say that, although his personal life was full of tragedy, nevertheless the world would be a much poorer and less magical place without the paintings of the Pre-Raphaelites.

Audience: I have Neptune square my nodal axis, and there are lots of spirits and other entities in my house. I am always trying to get rid of them because they are very disruptive.

Clare: If the nodal axis represents a threshold through which we have access to all of human emotion and experience, it may be that our task, with Neptune here, is to listen to these spirits and to find out what they want.

Audience: I spend most of my life doing that.

Clare: Well, in that case, it may well be that that is your nodal task.

Audience: But it's very exhausting. I have a friend who is a medium, who helps me to get rid of them, and I asked him once why they continue to plague me. He said that I should imagine standing in the middle of Wembley Stadium, which would be crammed with souls that can't move on. That image really helped me not to take it so personally.

Clare: With Neptune aspecting the nodal axis, we are likely to be very sensitive to, and possibly overwhelmed by, the other realms, because there is an enormous amount of grief and unresolved pain, brutality, cruelty, poverty and starvation in our collective inheritance. As individuals we seem to get our little piece of that inheritance, and there is work for us to do. This brings us back again to Chiron, because we are not born into a perfect world where everything is resolved. There is a balancing and healing which needs to be done on behalf of the collective, an integration of the sign opposites across which our nodal axis falls.

Finally, with Pluto connected to the nodal axis, somehow the individual has to live on the threshold between intense destructiveness and creativity, travelling into the psychic underworld on a regular basis, connecting to the life-force which resides there, and re-emerging before going down again. This is a very compulsive picture, and the issues can revolve around power and the surrender of power, as in the case of Tina

Turner.

Audience: Are these interpretations similar when someone else's planets aspect your nodal axis?

Clare: Yes, particularly in relationships which feel fated or inevitable in some way. For example, I have a friend whose ex-husband's Saturn is on her north Node, and that was immensely difficult for her because, in order to stay in that relationship, she had to deal with Saturn, to feel very alone in the marriage, and to learn some hard lessons. In the end she couldn't stand it any longer and bailed out, partly because she also has Venus in Sagittarius. But she is well aware that the marriage was part of her destiny, and the responsibilities continue because they have three children. The only way she could have stayed in the marriage would have been to change her relationship to Saturn, and in fact this nodal connection has forced her to become much more adult and self-sufficient.

Audience: I have that connection with my partner. Is there any hope?

Clare: It indicates that you have work to do together, building lasting structures, and it can also feel very safe.

Audience: What if your nodal axis makes an aspect to your partner's nodal axis?

Clare: Then I would imagine that your respective daemons have chosen to engage, whether you like it or not. There is a meeting of souls. Now that we live in such a rational, secular age, the daemons are having a hard time communicating with us because, as a general rule, we no longer believe they exist. This could be one reason why they appear to us as ordinary people – as guides, teachers, mentors and messengers – people who help us remember our soul's purpose.

Audience: But everything I have read about the Nodes is that they are directional, and that we are meant to leave behind what we are born into because it can hold us back.

Clare: I am not sure why we would want to cut ourselves off from that which supports and sustains us, unless we are deeply alienated from ourselves and invested in a heroic vision of personal progress and spiritual development or, equally possible, that we are victims of the 'tyranny of perfection' which is so prevalent in our culture. But you are right that this is a very common interpretation of the south Node, although every time we fall into the either/or trap – which is very easy to do, of course – then we have effectively got out a knife and chopped our psyches in half. This is exactly how the analytical mind works. My question is, 'Who or what says we are *meant* to do this?' There are no moral imperatives in astrology. But it is all too easy for us to take a judgemental stance which has nothing to do with astrology, but everything to do with our personal opinions, which are so easily affected by fear or by a kind of rigid adherence to what we believe to be the rules, whether we assume that these rules are temporal or spiritual. This is why I think it can be helpful to focus on the planetary rulers of the Nodes, their function in the chart, and their relationship with each other. This releases us from approaching the nodal axis as if it were primarily an axis of time.

As astrologers, it is particularly easy to fall into judgements. For example, we might think that Mars in Aries *ought* to be more considerate. Well, actually, no. Mars in Aries is Mars in Aries, and it is what it is. In its essence, astrology is descriptive, not critical. So we need to ask, instead, what does this Mars want? How does it act? Give it some space to be what it is. Let it off the leash; it can be a tremendously positive and powerful force in our lives. If we deny the liminal realms that are the meeting place of spirit, soul and earth as symbolised by the Nodes, then we lose the connection between opposites. If you are interested in this subject, then I recommend that you read Patrick

Harpur's book, *Daimonic Reality*, which is an absolutely splendid exploration of this subject. If our world-view is purely scientific or mechanical, a living relationship with an enchanted, living and densely inhabited universe is impossible because it does not exist for us. Our astrology becomes mechanical, and there will be no surprises to be found, just rules to be mastered. If our planets are not living gods assisted, each one of them, by a host of messengers and intermediaries, then we are no longer in dialogue with the *anima mundi*, with the intermediary realms. We are just very clever mechanics.

If we can accommodate the presence of the *anima mundi* in our astrology, then we can find a place for a magical dialogue, and many of the so-called afflictions of the mind, such as delusions, complexes, neuroses, depressions or paranoia, to name just a few, may not after all need to be pathologised or medicalised as they have tended to be in mainstream psychology. This is why Jung wrote, 'The Gods have become diseases'. As his work developed, he realised that the psyche was not just subjective, projecting all kinds of images onto the world, but that it was also objective – out there in the world as well. And synchronicity was his proof. When we are working with astrology, it is clear that the planets manifest both within us and outside in the world in the form of concrete facts and events. So it seems to me that astrology belongs absolutely to the daemonic realm and that, as astrologers, we have a daemonic function, as intermediaries and messengers standing on the threshold between the heavens and the earth. Ultimately, it is our function to help our clients to remember their pattern, their soul's purpose. For this reason it is always worth checking our client's nodal axis in relation to our own charts, to see how we might have a role to play in their lives.

The nodal axis in the houses

Let's look at some examples of the nodal axis in the houses.

Nodal axis in the 1st and 7th houses

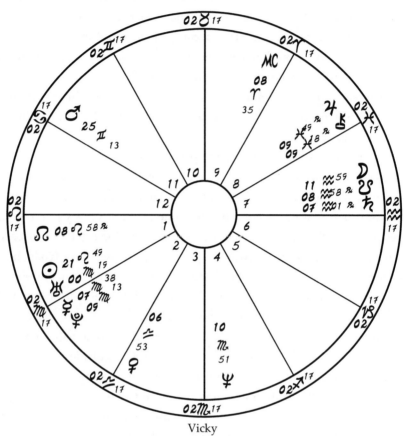

Vicky

Chart data omitted for reasons of confidentiality

Vicky: I have my north Node in Leo in the 1st house, and Saturn conjunct my south Node in Aquarius in the 7th house, and it doesn't feel that good.

Clare: Let's look first of all at the meaning of the Leo-Aquarius axis. Collectively, this has to do with finding a conscious relationship between the individual and the collective, between doing our own thing and contributing to group or community efforts and causes. Specifically, this has to do with discovering your unique and individual gifts and talents, and offering them to the world. Because this axis falls across your 1st and 7th houses, we know that it will be through personal relationships that you meet and grapple with these themes. With Saturn there as well, partnerships will be of particular significance in your life, involving difficult but valuable lessons to be learnt.

Audience: Is Vicky looking for a father figure, with Saturn in Aquarius in the 7th house?

Clare: That could certainly be the case and, because the nodal axis is here as well, then it is likely that Vicky will find herself in relationships which force her to develop genuine self-respect and personal authority, and to gain the support, respect and friendship of her partner. This is a parent-child axis, with the Leo end representing creative, spontaneous self-expression and the Aquarius end representing the adult qualities of detachment and objectivity. Leo without Aquarius can be fairly demanding and childish, and it seems that Vicky's eventual fulfilment is to learn to value and take responsibility for herself as an adult.

Vicky: I do have a real fear of being judged, and I hate to be criticised. I don't like anyone who challenges me.

Clare: If you find yourself polarising on the Leo end of this axis, you may feel more and more isolated and unappreciated, and afraid of the criticisms and judgements of others. But Saturn may eventually turn out to be your greatest friend, and there is much of real value for you to learn about yourself from others.

Nodal axis in the 2nd and 8th houses

The 2nd/8th house issues revolve around the theme of personal security and sharing our material and emotional resources with others. Life circumstances will force us to find the balance between developing our own values and learning to trust ourselves, and putting our trust in others without depending solely upon them.

Jane: I have the south Node in Aries in the 2nd house, and north Node in Libra in the 8th house.

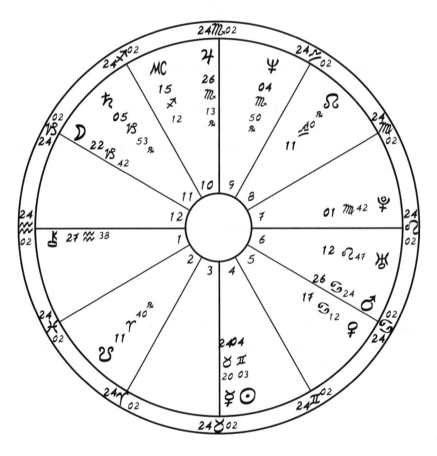

Jane
Chart data omitted for reasons of confidentiality

Clare: The Aries/Libra polarity concerns the relationship between independence and compromise. In the 2nd and 8th houses, the question is how you can learn to trust and share yourself with others, and yet not lose your autonomy and personal security in the process.

Jane: I kill myself trying to compromise, but it never seems to work. I find it fascinating to watch how other people manage their relationships as if they were easy things to do. My sister is a good example – she just met a guy, got together with him, got married, and now she has two kids. And I find myself thinking: 'How on earth do you do that?' The most scary thing in my mind is the thought of getting married.

Clare: Do you remember the Julia Roberts' film, *Runaway Bride*? That is a good example of the Aries/Libra dilemma.

Jane: That's right, I really get that. Give me the horse and get me out of here. But do you think that something just happens and you get helped along? I am fed up with trying and failing with relationships.

Clare: With the nodal axis there, yes, I do. It sounds as if you are trying to force yourself into a relationship because you feel it is expected of you. But perhaps your gift is that you are independent and focused and goal-oriented. I think your task is to enjoy this gift and give it full rein, knowing all along that, when the time comes, events and circumstances and other people will no doubt come along and open up whole new areas of your life which you never thought were going to be possible. It is not about applying the will, but about keeping your eyes and ears open for clues. I think this is something that will happen anyway, since it is already built into your chart and because Venus is square to your nodal axis, in Cancer in the 5th house, which indicates your desire for children.

Audience: So if we ignore either Node, then somebody or something will come along which will make sure we pay attention.

Clare: Yes, and that is the nature of the fated quality this axis seems to have.

Audience: This all sounds a bit like the outer planets. If we ignore them, then they will get us anyway.

Clare: Exactly.

Jane: So I shouldn't be trying so hard, but I should have more faith in the area of relationships?

Clare: That's right. I think the solution is just as likely to emerge from meeting people who constellate your south Node in Aries in the 2nd house – people who have, for example, emerged strong and independent and personally secure after a marriage breakdown or the collapse of a longstanding relationship, and who can say, 'I'm glad that marriage is over'. That could give you the confidence and faith to trust in life a bit more, knowing that if things don't work out it won't be the end of the world, because nobody has the power to take your sense of self away. That might be a great help, rather than standing on the brink, being terrified to plunge into a relationship.

Jane: That's very interesting, because when I was going through a difficult relationship a few years ago, I did meet a number of women who were just fine on their own.

Clare: There you are. And they demonstrated to you that relationships and marriage are not, in fact, the end of the world, or irretrievable in any way. Perhaps these women were performing the function of guides and mentors, who may not have been in your life for long, but who showed you the way forwards and taught you to have faith.

Audience: Is it true that the south Node is like a comfort blanket?

Clare: Not necessarily. It all depends on the house and the aspects made to it. If, for example, we have Saturn on the south Node, as Vicky does, then it can be a very uncomfortable place indeed – our so-called comfort blanket can be made of barbed wire. We may well feel utterly alone in the world, unsupported, cast out and abandoned, but our task with Saturn on the south Node appears to be to develop inner resources and personal mastery, and to learn to stand on our own feet. Our lives are a constant dance between opposites, so it is a question of finding a way to navigate the entire spectrum without either end taking over.

Audience: I have always found my south Node to be very powerful, so it is a relief to hear that I don't have to fight against it.

Nodal axis in the 3rd and 9th houses

Paul: What about the south Node in Leo in the 3rd house opposite the north Node in Aquarius in the 9th house?

Audience: Would that be about collecting information for teaching?

Clare: Yes, and we need to look at all the layers here. The Leo/Aquarius axis is the relationship between the individual and the group. And the 3rd/9th house axis concerns learning and teaching, so the theme here is the relationship between your personal ideas on the one hand, and collective beliefs on the other hand. And because the nodal axis is here as well, then we know these issues will be highly charged. We would also anticipate that your teachers, and your brothers and sisters and fellow students, are going to be especially important figures in your life.

Paul: What are the myths associated with the 3rd/9th houses?

Clare: This axis describes the powerful archetypal relationship that exists between the student and the teacher. It is about absorbing the essence of the teacher, incorporating what we have been taught, and passing on our knowledge to others. It is both our apprenticeship and our vocation.

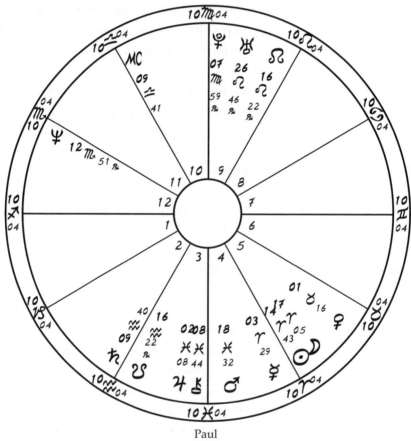

Paul
Chart data omitted for reasons of confidentiality

Paul: Could it also be writing about what you've learned?

Clare: Absolutely, because the writing process itself is about analysing and trying to understand your own relationship to the greater picture.

Nodal axis in the 4th and 10th houses

With the nodal axis in the 4th and 10th houses, it is likely that our parents, family, and ancestors may be our greatest teachers, mentors and guides. Or we may have a boss who sees our potential and who encourages us to develop it. We may have a particular function to play in the world, as well as a strong connection to family traditions and to history.

Lillian: What if you have the south Node in Sagittarius in the 4th house? Does that show what I will be moving away from?

Clare: Well, this means that you have the Nodes in Gemini and Sagittarius across your 10th and 4th houses, and the north Node in Gemini in the 10th house. Does anyone want to have a go at that?

Audience: This means that Lillian's vocation has to do with learning and teaching, and that she may be encouraged to do this by her family or by her boss.

Clare: We will find out more if we know where Jupiter is, as the ruler of that south Node.

Lillian: Jupiter is in the 9th house, in Taurus.

Clare: Well, in that case I think it may well be that you have inherited a particular belief system, religion or philosophy from your family, which sustains and supports you. It could also indicate that your family originated from another country.

Lillian: My parents came originally from Jamaica and settled in England. And it is true that I am interested in Jamaican culture and in the history of slavery.

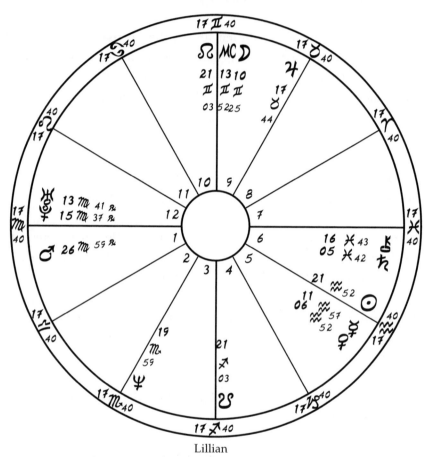

Lillian
Chart data omitted for reasons of confidentiality

Clare: Can anyone suggest what Lillian's north Node in the 10th house in Gemini might be about? The ruler is Mercury in Aquarius in the 5th house.

Audience: Struggling to be a writer?

Lillian: I keep hearing that – writing or teaching. But it doesn't register at all.

Clare: Would you like to be a writer or a teacher?

Lillian: I wish I could be – that would be great.

Clare: But it is very hard?

Lillian: Yes.

Clare: Well, we could say that this is your vocation, although it does look challenging because the planetary rulers of your Nodes are in square aspect to each other. But no doubt you will find yourself doing work or constantly running into people or circumstances that point you in this direction, no matter how difficult you feel this to be. It is also perfectly possible that the Gemini north Node in the 10th house indicates some kind of public communication or public speaking or teaching.

Lillian: That's all very well, but I am always asking myself what I am meant to be speaking about.

Clare: It may be that you are taking a rational or intellectual approach, since Mercury in Aquarius can be rather detached and objective. I suspect that it is through the Sagittarian end of this axis that you may discover what you are really passionate about, and what carries deep meaning for you. And since Jupiter is in Taurus, this could well have something to do with the land of your ancestors. Once you have allowed yourself to trust the vision and faith of the south Node, which will come from deep within you, and from your family or background inheritance, I suspect you will know what you need to speak about. I think this is about learning to trust that you will be given your direction and your voice.

Nodal axis in the 5th and 11th houses

When we are considering the 5th/11th house nodal axis, we are going to start thinking about the Leo/Aquarius themes of the individual and the collective, the heart and the head. Since the nodal axis always has a powerful charge, we know that life will present us with this dichotomy. This axis can also mean that our children and our work colleagues and friends may play a particularly important role in our lives, acting as our guides and mentors and teachers. We will feel ourselves equally pulled towards contributing to group situations and playing a part within a larger community, and yet finding enough time for ourselves to have fun, to do our own thing, and to enjoy the pleasures of life. It seems, in the end, that our function is to make some kind of unique contribution to the group, and we may well feel compelled to do so. We can get more information about the kind of personal contribution we need to make by looking at the sign and house positions of the planets which rule each of the Nodes, and also if there are any planets conjunct or square to the nodal axis.

Audience: But apart from that, we have to stay on the see-saw?

Clare: Yes. That is the whole point of all axes, and the nodal axis is no exception.

Nodal axis in the 6th and 12th houses

Penny: What about the north Node in Pisces in the 12th house? I also have Pisces on the Ascendant, but they are about 9° apart.

Clare: In the 6th/12th houses, the nodal axis will describe the tension between engaging with, and wishing to retire from, the world. There is also likely to be a struggle to find a balance between needing to be in control and longing to surrender control. Because the nodal axis is here, these themes will be particularly highly charged.

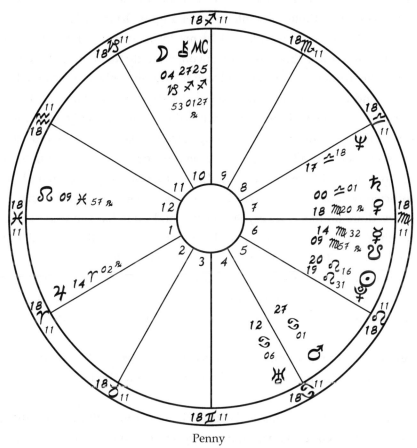

Penny
Chart data omitted for reasons of confidentiality

In the 12th house, there is likely to be a strong desire to retreat from the world, to avoid having to define oneself or be held accountable or responsible for one's actions. In the 6th house, there is an equally strong desire to develop practical skills and areas of personal expertise that can be put to use. The challenge of this axis is to dedicate our practical skills and talents in the service of something greater than ourselves – to construct a container or a vehicle for that which we serve, so that it can be made manifest in this world. It is like sweeping the steps of the temple, practical service as ritual through which we express our devotion. Without the content, we end up with empty jars.

This was once explained to me by a woman whose husband decided that it was time she got someone in to do the ironing, to relieve her of the drudgery. Her husband saw the ironing only as a meaningless chore, and my client was extremely upset about this because, for her, it was a practical expression of her love and care for her family, something she realised her husband did not appreciate. On the other hand, as a thing-in-itself, cut off from the Pisces end of the spectrum, having to do the ironing could well have made her feel resentful, put upon and not sufficiently appreciated, which can easily slip into a feeling of martyrdom. So this is a very subtle axis and quite hard to understand, certainly from the outside. With the nodal axis across the 6th and 12th houses, we will be called to find a way to serve both areas of life. And it is often very helpful to look at the position of the planets which rule both Nodes, which in your case would be Jupiter and Mercury, with Neptune also there on a collective level. Have you always worked?

Penny: Yes, I took six months off once and I was miserable. As soon as I started working again, just a few hours a week, I felt better.

Clare: It certainly seems to be true that a Virgo without something useful and practical to do is an unhappy Virgo. But that is not the whole picture, of course. There must be something calling to you from the Piscean 12th house north Node.

Penny: Yes, it is the longing to stop working!

Clare: Yes, what calls you is the desire to escape from the routine and all the demands of daily life. But, as you know from your own experience, giving up work is not the solution and doesn't solve the problem. Perhaps this indicates that you need to work at something you find really meaningful.

Penny: I think Vicky, my fellow student over there, was right when she said the reason I was doing this course was to become more of a Piscean. It has opened up a whole new spiritual realm for me. I do find it hard, but I am determined to do it. It is terribly important to get away from my everyday work and do something of this nature. This is a very big issue on my mind at the moment.

Lesson Six: Introduction to the Aspects, Part One

Now we have studied the planets, signs and houses, or the *what*, the *how* and the *where*, we are now going to look at the aspects. The reason I have left the aspects until now is that people often assume that they are difficult and complex, whereas in fact they simply follow on logically from what we already know.

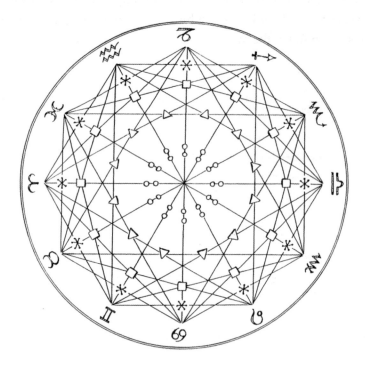

Aspects are about *relationships*. They are *dynamic*. They bring various chart factors – planets, Nodes, signs, angles and houses – into an active relationship with each other. But aspects are more than that – they are also beautiful, because they remind us that the birth chart is yet another expression of the sacred geometry that has always been a central feature in the mystery traditions. There is something inherently magical and fascinating and deeply satisfying about the shapes and patterns formed by mathematical division and proportion, and they can be found everywhere in nature, art, architecture, music and, of course, in the human psyche.

Rose window at Chartres Cathedral

We are already familiar with the symbolism of the circle and the square, the fundamental components of a horoscope. The circle is considered to be the most perfect shape of all, and is the symbol for pure spirit, eternal and unchanging. The square is the symbol for the earth, for all physical manifestation, and for our orientation on earth via the four directions, four seasons and four elements. The symbol for the earth and the structure of the horoscope show us that the earth is at the centre, surrounded by the circle of spirit, within which all of life is contained. One of the questions which has fascinated philosophers, theologians and mathematicians throughout history is how to 'square the circle'. In other words, how do we find a relationship between spirit and matter, between the gods and ordinary mortals, between the eternal and the temporal? An image which includes both symbols is proof of our dual nature. And in fact this is, of course, exactly what a horoscope is – in essence it is a wonderfully simple symbolic map that does in fact square the circle.

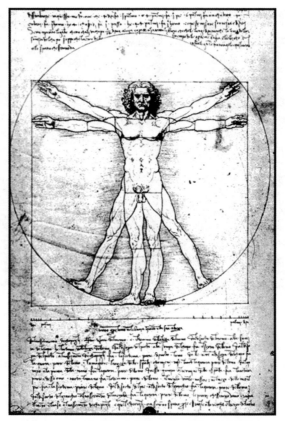

Leonardo da Vinci, 'Vitruvian Man' (1490)

Leonardo da Vinci's 'Vitruvian Man' is one of the most famous images of all times, and is still reproduced everywhere in the world today. The drawing symbolises the essential symmetry of the human body and, by extension, of the universe as a whole. Drawn by Leonardo around 1490, this beautiful figure first appeared in the second of three books entitled *Divina proportione,* or 'Divine Proportion', published by Leonardo's close friend, the mathematician Pacioli. It is a wonderful example of the integration of art and science during the Renaissance.

Audience: Do you know why this drawing is called the Vitruvian Man?

Clare: Vitruvius was an ancient Roman architect who wrote a series of ten books on architecture that, fortunately, survived into the Renaissance. In the third volume, he writes that the proportions of temples should be based on the proportions of the human body, because the human body is the model of perfection. He justifies this by stating that the human body with arms and legs extended fits into the perfect geometric forms, the circle and the square. This takes us back again to the Pythagorean number symbolism that is so fundamental to astrology, since it describes the inherently identical structure of all systems. Last term we looked at the *tetractys*, the symmetrical and well balanced model of the universe, which is reflected in the structure of the zodiac and which describes the generation of symbolic numbers out of the original unity.

Audience: Can you say more about this, Clare, since I am new to the class this term?

Clare: Simply expressed, the Pythagoreans believed that the nature of all things could be understood according to the powers of the one, the two, the three and the four as an unfolding sequence of creation. These numbers are not just quantities; they are also archetypes in their own right, so that 'oneness', 'twoness', 'threeness' and 'fourness' each have their own qualitative meaning. The astrological chart is an exact representation of the *tetractys*, being itself a one (the whole chart), a two (with each of the twelve signs of the zodiac being polar – active or passive), a three (the cardinal, fixed and mutable signs), and a four (the elements of fire, earth, air, water). The number twelve is a remarkably complete number in which the polarity is repeated six times, the three modes are repeated four times, and the four elements are repeated three times.

Number as an Archetype of Cosmic Order

Horoscope structure		Astrological aspects
Unity:		Conjunction
The whole chart	⬯	☌
Polarity:		Opposition
Positive/Negative	⬯ ⬯	☍
Three Modes:		Trine
Cardinal/Fixed/Mutable	⬯ ⬯ ⬯	△
Four Elements:		Square
Earth/Air/Fire/Water	⬯ ⬯ ⬯ ⬯	□

The Tetractys: 1 + 2 + 3 + 4 = 10

We are going to look at the aspects in exactly the same way as we looked at the structure of the horoscope last term – as an expression of the sequential division of the chart by One (conjunction), Two (opposition), Three (trine) and Four (square), in which One equals unity, Two equals division and separation, Three equals reconciliation and mediation, and Four equals manifestation. Every birth chart has its own particular shape, its own geometrical structure, its own unique physical and psychic patterning. And the most significant point about aspects and aspect patterns is that they bring the birth chart to life as a series of stories that help us transform our two-dimensional horoscope into a living, breathing reality. Have a look at this table, which lists the aspects that are most commonly used in modern astrology. You will see that these aspects are formed by dividing the 360° circle by two, three, four, and by the product of these first three numbers: six (which is 2x3), eight (which is 4x2) and twelve (3x4).

The Astrological Aspects

Division of the circle	Angle	Aspect formed	Orb	Symbol
1	0°	Conjunction	8°	☌
2	180°	Opposition	8°	☍
3	120°	Trine	8°	△
4	90°	Square	8°	□
6	60°	Sextile	4°	✳
8	45°	Semi-square	2°	∠
8 (3/8)	135°	Sesqui-quadrate	2°	⚼
12	30°	Semi-sextile	2°	⚺
12 (5/12)	150°	Quincunx	2°	⚻

All numbers have symbolic meanings, and it is perfectly possible, of course, to go on dividing the circle by five, seven, nine, eleven, and so on into infinitely greater divisions.

Orbs

You will see from the table above that each of the aspects has an 'orb', which means that each aspect holds for a certain number of degrees either side of exactitude. The closer the orb, the stronger the aspect. For example, an opposition between two planets 172° apart (8° orb) will not be as powerful or as intensely felt as an opposition between two planets 181° apart (1° orb). You will see that the orbs become smaller as the circle is increasingly divided. So we are much more likely to have major aspects in our chart (those with an orb of 8° or 4°) than we are to have minor aspects in our chart (those with a 2° orb), but when they do occur, they will be of equal importance.

Audience: Does this apply to all the planets? Sometimes you come across people who use a larger orb when the Sun or the Moon is involved.

Clare: The whole question of orbs is, like everything else in astrology, open for debate and subject to personal preference. Basically, because we need to start somewhere, it is useful to begin with some nice clear rules. Later on, we are of course free to experiment with the orbs for ourselves and to develop our own ideas.

In practice, we know that although the planets are caught in a 'freeze frame' at the moment of birth, they are actually moving all the time in relation to each other. So if, for example, the Sun is 9° behind Pluto in a birth chart, then it is an *applying* aspect because the Sun will make an exact conjunction to Pluto nine days after birth. Using the technique of progressions, the Sun will make an exact conjunction to Pluto nine years after birth. Naturally, this could be of immense significance, and we will be looking at the moving chart – transits, progressions and directions – in much more depth next term. So I think it is perfectly acceptable to stretch the orbs a bit when an aspect is applying. If the Sun was 9° ahead of Pluto in a birth chart, then it is already *separating* from the exact conjunction, which will have taken place nine days before birth, and I would be much less inclined to build it in as a factor in interpretation.

Audience: But presumably what occurred before our birth is also significant?

Clare: Absolutely right. This gets very interesting when we start looking at the planetary cycles, but all this will have to wait till next term, I'm afraid. The point to remember about aspects is that, if two or more planets or points in the birth chart are connected in any of these mathematical relationships, they can no longer work by themselves. They are unable to function without each other – their destiny is shared. It is helpful to study the aspects as two evolving sequences unfolding, respectively, out of the first odd and the first even number. In the Pythagorean system, the number two has the nature of *yin*, the first female number, and the number three has the nature of *yang*, the first male number. This system was developed by Aristotle in his famous Table of Opposites.

Male	Female
Limit	Unlimited
One	Many
Right	Left
Odd	Even
Resting	Moving
Straight	Curved
Light	Dark
Good	Bad
Square	Oblong

As you will see from this table, it is fortunate for Aristotle that he lived well before the age of political correctness.

Audience: But surely the number one is the first odd number?

Clare: That is a good point, and of course you are factually correct. But when this is seen symbolically, unity – or the One – is primordial. It is the original creative force of the universe, which pre-exists any kind of differentiation. The One is the seat of the original wholeness out of which all numbers emerge. All the principles in the table of opposites are included in the One, merged with their primal source. This explains why the conjunction is not, strictly speaking, an aspect at all. We can learn some interesting things from this Table of Opposites, particularly in view of the fact that it was the ancient Greeks who first constructed the system of the astrological aspects. Using the analogies and associations contained in this table, it is not so difficult to understand why *hard* aspects – those which unfold from the original even, female number two – have traditionally been interpreted as difficult, tense, effortful, challenging (moving), devious (curved), unfortunate, malefic, and just plain bad, whereas *soft* aspects – which unfold from the original odd, male number three – have been traditionally interpreted as easy (resting), pleasurable, straight, light, fortunate, benefic, harmonious and good.

G. Riesch, 'Margarita philosophica', Freiburg (1503)[24]

---

[24] Illustration from Lawlor, Robert, *Sacred Geometry* (London: Thames and Hudson Ltd., 1982), p. 7: 'Arithmetic is personified as a woman with the two geometric progressions on her thighs (symbolising the generative function). The first series, 1, 2, 4, 8, goes down the left thigh, associating the even numbers with the feminine side of the body. The second series, 1, 3, 9, 27, goes down the right

If we extend this analogy to equate matter with the feminine principle and spirit with the masculine principle, we can also see how the aspects emerging from the number two are *'doing'* aspects, engaged with actual manifestation and embodiment, providing the resistance, the reflection and the container for the inspiration, clarity and light of the male spirit. The aspects emerging from the number three are *'being'* aspects. As I mentioned last term, it is important to remember that the masculine-feminine, spirit-matter, active-passive, yang-yin polarities in astrology and in mathematical symbolism do not refer to our biology but to our psyches. So we may have a prevalence of 'doing' or of 'being' aspects, regardless of our gender.

For the Pythagoreans, the first union of the masculine and feminine principles does not occur until we get to the number five, which is two plus three. The quintile, which is the aspect of 72° created when the horoscope is divided by five, describes creativity, joy and

---

thigh, associating the odd numbers with the masculine side, an association which goes back to the Pythagoreans, for whom the odd numbers were male and the even numbers were female. The Greeks called these two series the *Lambda*, and Plato in the *Timaeus* uses them to describe the World Soul. On the woman's left sits Pythagoras, using an abacus system for computation. In this system, number notation is dependent upon spatial arrangement. Boethius sits on her right, using Arabic numerals in a modern system of calculation with which number notation has become an abstract system independent of its geometric origin.'

consciousness. The five-pointed star and the pentagram are sacred symbols in many cultures, and it is from this figure that the golden section is derived, a proportion which has been used in many sacred buildings, from ancient Greek temples to the Gothic cathedrals, and which creates a particularly pleasing sense of harmony and balance.

There is a point I want to make before we start looking at the actual aspects themselves. Although the symbolic numerical meaning of an aspect tells us something about the general nature of the relationship between two or more planets, at the end of the day the meaning of every aspect and every aspect pattern is unique to a particular individual and a particular chart. Whether we are interpreting aspects which belong to the two series or the three series of numbers, and whether or not we are thinking in terms of *being* or *doing* aspects, every single aspect and aspect pattern needs to be analysed entirely in its own terms, which will include the intrinsic meaning of the planets involved as well as the houses and signs in which they fall. What we are really looking for is the story, and if we pay good attention to all the factors involved, then the meaning of the aspect and the themes of the story will gradually come to life.

Audience: So does this mean that we shouldn't pay too much attention to the meaning of the aspect itself?

Clare: Well, I think it is important in the first instance, because it is the mathematical relationship that tells us that two or more planets are linked together in a certain way. But once we have identified that, then I think our focus should be to extract the unique story revealed by the planets involved, according to the signs and houses they are in. What I am really trying to say is that squares are not necessarily difficult and trines are not necessarily easy – it all depends on the context. Hopefully, as we go through some examples, this will become clearer.

The conjunction   ☌

We are going to start by looking at the conjunction which, strictly speaking, does not really qualify as an aspect at all. The conjunction signifies unity, undifferentiated energy, the merging of two or more planets in such a way that they always operate simultaneously. Whether or not the planets concerned are inherently sympathetic to each other, they are irrevocably joined together.

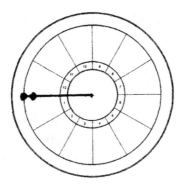

Two planets, or any two points in the chart, such as a planet and an angle, will be in a conjunction if they are within 8° of each other. This is a relationship of unity, of oneness – there is no separation or differentiation between them, and there is no objective awareness of either planet as a separate entity. For example if you have a Sun-Mercury conjunction, your identity is going to be connected to your thinking process; you cannot separate them. Planets in a conjunction aspect are normally in the same sign and house, which indicates a concentration or focus in the area of life associated with that house.

Audience: What happens if two planets are in conjunction, but they are in different signs or houses? How do you interpret that?

Clare: This is an example of an aspect breaking the rules – and I'm afraid it can happen with all aspects. In a nice simple conjunction, the planets involved will be in the same sign and house. But if, for example, one planet is right at the end of a sign or house, and the other planet is right at the beginning of the next sign or house, the conjunction is neither supported nor strengthened by the signs or houses in which it occurs. The mathematical symmetry is broken. In these cases, I think the intrinsic meaning of the aspect itself breaks down and our task is then to analyse both planets individually as separate entities, by sign and house, before bringing them together in our aspect interpretation. The technical term for these kinds of aspects is that they are 'dissociate' or 'dissociated'.

Audience: Can you give an example of this, Clare?

Clare: Let's assume, for example, that one planet is right at the end of Pisces and the other is right at the beginning of Aries. This means that the two planets will be coming from very different perspectives, and there will be a tension between them that is not normally present when planets are in conjunction. The interesting thing about adjacent signs and houses is that they have absolutely nothing in common. Pisces is a mutable water sign and Aries is a cardinal fire sign, so they are unlikely to be able to understand each other. So in this case, we have a 'dissociated conjunction' and the tension of that has to be built into our interpretation. A 'dissociated opposition' will occur, for example, if one planet is at 25° Gemini, and the other planet is at 1° Capricorn. In this case, the planets are still in opposition, with a 6° orb, but the symmetry is lost, because a natural opposition would be between planets in Gemini/Sagittarius or Cancer/Capricorn. Let's look at some actual examples. Who has a conjunction of two or more planets?

Moon-Venus-Neptune conjunction

Beth: I have Moon, Venus and Neptune conjunct.

Clare: That means that all three planets work together. This is a good example, because as you can see from the chart, Neptune is not strictly conjunct Venus because they are more than 8° apart, but the Moon is in between them, linking them both to each other. Let's see if we can find a composite image or picture for these three planets together. This is a *stellium*, which is the technical jargon for three or more planets in conjunction. It functions rather like a complex, and is certainly an area of focus and emphasis in the chart. What ideas come to mind?

Audience: Idealised emotion.

Audience: Generous and giving.

Audience: Deceptive

Audience: Do you drift around in a cloud?

Clare: With both the personal feminine planets involved here, this tells us something about you as a woman and your relationship with your mother and with women in general. With Neptune here as well, we might start thinking about being in love with love, possibly even addicted to love. There could be an idealisation of the perfect feminine, and even themes around sacrificial women. Would you say you had a romantic nature?

Beth: Yes, I think I do. And I see my mother as trying to fit into the wife role rather than being true to herself. She has always been concerned about how people see her, more concerned about other people's values than about her own.

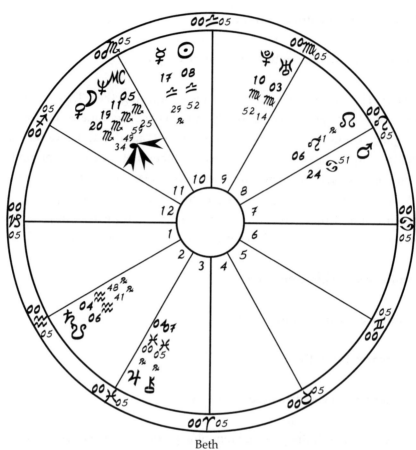

Beth
Chart data omitted for reasons of confidentiality

Clare: Do you find it rather hard to define your relationship with your mother, as if she was rather mysterious or unavailable to you in some way? She may also be a very devotional figure dedicated to serving others, particularly in her role as wife and mother. Let's add the sign and the house and see what additional information this stellium can give us. All three planets are in Scorpio in the 11th house, which makes the stellium more hidden and intense. Scorpio adds an underlying emotional intensity and complexity, so we might suggest that you, and perhaps your mother as well, derive your power as women through relationships, but equally, you may well feel that you sacrifice yourself in relationships. Do you recognise these themes in your own life?

Beth: Yes, I certainly think there are two sides to this Venus.

Clare: Moon, Venus, and Neptune in Scorpio are a powerful force, seductive, rather unearthly, and very mysterious. An image or story for this composite picture might be something like the sirens in Greek mythology, using their power and their beauty and their singing to hypnotise and seduce passing sailors, who would be pulled towards them in a trance and end up being drowned on the rocks. So it has a magnetic and rather dark aspect to it as well. In the 11th house we might imagine that your female friends are very important to you, since Scorpio generally makes few, but very intense, friendships. Since the 11th house is also about your social or political ideals, you may well find yourself involved in organisations which are concerned with women who may have been exploited or manipulated in some way.

Beth: Well, I generally find it easier to be friends with men than with women.

Clare: Perhaps you find women a bit dangerous?

Beth: I think it is important for me to fit in. To be accepted.

Clare: So we could say that you value (Venus) belonging (Moon) to the group (11th house), and perhaps you will do whatever it takes (Neptune) to be accepted.

Beth: This is a very difficult combination for me. I think Neptune is quite a negative influence, being connected to such personal planets.

Clare: As part of the Neptune in Scorpio generation, you will no doubt have a longing for, and an attraction to, intense emotional encounters, and with the Moon and Venus there as well, it is these kinds of experiences which will transform how you feel about and value yourself as a woman. No doubt you will experience many different manifestations of this combination during your life, which are likely to revolve around issues of both power and powerlessness, both in yourself and amongst your friends, and in your work.

Sun-Mercury Conjunction

Susan: I have a conjunction of the Sun and Mercury. They are in Gemini in the 11th house.

Clare: OK, let's see how that works. A general word first about the Sun-Mercury conjunction: You will remember that Mercury is the closest planet to the Sun, never more than 27° from the Sun, and prone to changing direction on a regular basis. This means that the Sun-Mercury conjunction is very common, and many of us will have it. In fact, the conjunction is the only exact aspect which can occur between Mercury and the Sun. Perhaps this explains why so many of us identify (Sun) with our ideas (Mercury) – to the extent that if someone criticises or disagrees with us, it is all too easy to take that as a personal criticism, rather than as a simple disagreement with our ideas. When Mercury is not conjunct the Sun, or in a different sign from the Sun, then it is easier to be more objective.

This particular conjunction in Gemini indicates that you are likely to be flexible, adaptable and articulate, and since it is in the 11th house, no doubt you are also sociable and friendly, quick to make connections, and functioning as a messenger or go-between or communicator in some way, particularly amongst your colleagues and in any groups with which you are involved.

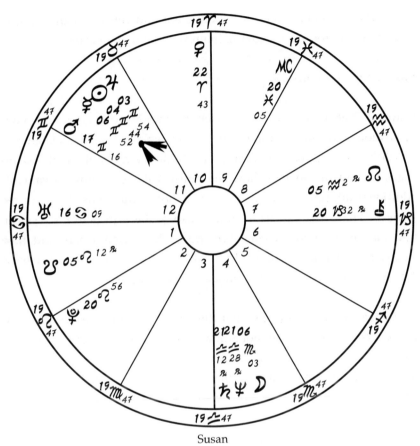

Susan

Chart data omitted for reasons of confidentiality

Susan: That's absolutely right, and in fact I am a teacher. But I also tend to find myself in the position of being an arbitrator between two people, husband and wife, for example. But, because I am a Gemini, I don't really want to get too involved, and actually I think I am rather flippant.

Clare: I would imagine that, because this conjunction is in your 11th house, you are not as flippant as you might imagine. This is a fixed house and, associated with the sign of Aquarius, so I suspect that, although you no doubt prefer to remain objective and detached, you are, perhaps, rather more loyal, consistent and reliable than you give yourself credit for. As a matter of interest, what do you teach?

Susan: I teach English.

Clare: That is perfect for a Gemini Sun-Mercury, because your profession is to communicate, and you are actually teaching a language, which is a vehicle of communication. While we are looking at Susan's chart, I want to illustrate how the house ruler can provide valuable additional information about the way a house functions. You will see from the chart that Taurus is on the cusp of the 11th house, so we can find out more about Susan's 11th house by seeing where and how Venus, the ruler of Taurus, is placed. In fact, her Venus is in Aries in the 10th house. What extra information does this give us?

Audience: I would imagine that this makes her more ambitious, and that she is a natural leader, not afraid to be an authority figure.

Susan: Funny you should say that, because I am actually head of the English department in the school where I work.

Sun conjunct Moon

Jan: I have a Sun-Moon conjunction in Libra in the 4th house, so I suppose that means my emotions and my identity are very tied up with each other. Does it mean that I am not able to observe myself objectively?

Clare: With a Sun-Moon conjunction, we tend to start by identifying with the Moon, because that is the child in us. So we start off needing (Moon) recognition (Sun). We need (Moon) to be seen and recognised (Sun). Gradually, there is likely to be a shift of emphasis as we begin to identify more with the Sun, and eventually, if we can make the transition, then we are likely to become (Sun) very nurturing and caring and giving (Moon). So, although these two planets are conjunct, there is usually a natural progression as we grow up from Moon identification toward Sun identification.

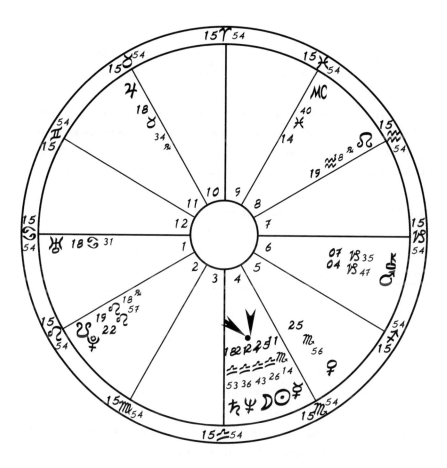

Jan
Chart data omitted for reasons of confidentiality

This conjunction also tells us that you were born at a new Moon, which is when the Sun and Moon come together. But these two planets are also parental significators, so I would imagine that your experience of your parents is that they function as one unit – that they are coming from the same place. For example, they may well have worked together at home, since this conjunction is in the 4th house. This would be an ideal placement if your parents ran a hotel, for example, or perhaps an art gallery, since both planets are in Libra.

Jan: Yes, they did both work together. They ran a business together from home when I was growing up, doing market gardening.

Clare: That is a perfect example of a Sun-Moon conjunction in Venus-ruled Libra, since Venus also rules gardening and flowers and all the fruits of the earth. It would be interesting to know where your Venus is, since it rules your 4th house as well as both your Sun and Moon.

Jan: My Venus is in Scorpio in the 5th house.

Clare: It looks as if the relationship between your parents may have been so complete and intense that there may not have been much space for you in there. Since your Sun and Moon ruler is in the 5th house, can you tell us something about your childhood and about your personal passions?

Jan: Well, I have devoted most of my life to self-growth in one form or another, and I have always interpreted my 4th house as more to do with the roots of consciousness. My life theme has been going inwards through therapy and meditation. I like my home to be beautiful, but I am not really a very homey person, and I have never lived in one place for a particularly long time.

Clare: So you need (Moon) to understand yourself (Sun) – to self-nurture (Sun-Moon), to find harmony and balance within, which would be the Libra. Like all conjunctions, this can be very subjective. And the

4th house, in your case, seems to be more about your private inner space – finding where you belong within yourself – than about your outer home.

Jan: Yes, that's right. I actually like spending a lot of time on my own.

The opposition 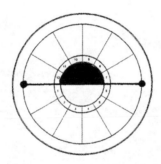 180°

Clare: Let's turn our attention now to the 'two' series of aspects. When the circle is divided into two, the result is the opposition between planets that are 180° apart.

We have already studied the whole principle of duality and polarisation in quite a bit of depth, and so we know that this is going to be an aspect of maximum tension, with the planets at each end of the opposition appearing to be mutually exclusive and yet at the same time complementing and balancing each other. As we have seen, the usual tendency with an opposition is to polarise and project, identifying with one side of the opposition and dis-identifying with the other side, which means that we are always meeting it in the form of outer events or other people. This aspect is particularly unstable and frustrating, and can lead to feelings of paralysis, of being caught between two poles. The attraction of opposites is the counter-tendency to this polarisation, and its resolution depends upon finding some kind of conscious relationship between the two poles.

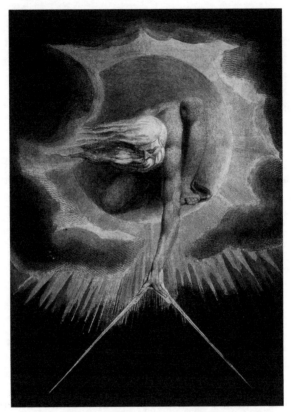

William Blake, 'The Ancient of Days' (1824)

Audience: So if you have an opposition, then your task is to recognise and then accept and integrate what you project outside?

Clare: Yes, although this is one of the hardest things to do. But our entire charts are constructed as a series of oppositions, opposite houses and opposite signs, so life itself seems to be an expression of this great drama of opposites. Having planets in opposition simply makes the drama more personal and immediate. However uncomfortable this may feel, nevertheless, planets in opposition ensure that neither side becomes too extreme. It is the nature of all the aspects created by the division of the circle into two, four or eight that the planets struggle and confront each other, which means that something can happen and the relationship between the two planets can become more conscious. And it is out of that tension that awareness is born. After all, there is no possibility of a conscious reconciliation if we don't have the struggle in the first place. Let's look at some oppositions, to get a feel for the way they work.

Mercury opposite Pluto

Sue: I have Pluto in Leo in the 9th house opposite Sun and Mercury in Aquarius in the 3rd house. I am obsessed with astrology – I have loads of books and am reading about it all the time, but I keep that part of my life very secret and never talk about it to anyone. Could that be because of Pluto?

Clare: This opposition is across fixed signs, and therefore particularly resistant to integration. The Sun and Mercury in the 3rd house indicate that learning is very important to you, and that you love being a student. You have a clear, rational and objective mind, and I would imagine that thinking astrologically comes very naturally to you, since Aquarius is very comfortable with the conceptual clarity of models and maps. It could even feel as if your fellow students are your true intellectual brothers and sisters.

The addition of Pluto to the picture adds intensity and describes penetrating thought and your sense of the immense power of words and of ideas. But it is clear from what you say that you feel there is something unacceptable or dark or dangerous about your interest in astrology. And that could be for religious reasons, since Pluto is in the 9th house.

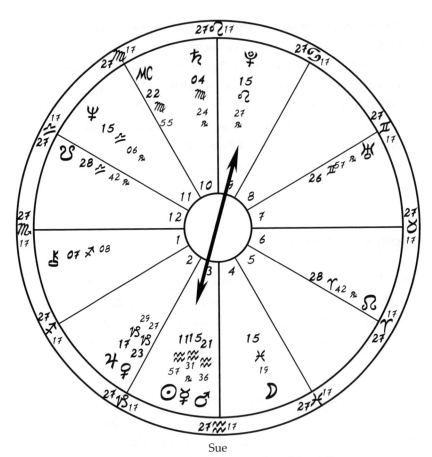

Sue

Chart data omitted for reasons of confidentiality

On the one hand, you are naturally attracted to unusual or unconventional ideas, and to the larger patterns that include us all. But on the other hand, Pluto in the 9th house no doubt appears to threaten your identity in some way, and to sabotage your studies. How would we interpret Pluto in Leo in the 9th house?

Audience: Breaking down the philosophy?

Audience: Total absence of belief?

Clare: Yes, a Sun-Mercury-Pluto combination describes someone who thinks very deeply, who is inclined to test their ideas to destruction, and who is not going to take anything at face value. We know that whenever you get into this 3rd house intellectual structure, you are also likely, in some sense, to feel you are being plunged into very deep waters which could even feel threatening and dangerous, because Pluto is always about survival. And it is to do with religion and philosophy, isn't it?

Sue: Well, I am a non-believer, but I do come from an Irish Catholic background.

Clare: This is a perfect description of Pluto in Leo in the 9th house. It sounds as if you have already tested your religious inheritance to destruction and rejected it, on an intellectual level at least. But Catholicism is a very powerful force, and no doubt there is a huge dilemma between pursuing your natural interest in learning, your belief in freedom of thought, and your fear of going to the devil – literally.

Sue: Yes, I think it was only a few years ago that the Pope forbade Catholics to consult astrologers.

Clare: You are very understandably caught in a conflict between your intellect and your instincts, and this opposition can easily feel like a kind of paralysis.

Audience: So Sue doesn't believe intellectually in God, but she does believe instinctively?

Clare: That certainly seems to be the case. Intellectually, there is no difficulty. Sue loves studying astrology. But if this is to become a powerful transformative aspect of her life and of her understanding, then she is going to have to find some kind of relationship between her love of astrology as a pure and clean, intellectual Aquarian discipline, and the issues which are haunting her about astrology being evil and dangerous. So the way she is dealing with this at the moment is to keep her astrology and her astrological studies secret, which is easier than 'coming out' because it means that her Sun-Mercury in Aquarius can just get on with studying, and Pluto can go underground. But, of course, it will always be there on some level. I imagine these are the kinds of things that you are going on for you.

Sue: Normally I am absolutely fine with this, but sometimes I have really bad nightmares about dreadful punishments and being burned at the stake and other things happening, and I don't seem to be able to shake them off.

Clare: That is exactly what one would expect. Having been consciously banished, Pluto is now communicating with you through your unconscious, while you are asleep. And, since this is a 9th house placement, whether or not you consciously believe in God, your God is becoming angry and destructive and you feel you will be punished for your ideas. The difficulty with this particular opposition is that Aquarius is so rational, civilised, detached and idealistic. The more extreme this becomes, then the more threatening, primitive and irrational the dark becomes. Your task, with a Sun-Mercury-Pluto combination, appears to be to recognise the real power of ideas by exploring whether true understanding of any subject might include both the light and dark, rational and instinctive aspects. We can find out more about this by looking at Saturn and the Moon, which rule your 3rd and 9th houses.

Sue: That's interesting, because I have Saturn in Virgo in the 10th house and my mother is a strict Catholic, very dutiful and into service.

Clare: With Saturn in the 10th house and ruling your 3rd house, mother is also, in some sense, the law.

Audience: Does that mean that Sue is going to have to reject her mother as well?

Clare: No. It means that she is going to have to become her own authority in these matters. Saturn is also the personal ruler of Aquarius, so it rules Sue's Sun and Mercury. This is about taking her own authority and giving herself permission to think what she thinks and to believe what she believes. And the transpersonal ruler of Aquarius, which is just as important, is Uranus in Gemini – the free thinker. We can begin to see where this particular struggle is going. It won't be easy, but Sue has Scorpio rising as well, so she is bound to live her life intensely, experiencing repeated periods of personal metamorphosis as she goes through the fires and regenerates herself. The other interesting feature of your chart is that your 9th house is ruled by the Moon in Pisces in the 4th house, so essentially we could say that you have an extremely devotional nature and that eventually you may be able to make peace with your God.

Sue: That is all really helpful, thank you. But it is also very hard.

Clare: Yes, particularly because this is a fixed opposition, so in addition to the compulsion to change, there is going to be a resistance to change. This theme is always present anyway in the sign of Aquarius with its two rulers – Uranus seeks change and Saturn resists change. If we have a cardinal opposition, we will feel challenged to actively resolve the tension. And a mutable opposition isn't going to be quite so tense or fraught, because both planets will be inherently more inclined to adapt and adjust and to be more flexible. But a fixed opposition will go on resisting until some kind of change is forced. And it can be a very stressful and tense experience.

Sue: I did in fact have a kind of mental breakdown when Pluto went over my Ascendant. That was a few years after my brother died in a car crash, and I completely lost my faith. It was a really difficult time in my life.

Clare: Learning astrology may well help you understand and come to terms with this very painful period in your life. You can see for yourself that the 3rd house describes your brother and your very close relationship to him, and how his death affected your faith. I think we can find great comfort from astrology, since it helps us make sense of the events that occur in our lives. After all, as Jung said, only suffering without meaning is unbearable.

Sun opposite Pluto

Tricia: I have something similar, with Sun in Aquarius in the 2nd house opposite Moon-Pluto in Leo in the 8th. Could we look at that?

Clare: Yes, and once again we will be working with the themes of light and dark, the intellect and the instincts. The Sun is how and where we seek to shine, to be recognised. However, with Pluto opposite the Sun, we can feel that our true identity is buried or sabotaged or somehow unacceptable. As a result we can build a kind of 'false self' which poses as our identity but which never feels completely authentic. With the Sun in the 2nd house of self-worth, no doubt your journey will be to learn to value yourself, just as you are, which will involve some kind of conscious integration between your Sun, Moon and Pluto.

Sun in Aquarius is clear, rational, detached, idealistic and very civilised. The Moon with Pluto is deeply instinctive, primitive and archaic, and in the 8th house it is not only deeply buried, but also likely to be projected onto mother and onto women generally. Again, this opposition is across fixed signs, and the Sun-Moon opposition points to a fundamental split between the masculine and the feminine principles, with the masculine being light and clear and the feminine being very intense, dark and mysterious. You may well have experienced this in your own life as deeply entrenched power struggles between your mother and father.

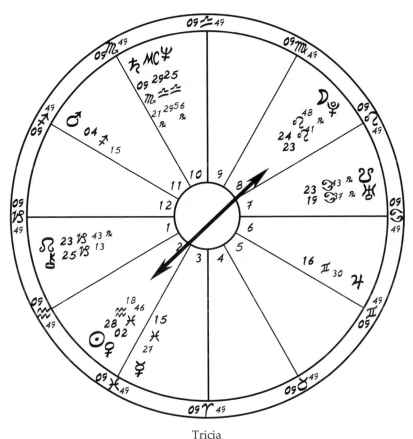

Tricia
Chart data omitted for reasons of confidentiality

Tricia: That's right, and I also experience this as a power struggle with women. I always get the feeling that women think I am too powerful and that they fear me, so they want to break me or subdue me, or something like that.

Clare: Yes, that is exactly the feeling you are likely to have. A useful image for Moon-Pluto in the 8th house is the witch, which can, of course, be both positive, in the form of the wise woman, or negative, in which case you may feel that women want to sabotage you or wipe you out altogether.

Tricia: Yes.

Clare: And that can lead to a powerful conviction that you are not allowed to be who you really are. And so, like Hades himself, you have to wear a cloak of invisibility and keep your true identity hidden.

Tricia: If I try and be sweet and nice, with my Venus in Pisces, then they think I am a wimp and walk all over me. But if I try to be strong, then they think I am a powerful, dominating bitch. Either way, I can't win. I don't seem to be able to find that balance. Although I am quite well balanced in myself, I always find that other people try to control me. I feel really strong within, and men always say they like strong women. Perhaps that is my own experience of the Moon-Pluto coming out.

Clare: Although power struggles are something you experience in relationships, we could say that this is something as yet unresolved within you, which is constellated in relationships. That is exactly how oppositions function. Outside the arena of relationships you can no doubt function quite comfortably as an Aquarian, and keep all your ideals intact. But it is close emotional relationships which plunge you into that Plutonic realm of power and survival and issues about who is controlling whom.

Tricia: Is there anything I can do about it?

Clare: Yes, recognise it, which ultimately means some kind of conscious relationship between your intellect and your instinctual nature, and learning to express your solar purpose and personal authority as an expression of your intense and passionate nature, rather than trying to be who you think you ought to be according to the values of others – which will never really work.

Tricia: I think I used to be much more intense and passionate, but nobody seems to be able to handle that. When I was younger, I was always being told not to be so intense.

Audience: I have been thinking about this during the week. If you have Pluto in aspect to your Sun or Moon or Venus or whatever, then when one is triggered, Pluto will be triggered at the same time. This can be quite a burden to carry.

Clare: Yes, it can, particularly if the Sun or Moon or Venus otherwise wants to be very light, detached and rational.

Audience: And there is nothing really that one can do about it, apart from trying to understand and accept it and work with it?

Clare: There is a tremendous depth to Pluto, and Plutonic people – by which I mean people with Scorpio rising, or Sun in Scorpio, or strong 8th house placements, or several Pluto aspects – are going to go deeper on an emotional level, and seem to have to spend periods of their lives in the underworld. But the underworld is a place of immense wealth, and the purpose of being there is to connect to the life force itself and to the wisdom which comes from that.

Tricia: It helped me to understand Pluto better when I started thinking of it more as a goddess than as a god. There is a whole other model of feminine power that is very ancient, but is judged and condemned in the world, or just not understood properly. You have to go right back into history, where the high priestess was honoured. I think that learning how to be powerful in a feminine way is an issue of our times, instead of trying to be like GI Jane and taking on male values. My favourite saying is that there is nothing so powerful as true gentleness, and there is nothing so gentle as true power.

Clare: Although I understand what you mean, it seems to me that this is your Aquarius Sun speaking, because it sounds so rational and detached, and because slogans are usually Aquarian things. There is an immensely destructive aspect to Pluto that has to do with the force of nature itself. For example, earthquakes, tidal waves and hurricanes are anything but gentle. They are absolutely ruthless and destructive. And there is nothing gentle about the dark and destructive side of human nature. The question is whether we can bear to look our own darkness in the face and accept that it belongs to us.

Tricia: Well, I know that when Pluto is active in my chart, it is always horrible and shocking. But at these times I also feel intensely alive and energised, in a way. When it is not active in my life, I tend to feel rather frozen and dead.

Clare: That is a good example of the black and white quality of Pluto. We cannot negotiate with Pluto; it is totally uncompromising. It will either be in its ice phase, completely cut off from our consciousness, or in its fire phase, in which we find ourselves burning – and there is very little in between.
Audience: In one of our lessons, you mentioned the word 'scapegoat' in relation to Pluto aspects. How does that work?

Clare: Scapegoating occurs whenever a group, family, tribe or society refuses, either consciously or unconsciously, to take responsibility for its own primitive darkness – in other words, for its own Pluto. In these cases, the darkness will be projected onto an individual or another group, tribe or race. They are blamed and scapegoated for the qualities that the group is not prepared to own. In families, there is often a kind of unconscious contract, in which one member of the family, usually the most sensitive one, lives out the family taboos because they can't bear the weight of the dishonesty or the poison of the unconscious collusion. This person will not only bring the taboos to the surface, but will also be blamed for doing so. This is where the idea of the 'black sheep of the family' comes from, which is another aspect of the scapegoat. Take, for example, the case of a white European family, outwardly civilised, well adjusted and morally upstanding. Suppose this family is secretly harbouring racial prejudices. With what seems like uncanny predictability, the adolescent daughter who takes on the role of the family scapegoat may find herself in a relationship with a young man from a different culture and with a different skin colour. Imagine, then, the scene when she introduces him to her family. Pluto has been evoked, and all hell will be let loose.

This same mechanism occurs with all kinds of collectives, and with countries as well. Other groups or nations or races will be scapegoated in an effort to maintain the moral high ground. Someone or something else has to carry the evil and the darkness that are not being recognised within. Jung wrote a great deal about this phenomenon in terms of racism, apartheid and religious hatred, and he believed that, until we are each prepared to accept our own individual burden of darkness, we will continue to see it only 'out there' in others, and not in ourselves.

Sun opposite Neptune

Laura: Can I ask something about Neptune? My Sun is in the 1st house in Pisces, opposite Neptune in the 7th in Virgo.

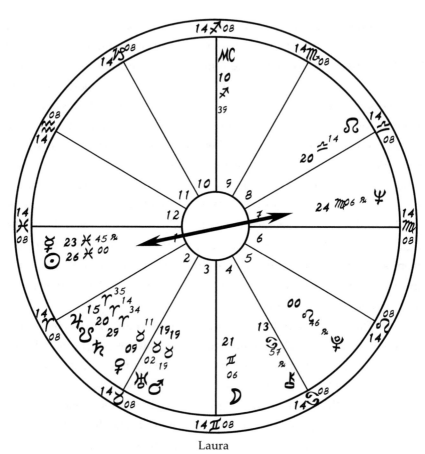

Laura

Chart data omitted for reasons of confidentiality

Clare: Well, let's start by looking at the Sun-Neptune principle. What does that say about our identity and about our experience of the masculine principle, which will include our experience of our father?

Audience: There is something nebulous and hard to grasp about this combination. Does that mean that Laura finds it difficult to reach her father, and difficult to find her own identity too? I have read somewhere that this could describe an alcoholic father.

Clare: Neptune is the dream. It describes ever-changing images and impressions and feelings. Neptune is our access to realms and landscapes that exist in the imagination. Questions of a clear or fixed identity are not really relevant to a Sun-Neptune person, because their identity is fluid, likely to change shape all the time, reflecting the environment they find themselves in. In so far as the Sun-Neptune aspect is associated with father, then we would expect that he was not around very much, certainly not available on a psychological or emotional level. It seems that he was lost to you in some way. This can lead to an idealisation of father and of the masculine, as well as a longing for him, since Neptune is where we are always thirsty. And, of course, this aspect may well describe more concrete manifestations, so your father may be a priest, or in the navy sailing the seven seas, or he could even be an alcoholic, as someone suggested.

Laura: My father was around, but he wasn't around. He was usually too busy.

Clare: And presumably you idealised him or adored him from afar?

Laura: When I was younger, I suppose. I didn't know him very well.

Clare: We are also talking about your own identity, of course, and with Neptune in the 7th house, it is unlikely that you received any kind of clear mirroring in your childhood. So on some level, you may even be a mystery to yourself. This means that you can easily find yourself becoming whatever other people want you to be, because you have no personal investment in being a particular shape, so any one identity may well be just as good as any other identity.

This is an immensely creative and artistic combination, ideal for photography, dance, acting, film-making or painting, for example, since you have a heightened sensitivity to beauty, form and shape. Because this opposition is across the 1st/7th houses, your sensitivity to others is also particularly strong, and you have a remarkable ability to devote yourself to the needs of others. The question is whether this devotion drains you or energises you, and this could go either way, depending on the strength of your personal ego container. With a strong enough ego you can choose whether and when to make yourself available to others. You can define your own boundaries, so that you are not left exhausted by others.

Audience: But isn't the opposition the struggle between the self and the other?

Clare: Yes, because we know that the theme of the 1st/7th house axis is to do with self-definition in relationship, and about discovering where the boundaries are between who I am and who the other is – defining what is me and what is the other. So it is particularly easy for Laura to seek to define herself through relationships, and in addition to that, with a Pisces Ascendant, the boundary between herself and her environment is likely to be diffuse. This adds to the general theme of the Sun in Pisces and Neptune in the 7th house. It is all so transpersonal and collective that we need to make it more personal by bringing in Jupiter, which is the personal ruler of the chart and of the Sun, and also Mercury, which is the ruler of the Descendant. This should help us get a better handle on the way this opposition works.

Audience: Why is Jupiter the ruler of the chart?

Clare: Because Pisces, the sign on the Ascendant, has two rulers. The personal ruler is Jupiter, and no doubt you can see how important Jupiter is, because it is also the ruler of the MC, which is in Sagittarius, so Jupiter rules both angles. With Jupiter in Aries in the 2nd house, the picture changes quite dramatically, because this indicates a particularly strong sense of self-worth and an ability to fight for one's own values and beliefs. In this chart there is a particularly strong relationship between the 1st and 7th houses, because there is a *mutual reception* between Neptune and Mercury. A mutual reception between two planets occurs when they are in each other's signs or houses. In this case, Neptune, the ruler of the 1st house, is in the 7th house, and Mercury, the ruler of the 7th house, is in the 1st house. Can you recognise these patterns in your own life, Laura?

Laura: Actually, I can't take too much – it's almost the opposite.

Clare: I wonder if the people you tend to attract are Neptunians – people with no boundaries, who are both unavailable but at the same time completely merged with you. You can feel drowned by their demands, and need to define the boundaries yourself.

Laura: That's true, but the strange thing is that they are not needy to start with, only when you get to know them.

Clare: Funny how that happens. And as you get to know them in all their Neptunian ways, you increasingly find yourself taking the opposite, Virgoan, attitude and becoming very boundary-conscious and self-contained.

Laura: That's exactly right.

Lesson Seven: Introduction to the Aspects, Part Two

The Square   □   90°

As we have already seen, the division of a circle by four brings about manifestation, as symbolised by the four elements, directions, and angles in the birth chart.

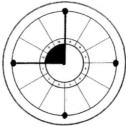

The geometrical symbol for the earth is the cube and, for Jung, the number four describes the way we make sense of the world, as can be seen from the universal fourfold structure of the mandala.

The square is an aspect of 90°, and planets in square confront and challenge each other. Squares are much more tangible than oppositions.

They symbolise resistance and motivation in equal measure. Although this does not necessarily feel comfortable, squares provide the energy and determination we need in order to make things happen and to achieve our goals.

The Labyrinth at Chartres Cathedral

Planets in square generally share the same orientation, since they will both either be in cardinal, fixed or mutable signs. As you can imagine, with planets in cardinal signs, the challenge of the square may well be rather welcome, because each planet will stimulate the other to express itself in a dynamic, focused and goal-oriented way. With a fixed square, on the other hand, each planet will resist the challenge of the other, and this can become very rigid and unyielding. A mutable square is much easier, since both planets are inherently more inclined to accommodate, adapt and adjust to each other. The tension of this aspect is explained by the fact that, although the planets will normally have the same modality, they will be in different elements, and so they will have a different way of processing information. This creates a friction between the two planets that may never be entirely resolved, but this tension also provides energy and motivation. Has anybody got any squares that they would like to look at?

Anna: I have a cardinal square between Moon in Libra in the 11th house and Mars in Capricorn in the 2nd house.

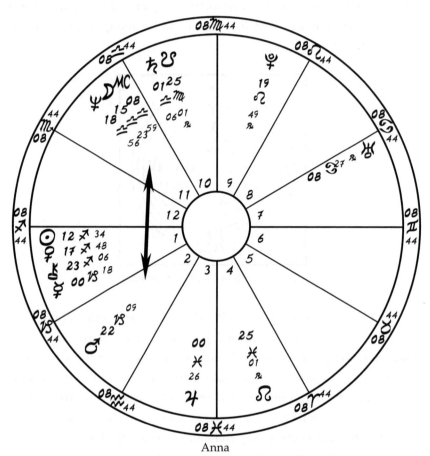

Anna

Chart data omitted for reasons of confidentiality

Clare: Let's start by looking at the Moon in Libra in the 11th house, which also happens to be conjunct Neptune and the MC. What does everyone think that Anna needs (Moon)? What kind of public image does she project (Moon conjunct MC)? What are her dreams and ideals (Neptune), and what nourishes her and makes her feel safe and comfortable?

Audience: I should imagine that Anna's public status as a wife and mother is very important to her, and that she may well do whatever is necessary to achieve this dream. I would also image that she needs everything to be nice and harmonious, and she will probably also need a partner who is also a friend, in order to feel complete. Perhaps she is nourished by her friends, or by being involved in social events. I should think she gives great dinner parties.

Clare: How are we doing so far?

Anna: So far, so good. That is definitely an aspect of my role as a wife and mother.

Clare: Now let's have a look at Mars in Capricorn in the 2nd house. What do you think that is about?

Audience: Since the 2nd house is about self-worth, I would imagine that Anna is ambitious and hard-working, and her self esteem is connected to earning her own money and standing on her own feet financially.

Clare: Exactly. But there is an inherent tension between Libra and Capricorn because, although they are both cardinal signs, Libra is an air sign and Capricorn is an earth sign. I would imagine there is a struggle for Anna between her rational principles (air) and her need to achieve something practical and concrete (earth). How can she reconcile her need to be there for other people, for her husband and children, and her need to stand on her own feet and earn her own money? I suspect that when you are achieving your goals (Capricorn), you may well feel energised (Mars) but guilty, because you are not looking after the needs of your family. On the other hand, when you are in your wife and mother role (Moon in Libra), you may well find yourself feeling angry and frustrated because you are not doing your own thing.

Anna: That's right – you have just put one of my major dilemmas into words. And what I really don't like about it is how angry I end up feeling.

Clare: Well, the two planets involved are Moon and Mars, so it is not surprising that the tension of this square can be expressed as anger, a kind of emotionally fuelled rage. Let's see if we can find out a bit more about this. Can you tell us where Venus and Saturn are in your chart? These are the two planets which rule your 11th and 2nd houses, and which also rule your Moon and Mars.

Anna: I have Venus in the 1st house in Sagittarius, and Saturn in the 10th house in Libra.

Clare: This tells us that your Moon ruler is expansive, restless and adventurous (Sagittarius), and Venus is going to feel trapped and frustrated unless she is on the move and having fun. But your Mars ruler is particularly ambitious, because Saturn is in Libra in the 10th house. This is a dutiful and responsible placement, and it is very important for you to be respected as a professional woman (Saturn in the 10th house). How can you bring both these things together in your life – professional achievement and status on the one hand, and the constant broadening of your personal horizons (Venus in Sagittarius in the 1st house) on the other?

Anna: I am an anthropologist by training, and have lived in many different countries, studying the social behaviour of different tribes. There is so much more work I want to do on this, and yet since I had children, all that has had to stop. I am beginning to think I am going to need to find space in my life for both things.

Clare: That's right, and although that may never feel completely comfortable, nevertheless you will at least be living both ends of your square. And that can be a dynamic and successful combination. If you are working, the energy of Mars can be used to achieve your goals, rather than having nowhere to go and ending up with you feeling angry and frustrated and venting your rage on your family or on yourself.

The T-square

Maria: I have a T-square in my chart. What does that mean?

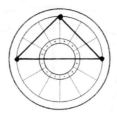

Clare: The T-square is one of the major aspect patterns that can be found in the birth chart. A T-square is formed when there are two planets in opposition and one planet square to the opposition. Once again, T-squares are likely to be either cardinal, fixed or mutable. The planet at the apex, which squares both ends of the opposition, functions as the catalyst, mediating between the planets in opposition. This is an open, unstable, stressful aspect pattern but, like all aspects in the 'two' series, it is often extremely effective and dynamic. Let's have a look at your T-square. Would you like to describe it?

Maria: It is a really horrible one. I have Uranus in Leo in the 8th house, opposite Venus in Aquarius in the 2nd house, and both are square to Moon in Taurus in the 5th house.

Clare: Before we go into the details, what kind of story are we looking for, with a Moon-Venus-Uranus cast of characters?

Audience: We have the two feminine planets at war with each other in some way, since they are square to each other, and Uranus makes the whole thing more edgy and unpredictable.

Clare: Yes, the square between the Moon and Venus is always interesting, because it describes some kind of tension between our basic security needs and our adult desires. In a woman's chart, this often seems to manifest as competition between mother and daughter, the grown woman (Venus) and the young girl (Moon).

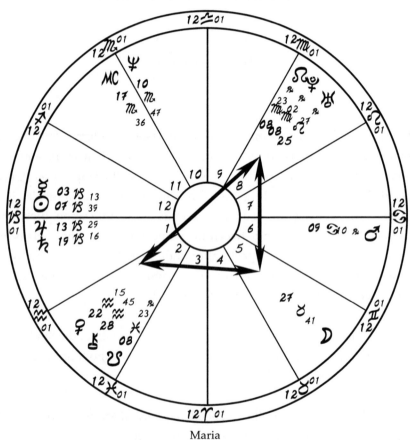

Maria

Chart data omitted for reasons of confidentiality

This square seems to be particularly powerful during adolescence, when Venus becomes active and the girl begins to grow into her womanhood, which can be seen as a threat to the mother. The presence of Uranus in this picture suggests that one, if not both, of these aspects of the feminine may well be cut off, in an effort to avoid confrontation. If this is the case, then Uranus is likely to wreak havoc from the unconscious, creating all kinds of emotional chaos. But first of all, let's find out more about these two aspects of the feminine. Can you think of some images for Venus in Aquarius in the 2nd house?

Audience: Is this a love of ideals?

Audience: I think it is objective and friendly. I would imagine that Maria values honesty, and that she values her friends.

Clare: Yes, this is a very rational, fair-minded, intellectual, objective and adult Venus. I would imagine that you value quite a bit of personal space and autonomy.

Maria: Definitely.

Clare: What does Moon in Taurus in the 5th house need?

Audience: Security and the time to do what one wants.

Clare: Yes, this is a fixed square, and the tension is between the elements of air and earth, between thinking and doing. Does that describe your relationship with your mother in any way?

Maria: Well, actually, I find her rather mad. She seems to be completely cut off from her feelings, and she is very unpredictable. She has had loads of relationships, but none of them have worked out. I am afraid I am going to end up like her.

Clare: All right, we now have Uranus in the picture, and it looks as if you are living out the Moon in Taurus and she is living out what appears to be a negative expression of the Venus-Uranus opposition. Does that seem likely?

Maria: That's certainly how it feels. I have always felt as if it was my job to look after her and to provide some kind of security and stability in her life. So I can definitely relate to the Moon in Taurus. In fact I think I have always played the role of mother in our relationship.

Clare: So you find yourself holding the apex planet in this T-square, in order to provide an element of stability for your mother. This is a very graphic picture, and the challenge is to find some kind of positive relationship between these three planets for yourself and in your own life.

Maria: But I really don't believe in the way she conducts her relationships. She has always been very promiscuous, and I believe strongly in commitment and in having a stable family life.

Clare: I can hear both your Venus in Aquarius speaking here, in terms of your beliefs and ideals, and also your Moon in Taurus, in terms of your need for a stable family life. But I can't hear Uranus, which is perhaps not surprising, since it is buried in the 8th house and most likely to be projected onto others. You may experience others as unstable and unpredictable, rather than seeing this as part of your own nature. I don't mean to say that you are either unstable or unpredictable, of course, but you may not be recognising your own need for space and freedom and autonomy, so you will be confronted by this kind of behaviour in its negative manifestation in people who are close to you.

Maria: That's what I mean about this being a horrible T-square. I thought I had managed to create a stable family life of my own, but then my husband just upped and left, so I have been a single mum for years.

And I haven't been able to find a stable relationship since, which is why I am afraid I will end up like my mum.

Clare: Well, fixed T-squares are never going to be easy, but no doubt you have found great fulfilment in your role as mother, and I would imagine, with Moon in Taurus in the 5th house, your children have grown up feeling very safe and secure. Perhaps you will soon have some more space and time for yourself. A Taurus Moon in the 5th house can be very creative, and you could get great pleasure from gardening, singing, sculpting, or any other kind of Taurean pursuit.

Maria: I really hope so. Thank you for that, it was very helpful.

The grand cross

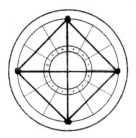

Clare: A grand cross is another aspect pattern that is created from squares and oppositions, and this configuration consists of two oppositions at right angles to one another. The oppositions are related to each other by squares, making this a closed aspect pattern that is particularly dynamic, self-motivated, and fiercely self-sufficient. People with a grand cross are very driven, and do not tend to rely on anyone other than themselves. It is a very resourceful and willful pattern, and people with this configuration often relate to the world as if it was a series of challenges and obstacles demanding to be conquered, which can lead to remarkable achievements.

Mary: I have a cardinal grand cross in my chart, with Chiron and Mercury in Capricorn in the 10th house opposite Uranus in Cancer in the 4th house, and Jupiter in Aries in the 1st house opposite Saturn in Libra in the 8th house.

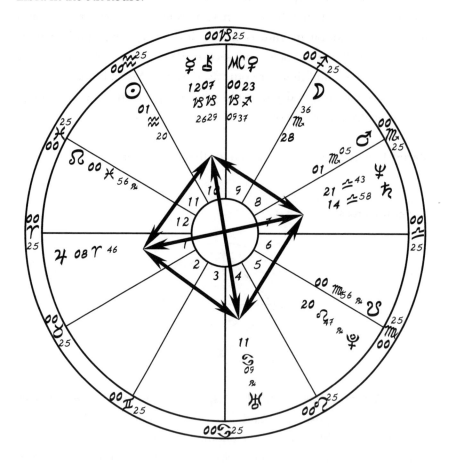

Mary
Chart data omitted for reasons of confidentiality

Clare: Before we look at this in more detail, let's just think about a story in which Chiron, Mercury, Uranus, Jupiter and Saturn all have a part to play. Does anything come to mind?

Audience: Jupiter and Saturn are the social planets, so that is about opportunities and restrictions, the tension between expansion and contraction. And Chiron and Uranus are outsiders, so there might be a theme about doing the right thing and gaining acceptance in the eyes of the world, and doing your own thing, regardless of what other people think. And Mercury is the mind, trying to make sense of all this, to mediate and bring all these things together.

Clare: That's excellent, and I think it helps us to start understanding the tensions and possibilities in this combination, in the most general sense. Now let's consider the houses in which this drama will occur. We have the 10th, 4th, 1st and 8th houses here.

Audience: The 10th and 4th houses are about family and the world, public life and private life. The 1st house is about fulfilling your personal goals, and the 8th house is about sharing.

Clare: So we are already getting a general sense of the story. Focusing in on more detail now, we could consider the Jupiter-Saturn opposition across the 1st and 7th houses in Aries and Libra. What kind of story do we have here?

Audience: Jupiter and Saturn are the principles of expansion and contraction, so Mary will feel caught between these two things. Perhaps her personal goals seem to be incompatible with her responsibilities and duties to her partner.

Clare: That's right. And because Saturn is in the normally projected 7th house, Mary is likely to feel that her partner restricts her or criticises her whenever she tries to do her own thing. In actual fact, this is an inner conflict that is difficult to resolve. How can Mary be free to follow her own path and direction and yet at the same time be a dutiful and responsible partner or spouse?

Mary: I would love to know the answer to that. My husband always comes up with loads of very sensible reasons why I can't do what I want to do, and it drives me crazy. Sometimes I feel that the only solution is to leave the marriage, but we have worked hard at it and, apart from the frustration, he is a good provider and a responsible father.

Clare: I think we can all understand how paralysed this opposition makes you feel. I suspect that you find yourself oscillating between these two positions. With Saturn in Libra in the 7th house, you will be aware that a successful marriage demands hard work and commitment. But it also feels constricting and limiting from a personal point of view. Jupiter in Aries in the 1st house is independent and goal-oriented. With Uranus squaring both Jupiter and Saturn from the 4th house, it is not surprising that, when the tension of the opposition gets too much, you have a strong urge to escape altogether by leaving the marriage and your home. The Jupiter-Uranus square needs space and freedom, and the Saturn-Uranus square indicates a struggle between staying the distance in your marriage, and escaping from its confines. But let's have a look now at the Mercury-Chiron conjunction in Capricorn opposite Uranus in Cancer across the 10th and 4th houses. What does everyone think this is about?

Audience: This describes the parental relationship, doesn't it? Mercury in Capricorn in the 10th house indicates that Mary has conventional and traditional ideas, particularly about being a responsible member of society. But at the same time, there is something very unconventional about her, because the Chiron-Mercury conjunction means that she thinks differently from other people, and she probably finds it hard to be understood. The Mercury-Uranus opposition describes an unusual mind, with sudden flashes of insight, and the Chiron-Uranus opposition is the mark of the outsider.

Clare: Yes, we have a theme here that indicates that Mary both believes and doesn't believe in traditional values and roles. This is supported by the fact that Uranus is in the 4th house. This is likely to be a reflection of the tension between her parents, and it may well be that, in her own marriage, she has found herself repeating the parental pattern, since the grand cross involves both the relationship houses and the parental houses. In this case, the ruler of the MC is Jupiter in the 1st house in Aries, so it looks as if Mary's mother was a free-thinking and independent woman who never really felt comfortable in her role as wife and mother. And with Uranus in the 4th house and Mercury, which rules the IC, in the 10th house, perhaps her father was also unconventional in some way. However, with Jupiter opposite Saturn and Mercury square Saturn in the 7th house, perhaps Mary's parents felt judged or constrained or limited in some way. And because this is in your chart, you have inherited a story that they have been unable to resolve in their own lives.

Mary: This is rather alarming, because I can now see how closely I am repeating the family pattern. In my childhood I was always embarrassed by my parents, because they were never like everyone else's parents – they thought differently and didn't follow the rules. My father was a university lecturer who taught politics, but he was also an activist and lost his job in the sixties when I was still very young. This caused real hardship and disruption in the family. I have spent most of my marriage trying to conform to everyone else's expectations, and it has just made me miserable and frustrated.

Clare: Now that we can see the whole picture, perhaps this makes it easier for you to appreciate that this cardinal grand cross represents a dynamic and potentially extremely creative inner challenge, rather than just a problem that can be projected onto your husband or onto your marriage, or solved by leaving the marriage. I think it is clear from this grand cross that you need to find more space in your life to develop your own ideas and direction, and there is no reason why this cannot be achieved within your marriage. Jupiter in Aries in the 1st house is your ruling planet, so this is about developing personal courage and self-belief. And the Mercury-Chiron conjunction square Saturn encourages you to develop your own ideas, whether or not they are judged or misunderstood by others.

Mary: Thank you for all this food for thought, which is really helpful. As I get older, I am beginning to admire my father for his courage and convictions, although they made me deeply embarrassed when I was younger. I used to be a teacher myself, but I left the profession because of all the government interference in education. In fact, I think that coming to this astrology class is a significant first step for me. Although my husband can't understand my interest in astrology and thinks it is a waste of time and money, I have told him that it is very important to me, and he is beginning to accept that this is what I now do on Wednesday evenings.

Semi-squares ∠ 45° and sesqui-quadrates ⬤ 135°

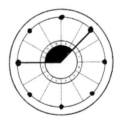

Semi-square   Sesqui-quadrate

Clare: Let's move on to the aspects that are created when the circle is divided by the number eight. Planets 45° apart are in semi-square aspect, and planets 135° apart are in sesqui-quadrate aspect. Like the opposition and the square, these aspects have the nature of twoness, and are therefore active and challenging. Although they are deemed to be minor aspects, with an orb of only 2°, they are nevertheless very dynamic and effective, because they do not suffer from the paralysis of the opposition or the same level of resistance as the square. They are easier to manifest and to work with.

Audience: Do you consider them to be as important as the square?

Clare: Yes, they are extremely effective and productive aspects. Do you have an example you would like to discuss?

Audience: I have Pluto at 8° Virgo in the 2nd house, and Saturn at 23° Capricorn in the 6th.

Clare: That is a sesqui-quadrate, with the planets three and a half signs apart. The planets are both in earth signs, so there is a similarity between them in that respect. Saturn in Capricorn in the 6th house indicates that you take your work seriously, and this could be driven by the fear of not being good enough, or by your need to get everything right. Together, these two planets can be a very powerful and effective force. There are also messages here about your health and about your body, since these planets are both in earth houses and signs. Does any of this make sense?

Audience: I have always been accused of being a hypochondriac, and I am always careful about my diet. I know I can be really disciplined about my body, and I used to work obsessively, but I am trying to get away from all that now.

Clare: Perhaps you are afraid of getting stuck in routine, and yet in a sense you need it as well.

Audience: So how would this work if it was a square? Would it be more difficult?

Clare: Yes, much more difficult, because there may well be a sense of being sabotaged or undermined or undervalued at work. This could either lead to a refusal to work because of the issues that always seem to arise, or alternatively, the challenge would be to accept the power and control and ruthlessness of the Pluto-Saturn square and use it to become an authority at work. It would depend on the individual chart. With a sesqui-quadrate and a semi-square, the two planets will work together more easily.

Audience: I have Moon semi-square Uranus in my chart.

Clare: What happens when we put the Moon and Uranus together?

Audience: An unusual woman or an unusual mother? Perhaps an intellectual mother.

Audience: Wanting to belong and wanting to be free?

Clare: Yes, there is something high-voltage and unpredictable about our emotional responses. This often describes inconsistent mothering at an early age. For example, when we are in our primal, lunar, baby stage of life, our basic sense of safety and the way we learn about the world depends on our mother's emotional responses to our needs. With a Moon-Uranus aspect, we may never have experienced a basic feeling of safety, which can leave us in a state of emotional shock, a high level of emotional tension.

Audience: Everyone in the family has lots of water in their chart, apart from my mother, who doesn't have any. So she is always having sudden eruptions that the rest of us have to deal with. I can certainly relate to what you said about not feeling particularly safe.

Clare: The semi-square between Moon and Uranus indicates that you can work very positively and effectively with this aspect. Your need is for freedom and autonomy, and you probably have unconventional or original ideas about the role of women or of families, or the care of children, which you will want to do something with, since this aspect is active and effective. And you may have some ambivalence yourself about becoming a mother.

Audience: I have never wanted children, but I have been involved in setting up a crèche at work, so that mothers can continue to work when they have children.

Audience: How would the Moon-Uranus square and opposition work?

Clare: With a Moon-Uranus square, the challenge would be harder to resolve, and you may have more difficulty resolving the freedom-closeness dilemma in your life. With a Moon-Uranus opposition, it is likely that you could swing between the two poles, either cutting yourself off from your needs and feeling frustrated about other people's neediness, or alternatively feeling that your security is always threatened by others, who are likely to be perceived as unreliable and disruptive.

Before we finish tonight, I just want to introduce you to two other aspect patterns that are formed from hard aspects. As with all aspects and aspect patterns, each configuration will be unique, depending on the planets involved, as well as the signs and houses they are in. The approach is to analyse each combination in its own terms, knowing that all the planets involved are linked together and cannot function separately. The first is known as the 'Finger of the World', a pattern which involves two planets in square to each other, both of which form a sesqui-quadrate to a third planet. The focal planet here is the one that makes two sesqui-quadrates, which will drive the individual to integrate and actively resolve the challenge of the planets in square.

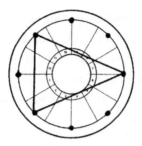

'Finger of the World'

The second is known as the *'Hard Rectangle'*, consisting of two oppositions, the ends of which are joined by two semi-squares and two sesqui-quadrates. Like the grand cross, this is a closed aspect pattern, which means that it is self-contained and fiercely self-sufficient, although there is less resistance than with the grand cross because the hard rectangle belongs to the eight series of numbers.

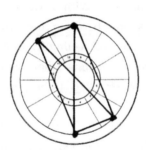

'Hard Rectangle'

All the hard aspects and aspect patterns are tense and stressful in their own particular ways but, as you will see when we compare them with the soft aspects next week, they do force us to grapple with the resistances and difficulties we encounter in life, without which we are unlikely to develop our full potential or sense of personal mastery. Hard aspects and aspect patterns can lead to significant achievements, personal growth, increased consciousness and self-knowledge.

Lesson Eight: Introduction to the Aspects, Part Three

The 'three' series of aspects emerges when the circle is divided by three, six and twelve. Symbolically, three is the number of reconciliation and mediation, creating a harmonious relationship between opposing forces. In astrology, the three modalities are known as cardinal, fixed and mutable, or initiating, resisting and mediating. It is the third force that creates harmony and balance.

The trine △   120°

When we divide the circle by three, we have three sections of 120°, the aspect of the trine.

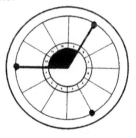

When planets are in trine, there is an easy, flowing, pleasurable relationship between them. The planets will be in the same element, and so they understand, accommodate and support each other. Two planets in a fire sign trine, for example, will share the same qualities of enthusiasm, optimism and faith. Two planets in an earth sign trine will share the same practical, realistic approach to the world. Two planets in an air sign trine will share the qualities of detachment and objectivity. And two planets in a water sign trine will flow and merge together in a harmony.

Audience: I read somewhere that the difference between the hard and soft aspects is like the difference between the carrot and the stick. Squares and oppositions force us onwards, and trines and sextiles are something we enjoy, and therefore something we want to move towards.

Clare: Yes, I think that is a very helpful image, since it illustrates the fundamentally different motivations in the soft and hard aspects. As far as I know, nobody has ever visited an astrologer about their trines. In fact, we almost always take them for granted, which is a pity, in a way, because they are gifts indicating real talent and the easy, joyful expression of that talent. I am sure you can all think of people you know who seem to take their talents and gifts completely for granted.

Let's use an example. Imagine two people planning a trip abroad, one with a Mars-Jupiter trine and one with a Mars-Jupiter square. The person with the Mars-Jupiter trine will find it easy to put their plan into action, since action and vision flow easily together and there is no resistance or hesitation. No doubt the bookings will fall into place effortlessly, and the journey will be dynamic and enjoyable. The person with the Mars-Jupiter square, however, may well find the planning process extremely frustrating. They may not be able to find exactly what they want, spending many frustrating hours on the internet, or they may end up getting very angry with the travel agent, who seems to be obstructive and difficult, so that the whole thing can be a tense and stressful experience. When I describe to my clients the inherent gifts and talents indicated by their trines, they usually find my comments easy to accept but of no real consequence, nothing special, since surely everyone else can do this too. Of course, that is just not the case. Trines are very accepting and allowing, and are an important factor in generating self-esteem and self-acceptance. They are so self-accepting that we can even say things like: 'I'm hopeless at this', or 'I'm useless at that', without it being an issue. With planets in square, on the other hand, there is a real issue – there is a complex. The challenge or struggle inherent in the square strikes to the core. It is sensitive and vulnerable, and definitely not something to be taken lightly. Has anyone got any trines they would like to look at?

Audience: I have a trine between Jupiter in Gemini and Mercury in Aquarius.

Clare: So here we have an air trine. First of all, how would we interpret a Mercury-Jupiter connection?

Audience: Expansive intellect, big thoughts.

Audience: Lots of talking. Perhaps lots of travel.

Clare: Yes, this has a kind of Bill Bryson feel about it. Jupiter in Gemini is going to be very communicative, full of ideas. And Mercury in Aquarius is detached and objective. The two principles will flow easily together.

Audience: I have a Mercury-Pluto trine.

Clare: Then I would imagine that you are naturally a very good listener, and that people trust you with their deepest thoughts.

Audience: I have Saturn in Capricorn in the 1st house, trine Moon in Taurus in the 5th.

Clare: This is an earth trine, naturally stable, realistic and practical. Saturn is in its own sign, so it is strong and comfortable there. In the 1st house, no doubt you have a real sense of your own personal authority and self-sufficiency. The Moon in Taurus works in harmony with Saturn; it is comfortable and well grounded, and in the 5th house it indicates the joy and pleasure you gain from the simple, tangible things in life, like children, for example. Your gift is that you are naturally reliable and stable. This doesn't need to be worked on, and people will value this quality and respond positively to it. A Moon square Saturn, on the other hand, would be much more hungry, much more inclined to feel isolated and needy and abandoned. In the case of a square, there is a conflict between the neediness of the child (Moon) and the responsibility of the parent (Saturn). With the Moon trine Saturn, it is much easier to be a grownup, an adult, so I imagine that this trine is no big deal for you.

Audience: No, it's not. You might like to know that I am the principal of a nursery school, so working with and looking after children comes very naturally to me.

Grand trine

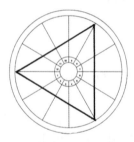

Clare: Grand trines occur when three planets are in trine to each other, so they will share the same element. All 'closed' aspect patterns have a feeling of self-sufficiency about them, and the grand trine is so whole and complete that it tends to cancel itself out. In our culture, which values the work ethic and the achievement of goals, the grand trine tends to be on the receiving end of judgements such as laziness, inertia, a lack of self discipline, and the avoidance of responsibility. These criticisms do not allow for the inner sense of harmony, wholeness and completion which is such a positive feature of the grand trine.

Audience: Would you say that the grand trine is unconscious?

Clare: I certainly think it can be. The way I have come to think about them, mainly because this does seem to be recognised by my clients, is that they represent an inner reservoir of immense strength that we don't know is there until we need it. Let's look at this in terms of the different elements. If you have a grand trine in fire, for example, this would indicate that, when all else fails, you will find within yourself an inner reservoir of faith and optimism which supports you through difficult times. You can draw on it when you need it. In the normal course of everyday life, however, it is unlikely that you will even notice it is there.

Audience: So, until everything falls apart, you are not going to bother about your grand trine?

Clare: Yes, I think that is right. A good example of a grand trine in fire is Winston Churchill. As you may know, Churchill suffered from periods of intense depression, which he called his 'black dog'. And yet I imagine that during these periods, he was able to draw on the deep faith of his grand trine, trusting that he would pull through again, no matter how black they were at the time. A grand trine in earth does not necessarily mean that the individual will find it easy to cope with life on a day-to-day level, or to make a living. These things demand work and effort. It seems to me that cats must have grand trines in earth – they are content simply to be, to find the sunniest and most comfortable spot and to sleep for anything up to twenty hours a day. But if you have a grand trine in earth and everything is stripped away from you, then you will find that you have a strong inner stability and confidence that will support you. We are just talking theoretically here, because I have never seen a grand trine just on its own which is not connected by other aspects to the rest of the chart. Aspects to the grand trine will immediately make it less passive and inert, since they provide the grand trine with an outlet.

Audience: I have a grand trine in water – Jupiter, Chiron, Neptune.

And Jupiter is on the Ascendant.

Clare: A grand trine in water indicates a deep reservoir of emotional support when we need it. In times of emotional difficulty or trauma, I suspect that your emotional strength will support you. In psychological terminology this is known as the ability to 'self-soothe', which enables you to find comfort within, even when you are feeling abandoned or alone. This is the resource that enables people to get through difficult emotional periods in their lives without cracking at the seams or falling apart.

Audience: How does a grand trine in air work?

Clare: Well, this would be the gift of detachment and objectivity under stress. I suppose it would be like being lost in a desert and running out of water. Rather than giving in to the situation and lying down to die, the individual with a grand trine in air is more likely to draw on their thinking process to deal with the situation. They are likely, for example, to work out which direction to go in, from observing the Sun's position during the day and the stars at night. In order to survive, they would use their intellect.

Audience: So they would deal with a difficult situation by becoming detached and rational.

Clare: Exactly right. Rather than getting caught up in the fear, they would try to stand outside this and look rationally at it, and work out a way to get through. This would be an extremely valuable gift. But in ordinary life, a grand trine in air might indicate a kind of mental inertia. Perhaps it might describe a perpetual student, since that comes easier to them than going out and getting a job.

Dividing the circle by six

The next division of the circle in the three series is the division by six. The number six is the product of the primal feminine and masculine numbers, two and three, and the six-pointed star and the sextile are both examples of harmony and balance in action, representing a synthesis of male and female. The upward-pointing triangle is the masculine triad and the downward-pointing triangle is the feminine triad.

The meaning of the number six is not unlike the meaning of the sixth sign and the natural 6th house of Virgo. It is both active and stable. It combines the ease and natural talent of the number three with the energy of the number two. It always reminds me of the industrious and productive activity of bees, whose honeycombs are constructed in the form of six-sided hexagons.

The sextile 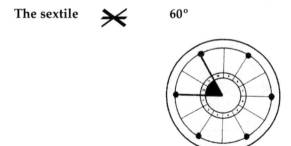 **60°**

The sextile, which is the 60° aspect created when the circle is divided into six, is not as passive as the trine. Sextiles, like bees, are industrious, practical, energetic and skilful. Planets in sextile aspect work rhythmically, fluidly and effectively together. This is an active, productive and talented aspect which functions with ease. There is an interesting feature with these two unfolding number sequences. As the two series unfolds from the opposition to the square to the semi-square and sesqui-quadrate, the aspects gradually become easier, less paralysed and tense, and more effective. As the three series unfolds, on the other hand, from the trine to the sextile, to the semi-sextile and quincunx, it becomes less passive or inert, and more dynamic and active and, eventually, stressful. Planets in trine share the same element, and planets in sextile share the same polarity, such as fire and air, which are both yang energy, or earth and water, which are both yin energy. So you can see that the sextile combines elements which are not identical but complementary.

Grand sextile

On very rare occasions, a grand sextile forms in the heavens, with six planets evenly distributed around the chart at 60° angles from each other. This is a very beautiful pattern, of course, and there is something particularly pleasing, harmonious and well balanced about this aspect pattern. However, it is extremely rare and I have yet to see a chart with a true grand sextile.

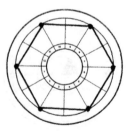

Because this is such a desirable pattern, people will sometimes bring in asteroids and fixed stars and all sorts of other celestial bric-a-brac in order to force a grand sextile out of their charts, but I am not sure this works because, by its nature, this pattern is inherently joyful, gracious and immensely talented. I think it is a gift which is either given to us in its entirety in the form of six planets in sextile to each other, or not at all.

Audience: But do you think it would be valid to include Chiron, the Nodes and the angles?

Clare: Yes, that would be worth considering, but as I said, I have never seen one, even including these extra points, so it is outside my personal experience.

Kite

Our next aspect pattern is a development of the grand trine, and occurs when a planet makes sextiles to two of the planets in the grand trine. This means that it will also be opposite the third planet in the grand trine. That is a kite. The planet at the apex of the kite provides an active and talented outlet for the otherwise self-contained grand trine. The apex planet will, of course, be opposite the remaining planet in the grand trine, but this opposition is not isolated or unresolved because each end is fed back into the kite. In fact, the opposition provides the backbone of this entire pattern, just as it does with a real kite. Without the central post, the kite would clearly not be able to fly.

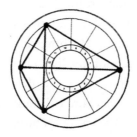

Audience: Can you give an example of the way a kite works?

Clare: Yes, although no matter what the general rules are, every aspect and every aspect pattern needs to be individually analysed and interpreted entirely in its own terms. This means that we need to examine and try to understand how each unique combination of planets, signs and houses comes together to create a particular story. I have some examples here, and maybe you will find a kite in your own charts. Am I overwhelming you? Is this all too much to take in at once?

Audience: No, it's getting interesting.

Clare: Here is a woman with a grand trine in air, with the Sun in Aquarius in the 10th house, Uranus in Gemini in the 2nd house, and Neptune-Chiron in Libra in the 6th house. The apex planet that forms the kite is Pluto in Leo in the 4th house. A grand trine in air is very intellectual, isn't it, and there is something particularly electric about this one, since we have the Sun in Aquarius, and Uranus, which is the ruler of the Sun, in Gemini.

   This represents a high level of mental energy. And the high energy of those planets flows into Neptune in Libra, which longs for beauty, harmony and balance. The presence of Chiron with Neptune describes her sensitivity to beauty and her devotion to her work. With an Aquarian Sun in the 10th house, she will want to 'break the mould' in her profession, and gain recognition for being unusual or innovative in some way. Uranus in Gemini in the 2nd house indicates not only that this is a free thinker, but that she is a free agent, living by her wits and working for herself. Neptune and Chiron in the 6th house indicate that she will devote herself unconditionally to her work, but also that she is physically vulnerable in some way. All this sensitivity and electricity will find an outlet and be anchored through Pluto in Leo in the 4th house, which intensifies the entire pattern and gives her a rather obsessive Sun-Pluto opposition. Incidentally, Pluto is the only planet in a fire sign, so it carries all the intense, creative energy of fire in her chart. This also indicates the importance of her family.

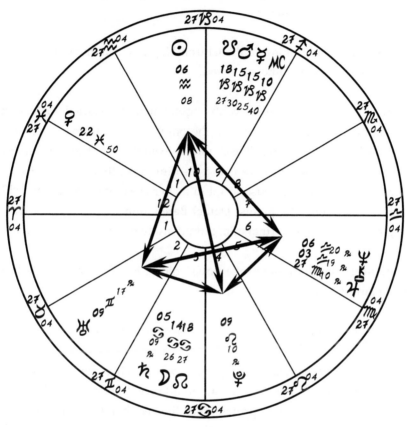

Jacqueline Du Pré
26 January 1945, 11.30 am GMD, Oxford, UK

This kite belongs to Jacqueline Du Pré, the cellist, who was an exceptionally talented musician and a very powerful performer. If you have ever heard her play Elgar, you will know what I am talking about. It is an astonishing experience, quite electrifying. With her Sun in Aquarius in the 10th house, it is not surprising that there is a biography about her called *A Genius in the Family*, and it is also interesting that Jacqueline's mother was her first teacher, no doubt recognising her unusual talent at a very young age. Jacqueline went on to have an extremely successful career, performing all over the world and receiving a host of awards and prizes.

Audience: I am thinking of the Chiron-Neptune conjunction in the 6th house, because of the illness she had.

Clare: Yes, she was only twenty-eight when she started to lose the feeling in her fingers, which was the onset of the multiple sclerosis, a progressively debilitating illness, which eventually led to her death at the age of forty-two. But we could also interpret this Neptune-Chiron conjunction in the 6th house in Libra as her close working relationship with her husband, the pianist Daniel Barenboim. No doubt this was a magical and creative partnership, but intensely painful for her as well.

Audience: The marriage broke down, didn't it? That must have been very painful for her.

Clare: Yes, although they stayed married until her death.

Audience: Have you seen *Hilary and Jackie*, which is the film about her life? According to the film, she had an affair with her sister's husband. All the pressures of her professional life led her to a near nervous breakdown, and the affair was her way of escaping from all the demands and trying to create a private life of her own. Unfortunately, the private life she wanted already belonged to her sister.

Clare: Pluto in the 4th house is not going to be simple, indicating hidden and taboo issues in the family, and no doubt an element of intense jealousy and rage as well. Hopefully, you can see from this particular example that every aspect pattern needs to be carefully interpreted in its own terms. Although we are likely to think of kites as fortunate patterns, and there is no doubt that they describe inherent talent and the opportunity to express that talent through the apex planet, you can see that, in this case, it was also extremely difficult and painful.

The minor grand trine

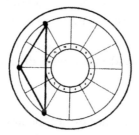

More common than the kite, the minor grand trine is composed of two planets in a trine aspect, which both make sextiles with a third planet. Here, the ease, enjoyment and talent of the trine is activated and expressed through the apex planet.

Grand rectangle

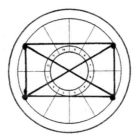

There is another aspect pattern which is comprised entirely of sextiles, trines and oppositions, and this is usually known as a 'mystic rectangle'. Personally, I think this is a rather confusing and unhelpful name for this aspect pattern, since the word 'mystic' always seems to throw us off track, and I can see no reason why this pattern is any more 'mystic' than anything else in the chart. So I am going to use some artistic licence and call it a grand rectangle. This is not a particularly common aspect pattern but, like the kite, it is potentially creative and talented. By themselves, the two trines are not particularly active, but they are put to work by the two sextiles, and two oppositions lend dynamism to this rather pleasing pattern. This is a particularly well-integrated shape in which the planets occupying the four corners are harmoniously linked and able to function extremely effectively together.

Audience: Is it still a grand rectangle if the angles make up one of the oppositions?

Clare: The question of whether or not the angles and Nodes should be included in aspect patterns is open to debate. There are certainly many astrologers who consider that it is only the planets that form aspect patterns. Personally, I think each chart has to be considered carefully in its own terms, and sometimes it seems as if the nodal axis and angles should be included, and sometimes not.

Dividing the circle by twelve

The number twelve is of particular significance in astrology, of course, since we have twelve signs and twelve houses. The number twelve is the product of spirit and matter combined. If we take the trine of spirit and multiply it by four, then we have spirit made manifest. If we take the cross of matter and multiply it by three, then we have matter spiritualised.

 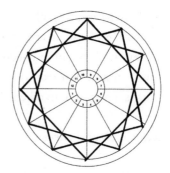

Spirit manifested   Matter spiritualised

The number twelve reveals, once again, astrology's central concern with the marriage of spirit and matter, the marriage of the heavens and the earth. And it is the tension between spirit and matter that is expressed in the two new aspects which emerge when the circle is divided by twelve. These two new aspects are the semi-sextile and the quincunx, or inconjunct aspect. These are awkward aspects, because it is difficult for the planets involved to recognise and therefore to accommodate each other.

Semi-sextile ⚹ 30° and quincunx ⚻ 150°

 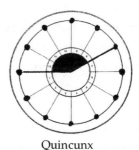

Semi-sextile   Quincunx

In the case of the semi-sextile you can see visually that the two planets only exist in each other's peripheral vision. They don't see each other clearly. They will also be in adjacent signs and, in the Equal House system, they will be in adjacent houses. And adjacent signs have nothing in common. For example, Aries is a positive, cardinal fire sign, and Taurus is a negative fixed earth sign. What is their relationship?

Audience: Chalk and cheese.

Clare: Exactly. The semi-sextile and the quincunx are awkward and vaguely annoying aspects because the two planets have nothing in common. They can't function separately because they are in aspect, but at the same time, they don't recognise each other.

Audience: That certainly sounds like the relationship between men and women.

Clare: When it comes to the quincunx, let's use the example of Aries and Virgo. In the Equal House system, this also describes the natural relationship between the 1st and 6th houses. Aries and the 1st house are about identity, action, movement, self, focus. It is not going to be very happy with Virgo and the 6th house, which is modest, self-effacing and conscientious. Aries doesn't care about that; Aries wants to act. Virgo wants to get it right. Aries to Scorpio is another example. Scorpio is sensitive to and aware of the environment, picking up underlying nuances and hidden emotions. Aries doesn't even notice. Aries is positive cardinal fire, and Scorpio is negative fixed water, so there is an immediate tension, since Aries wants to act and Scorpio wants to stay put.

Audience: I have that. I have Neptune in Scorpio in the 3rd house, and Sun-Mercury in Aries in the 8th.

Clare: Neptune in Scorpio in the 3rd house is imaginative, and indicates a kind of subtle, diffuse awareness. Mercury in Aries in the 8th house describes focused precision and penetrating thought. These two planets do not confront each other, as they would with a square, or support each other, as they would with a trine or sextile, but they are connected in a rather awkward and unsatisfactory way.

Audience: I have Chiron in Aquarius in the 8th house, quincunx Sun in Virgo in the 3rd.

Clare: Just putting Sun and Chiron together, what do we have?

Audience: A wound around our identity?

Audience: Self-expression as a healer or teacher?

Clare: The Sun in Virgo in the 3rd house indicates that you identify with your analytical skills, and with your ability to communicate them. But Chiron is the outsider, so you may feel that, in some way hard to define, it is not acceptable to be yourself or to say what you think. Since Chiron is in Aquarius in the 8th house, perhaps you sense that you could be scapegoated for your ideas and opinions, excluded from the group. Do you sense that?

Audience: I have always felt that. I have never really been able to say what I think, because people never seem to be able to understand what I am talking about.

Clare: Has anyone got any semi-sextiles we could look at?

Audience: Yes, I have Mars in Taurus and Moon in Gemini.

Audience: Does that mean that Mars lives in the body, and the Moon lives in the head?

Clare: Yes. Mars is practical, and the Moon is intellectual. Mars wants to act, and Moon wants to think. Does that feel right?

Audience: Probably, but it is difficult integrating them.

Clare: Yes, and that is the whole point about semi-sextiles and quincunxes. They feel awkward, as if there is something we can't really get to grips with although we know they are there. They describe a kind of background tension and aggravation, and there is no nice, clean resolution.

Audience: That's what it feels like, but I have been unable to put my finger on it. It's like feeling that something isn't quite right, that I must have forgotten something.

Yod

Clare: The aspect pattern formed from two quincunxes and one sextile can provide a synthesis, because it creates balance where there was no balance before. This is known as a yod, or as the 'Finger of Fate', which can be quite dramatic and dynamic. As you would imagine, the focal point of the yod is the active planet at the apex of the two quincunxes. This planet functions like a pivot point, like a point of destiny around which our lives can change direction.

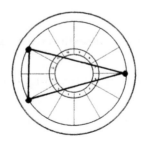

Audience: What happens if you have a planet right in the middle of the sextile, in semi-sextile to both the planets in the sextile and opposite the focal point of the yod?

Clare: Then you have a kind of 'dart', with three planets in a row exactly 30° apart, and an opposition. There is a very nice symmetry here, although I am not sure if it has been named as an aspect pattern. Once again, we would need to examine the specific configuration in its own terms, but I suspect that the planets in opposition will be of particular significance. I thought you would be interested to know that we have a yod in our own chart, which I drew up at the beginning of our class last term. We have Jupiter at 11° Gemini as the focal point, inconjunct to both the MC at 12° Capricorn and Venus at 12° Scorpio. And, as it happens, we also have Pluto and Chiron in Sagittarius in the 8th house, opposite the focal Jupiter and semi-sextile to the MC and Venus. This is, in fact, the dart pattern you mentioned.

We have all come together to give substance (2nd house) to our learning process, because that is what we value (2nd house). Jupiter in Gemini is very busy and active, and believes in learning about philosophical subjects and expanding the mind. Jupiter is in quincunx to the Saturn-ruled MC in Capricorn, so our purpose, the direction we are going in, is to work hard and to build an intellectual structure. There is a real focus to this cardinal, Saturn-ruled MC. The other quincunx from Jupiter is to Venus in Scorpio in the 7th house, so we are here to meet each other (7th house), and because we value deep feelings and have chosen to explore the depths of the psyche together (Venus in Scorpio). This yod describes what we are about and what has drawn us together. It describes our destiny as a group.

Even more to the point, Pluto and Chiron are in Sagittarius in the 8th house and opposite Jupiter. I would say that there is something very powerful going on here for all of us, as we explore the depths of our own personal psyches. Astrology is a powerful philosophical system, and Pluto in the 8th house is no doubt taking us all very deep.

This is a private area for us, and maybe our experiences are both painful and healing, as we process and integrate what we are learning. No doubt there are many personal discoveries taking place that are not being talked about in the group, and this is quite right, since it is going on in the 8th house. Does this ring any bells for you? Many of us will be having profound personal insights, and the group itself is containing that.

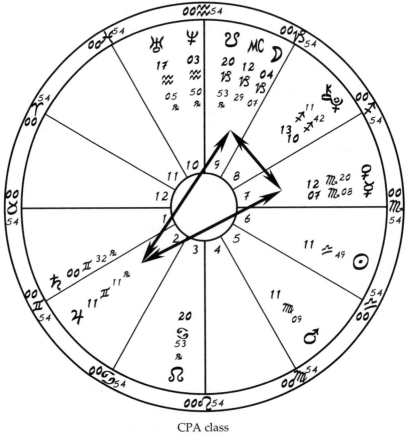

CPA class
4 October 2000, 7.00 pm BST, London

Audience: You can say that again. There are so many things going on for me personally as a result of what I am learning, but it is very hard to define what is actually happening.

Clare: Because we have a yod in the chart, I imagine that many of us will look back on this class in years to come and realise that, in many ways, it was a turning point in our lives, a kind of fated encounter. We have not found ourselves in this class by accident. And, of course, we will all have our own personal reactions and responses to this group, which will depend on the way our own charts pick up the group chart. Next week I want to start looking at what is not in the chart, which seems like a contradiction in terms, but which in fact provides extremely useful information. We will be looking at the lack of an element or modality, and at unaspected planets.

Lesson Nine: Chart Imbalances

Until now we have been looking at what is in the chart, finding the emphasis and focus and the living energy. We have seen what happens when planets are brought together in a dynamic way by the aspects and by the aspect patterns, and we have looked at some of the stories that emerge. But what I want to do tonight is to turn everything on its head, and to look at what is missing from the chart, because that is important, too. In every birth chart there will be empty houses, and there may be whole areas of a chart which are empty, or elements or modes which are absent altogether or under-represented, or planets which make no aspects. We need to pay proper attention to anything which is absent or lacking in a chart, because it is likely to exert a powerful unconscious influence over us. If you would like to follow up this idea in more depth, then I would highly recommend Richard Idemon's book, *The Magic Thread.*[25]

Audience: I am not sure what you are saying here, because it sounds as if everything is equally important, whether or not it is in the chart.

Clare: That is a good point, and I will try to explain what I mean. Let's start with what is actually there in the chart. No matter how challenging our birth charts may be, they will feel familiar to us because we have been inhabiting them all our lives. The birth chart defines our personal experience of the world, and tends to be more or less under the control of the ego, to the extent that it can be made conscious. For example, if we have several personal planets in air, we are likely to have a well-developed thinking function which we will use to navigate and make sense of the world. As far as we are concerned, that is normal. And if we have several personal planets in mutable signs, we will be naturally

---

[25] Idemon, *The Magic Thread.*

flexible and adaptable. And if we have several aspects to our Mars, we will know very well how to assert and defend ourselves. All of these ways of being feel normal to us. By contrast, anything which is not in the chart will be outside our conscious or ego control. But that does not mean that it doesn't exist. In fact, the way this seems to work is that whatever we don't have inside, in our birth charts, somehow has to be manifested out there in the world. In other words, every void or imbalance within seeks to be filled or balanced in the outside world. This is another example of the compensatory nature of the psyche.

However, there is a noticeable difference in expression, emphasis and intensity between what is within our charts and what lies outside, and we seem to have a particular blind spot about what is not in our birth charts, with the result that whatever is lacking functions autonomously, like a complex. And we do not have complexes – complexes have us. When a complex is activated, it takes us over, which is why we are prone to finding ourselves in the grip of anything which is not in our birth chart.

Audience: Can you say a bit more about complexes, Clare, so that we can understand how they function?

Clare: Yes, and I am taking a particularly psychological approach here, because I think it makes the subject of chart imbalances very clear and easy to understand. Complexes are powerful, compulsive, autonomous driving forces. However, because they exist outside ego consciousness, they are only experienced in projection, and are never really 'owned'. They are highly charged – affect-laden – and seem to have a life of their own, acting independently and often inappropriately or out of proportion to the objective reality of a situation. One of the easiest ways to recognise complexes is that they lack a sense of humour. I am sure you have all noticed how perfectly reasonable and relaxed people can suddenly become rigid and defensive and start speaking in an authoritative or strident voice which is not normal to them. Suddenly, in the place of the person you know, there is an inflexible, intolerant, rigid, fanatical individual who is completely certain that they are right. If that has happened to you, then no doubt you have unwittingly stepped on their complex. Does this make sense to you?

Audience: Yes, I can think of one or two examples already.

Clare: Just to take this one step further, singletons and missing functions constellate a variety of different psychological defence mechanisms, which is the ego's way of trying to keep control. We may well attempt to deny what we lack by using another function instead. For example, we may try to feel with our thinking, air function. Or we may try to achieve concrete results with our fire function. Alternatively, we may consciously devalue, neglect and criticise what we lack, and at the same time work hard to achieve it. This would mean that we both deny and over-compensate for what we lack at the same time. Another way of balancing ourselves is to enter into relationships with people who have plenty of what we lack. This is why it is so easy to fall into the habit of criticising our partners for expressing the qualities we lack, while at the same time being dependent upon them because they balance and complete us.

Audience: I have no earth in my chart, but I do have an angular Saturn and several planets in the earth houses. Does that compensate for my lack of earth?

Clare: Your reaction is not uncommon, but it could be interpreted as a denial or defence mechanism, an example of the ego trying to defend itself, since it is an attempt to give yourself some earth. The same thing might be said, for example, of a chart with no water but with an angular Neptune, or many aspects to Neptune or planets in the water houses. The point here is that neither your angular Saturn nor its ruler will be in an earth sign. The same thing is true of your planets in the earth houses

– they will not be in earth signs, and neither will the planetary rulers of the earth houses, so I am sorry to say that we cannot manufacture an earth function for ourselves if none of the planets are there.

But the main point I want to make is that our greatest gifts can come from the imbalances in our charts. The energy that clusters around a complex can be immensely creative, for the very reason that it lies outside the control of the ego. It is important to remember that obsession and compulsiveness are not necessarily negative. After all, if we were all perfectly balanced, it is unlikely any of us would bother to get out of bed, let alone work obsessively on a scientific discovery, climb Mount Everest, write a symphony or a book, or paint a great painting. It is through what is lacking in our birth charts that we may make our greatest contribution to the world.

Here is a crib sheet which may help you to identify quickly how the various imbalances in a chart might function.

Rough Guide to Interpreting Chart Imbalances
What is Absent or Singular in the Birth Chart

<u>Chart shaping:</u>
ASC/DESC axis (public life/private life)
Marked emphasis either above or below the horizon will lead to a fascination/obsession to explore the opposite hemisphere.
MC/IC axis (self/partner)
Marked emphasis either east or west of the Meridian will lead to a fascination/obsession to explore the opposite hemisphere.

<u>House/Sign Emphasis:</u>
Lack of planets in first four houses/signs:
Intense involvement with all that is personal & subjective
Lack of planets in second four houses/signs:
Intense involvement with social life and relationships
Lack of planets in last four houses/signs:
Intense involvement with collective or public life

Modalities:
Lack of planets in cardinal signs:
Tendency for sudden action, impulsiveness, leadership
Lack of planets in fixed signs:
Tendency towards resistance, rigidity, perseverance
Lack of planets in mutable signs:
Tendency towards confusion, drifting, deviating from purpose

Elements:
Lack of planets in earth signs:
Powerful emphasis on/obsession with body, sexuality, food, money, *e.g.* the businessman, naturalist, body-builder
Lack of planets in air signs:
Powerful emphasis on/obsession with education, learning, writing, communicating, *e.g.* the writer, philosopher, actor
Lack of planets in water signs:
Powerful emphasis on/obsession with feelings, relationships, *e.g.* the musician, psychotherapist
Lack of planets in fire signs:
Powerful emphasis on/obsession with meaning, faith, adventure, risk-taking, *e.g.* the entrepreneur, the explorer, the preacher

Unaspected planets and singletons:
Driving motivation, autonomous, compulsive expression of the archetypal qualities of the planet concerned

---

Audience: What happens if you only have one angle and one planet in an element? Is that still an imbalance?

Clare: Yes, there will still be a sense of deficiency that seeks to be balanced. However, in a case like this, there is usually an element of awareness of the imbalance – it is more accessible. When someone has a total lack, it will be immediately obvious to everyone else, but the person with the total lack can be oblivious of the fact.

Audience: What about the outer planets, Chiron, and the Nodes?

Clare: Well, the same thing applies. In charts where only an outer planet, Chiron, or one of the Nodes is in an element, the individual will be expressing the collective charge of that planet or point in its purest, most autonomous and archetypal expression. The particular individual expression of this influence will be experienced in the house in which it occurs.

Audience: I'd really like to get this counting thing straight. I know you only use the seven traditional planets, but do you also count the angles?

Clare: No, because the angles are not planets. For example, if you have Sagittarius rising, then, although your Ascendant is in fire, it is the element of the ruling planet which we will be looking for. I think it is unfortunate that computer programs always include the outer planets in the mode and element count, because this encourages us to think of them in the same way as the seven traditional planets, whereas they belong to another order altogether, to a different dimension. I think we need to count again and to take them out, but that is only my view, and you are welcome to make up your own minds about this.

Audience: What happens if you have two planets in an element?

Clare: That is fairly average, and wouldn't register as a lack. Let's have a look at the element imbalances to see how they work.

Element imbalances

Lack of fire

How would we describe someone who has a dominant fire element, with several planets in fire signs?

Audience: They will be optimistic, dramatic, radiant, forward-looking, and they will believe in themselves.

Clare: Yes. For people with several planets in fire, these qualities will be an intrinsic feature of their conscious psyches. They have 'fire within', or true fire, which means that they will usually have plenty of faith in themselves, and an instinctively optimistic approach to life which feels natural, comfortable and relaxed. They have nothing to prove. People with a lot of fire don't have to make an effort to be optimistic; they are just naturally optimistic, because that is how they are wired. And they don't need to preach optimism and faith, because neither of these things are a problem for them.

   With a lack or absence of fire, however, then the *quality* of the fire expression will be significantly different. Someone with a lack of fire within will need to find their faith and meaning out there in the world, and this may well drive them in a fanatical, compulsive and extreme way which can actually be quite exhausting for that person, and even burn them out. This is an example of false fire, which can never be easy or comfortable, and which cannot be taken lightly or joked about. There is an important and very noticeable difference in the quality of these two types of expression. A lack is harsh, exhausting, and obsessive, which immediately gives us the clue that this person may not have that element.

Audience: This sounds like the difference between trines and squares.

Clare: Yes. A strong element is like a trine, relaxed and comfortable. An element lack or imbalance is like a square; there is a confrontation, a striving to resolve and manifest something in the world, and it is out of this struggle and tension that the most amazing achievements come. A shorthand way of thinking about the issues that might arise with a lack of fire in the chart is to think about the themes that belong to the signs of Aries, Leo and Sagittarius. Some fire words would therefore be: passion, competition, fame, recognition, self-belief, self-expression, risk-taking, the excitement of the chase, enthusiasm, optimism, and adventurousness. Without these qualities as conscious components of our own psyches, we will be driven to demonstrate them in the outside world. It is no accident that many famous people and film stars, such as Elvis Presley and Sean Connery, are lacking in fire, because there can be a tremendous drive for recognition by the outside world. Or that successful entrepreneurs and risk-takers, such as Aristotle Onassis, lack fire. Or that cult figures, visionaries or religious leaders, those who fire our imaginations and give us faith – anyone who is consumed by a cause – may lack fire. Inner faith does not have to be preached, it just is. Nostradamus, who had a lack of fire in his chart, was overwhelmed by powerful visions of the future.

Audience: Does this kind of overcompensation sometimes take a long time to show up? I know several people who are lacking in fire, but they are very passive and earthy. They are procrastinating all the time, and dreaming about doing things but never actually doing them. They don't seem to have any driving energy. I keep wondering if this will come later on.

Clare: It may be that they are already living the fire in their imaginations and dreams, and perhaps it is these dreams and fantasies that are more important to them than reality itself. Their driving energy may well be going into the imagination. Alternatively, they may have fiery partners who are living this out for them.

Audience: Let's say you are doing a chart for someone who has no fire. Do you assume that they will be lacking in basic energy and faith and self-belief, or do you assume they are going to be all fired up with some kind of goal? How do you approach this?

Clare: I think both are true. Most of what I am talking about tonight has been drawn from my own experience of working with clients. When I first started seeing clients and, for example, had a chart with a lack of fire, I might suggest that they had a lack of basic optimism, faith or energy. And I learned very quickly that this was not the right approach, because there was almost bound to be a kind of rigid defensiveness, a flat denial or over-compensation going on, and the client would often feel offended and start saying things like: 'No, I haven't', and then go on to give many instances to prove that what I had said was not true.

Audience: I was doing the chart of a friend of mine the other day, and I explained that she had no fire. She said that everyone was always telling her how fiery she was.

Clare: Yes, that tends to be the response you will get – something along the lines of, 'What do you mean?', or 'How can you possibly say that?', because it is a sensitive issue.

Audience: It is interesting that you say that Elvis Presley had no fire, because to me he is the archetypal fiery character. And yet he was a Capricorn Sun, wasn't he?

Clare: Yes, and yet he is one of the most famous cult figures of all time. He has become mythic, almost godlike, which is also a common theme with people who have a lack of fire.

Audience: And he was, in fact, very interested in religion, because a lot of his music was based on gospel music.

Clare: For some reason it seems that exceptionally talented people with a lack of fire can also die young, but at the same time become immortal, because they take on a mythic quality. This was true of both Kurt Cobain and Mozart, to take two extremely different examples. One of my favourite examples is that of Johannes Kepler, the sixteenth century astrologer and astronomer. Kepler had no fire in his chart except for the north Node in Leo. In spite of having double vision, he worked obsessively on the planetary orbits, producing 900 pages of tiny writing on the orbit of Mars. This is a good example of unbalanced behaviour, but his work led him to the discovery of the three great laws of planetary motion, which made him famous. What drove him was his desire to prove mathematically that the cosmos was an expression of divine perfection and harmony. We can achieve tremendous things where there is a lack in the chart, but they are never achieved easily, or without stress or tension.

Audience: Bruce Willis is another one without fire, isn't he? And yet he is out there being heroic and saving the world all the time in his films.

Audience: And I think there is a film where he actually goes out into space to blow up an asteroid that is heading for the earth. That is a combination of the extreme adventurer and risk-taker acting as the saviour of the world.

Clare: Quite. And we could certainly see this as a good example of over-compensation. But films – particularly science fiction – are flights of the imagination, so they can be a fiery medium, and it is through film that he achieves the fame and recognition he is seeking.

Lack of earth

With a lack of planets in earth signs, we can start to think about the kind of issues associated with the earth signs of Taurus, Virgo and Capricorn. These will include money, security, the body, sexuality, food, health, work, practical skills, professional status, and responsibility. But I have learned never to say to someone with no earth that they may have issues about money, or about their bodies or their careers, because they are most likely to deny it, and say things like: 'I am very embodied – I go to the gym eight times a week'. The point about this is that it does not prove they have a good relationship to their bodies – it just proves that they have an obsessive relationship with their bodies, because it is not normal to go to the gym eight times as week. This will be a sensitive issue, but the point is that it is this kind of obsession which makes exceptional gymnasts or dancers or athletes, so it can be very creative.

Audience: I have a friend who is a great nutritionist, and she only has one planet in earth.

Clare: That is a good example of two earthy themes, work and food, coming together. And I would imagine that she is quite obsessive in her own life about food and diet, so working as a nutritionist is a very good way to earn money and to be of practical service, while at the same time, it gives her a reason to focus on the thing which obsesses her.

Audience: Yes, that's right.

Clare: I have often noticed that people with a lack of earth can have real issues about authority figures or professionals or people who represent structure and organisation. There can be a rather fanatical mistrust or despising of people in authority, and yet at the same time, the individual often longs for a position of authority and professional recognition themselves. Having a lack of an element often means that we will simultaneously despise and crave those things that are associated with that element. It sounds irrational and it *is* irrational, but it is very useful to understand that this is an important component of human nature.

Audience: That sounds fairly similar to the way oppositions work.

Clare: Yes, that's right. Bill Gates is an example of someone with no earth, who is one of the wealthiest men on earth and who has built a huge empire. And now that he has become a philanthropist, a great deal of his money is being spent on medical research, which is an interesting manifestation of a lack of earth and a corresponding interest in health issues.

Audience: It's as if he is not actually interested in the money itself.

Clare: That's right. He may well despise wealth and status on some level, and yet, on the other hand, work fanatically hard to achieve it. This can be a very useful way of helping us to see and accept our inner contradictions. This is not easy to do, but very helpful in understanding ourselves more fully. Bill Gates has now made himself whole by 'finding his earth' out there in the world. But that still doesn't give him any earth within. So, if he was your client and you mentioned 'money issues' during the consultation, he would probably agree with you – unless, of course, he had an unconscious complex about money, in which case he would feel offended and defend himself rigorously.

Audience: I only have Mercury and Chiron in earth, so I suppose that means I have a problem with the earth function.

Clare: It means that the earth function will be extremely important. You will find yourself driven to achieve something concrete and useful and practical, and that is where your particular gifts and talents may lie.

Audience: What I really hate is when people are tight and mean.

Clare: It sounds as if you judge people who hold on to their money, and yet, no doubt, you also work hard to build up enough of your own and to hold on to it, because this represents personal security for you. This could be an example of the kinds of contradictions that are inherent when we have a lack or absence of an element. Does this make any sense to you?

Audience: Yes, you are right.

Clare: I will just mention a few more examples of people with a lack of earth in their charts, before we move on. As I mentioned before, this can be a feature in the charts of people with highly developed and controlled bodies, such as athletes and ballet dancers. Or we might see this in people's life work – for example, Charles Darwin, whose life was devoted to studying nature, and Thomas Hardy the writer, whose novels strongly evoke the seasons and the English countryside, and Rodin, the sculptor. Or even the model Elle Macpherson, who has no earth in her chart, but who is known as 'the body'. An extremely unpleasant example is that of Dennis Nilson, the serial murderer who was obsessed with bodies, chopping his victims into pieces.

Lack of air

How are we going to approach a chart with a lack of air?

Audience: Will they have difficulty with detachment and with thinking logically?

Clare: That's right, and they are likely to have difficulty with intellectuals, or with the education system, or with people who are experts in their field, while seeking to be respected for their intelligence and ideas themselves. An air complex is likely to be fanatical, opinionated and rigid. Or they may well try to do their thinking by using one of the other elements, which is not the same thing as true air. For example, there may be a passionate drive or desire to communicate (fire acting as air), particularly strong feelings about relationships or social issues (water acting as air), or an obsession to objectively prove one's intellectual ability to the world by learning several languages or gaining several degrees or doctorates (earth functioning as air), none of which are ultimately the same thing as the thinking function itself, which is cool and logical and rational. All of these functions masquerade as the air function, but none of them is capable of genuinely replacing or truly compensating for the lack of air in the chart. But if we are comfortable with our intellects, we don't need to prove our intelligence to the outside world.

Audience: My boyfriend only has his Ascendant in an air sign, and he is obsessed with studying.

Clare: And no doubt he has made great achievements intellectually?

Audience: Yes, he has.

Clare: I think it is important not to see this as some kind of handicap, but as the source of our unique talents and achievements. The issues are likely to be those which are associated with the air signs of Gemini, Libra and Aquarius. This is not just about learning and studying, but it also includes the principles of equality, justice and harmony, relationships and involvement with social or political issues. And it is certainly true that there is a long list of famous scientists, writers, thinkers, politicians and philosophers who have a lack of air in their charts. When the air function erupts from the unconscious, it can bring real genius and brilliance, although the lack of an integrated air function can also mean difficulty functioning on the ordinary levels of thought and communication. The philosophers Bertrand Russell and Descartes lacked air, as did the writers Tolstoy, Goethe and Walter Scott, to name just a few examples. This can also be the case with brilliant scientists, such as Albert Einstein, whose only planet in air was Jupiter. I believe that he was literally unable to work out how to tie his shoelaces.

Lack of water

A person with several planets in water is likely to be in constant touch with the natural ebb and flow of their emotions. They are sensitive to changing rhythms in themselves and in others, and normally able to ride the emotional waves as they rise and fall. A lack of water, on the other hand, can describe someone whose emotional responses can be rather inappropriate, absent, or overwhelming. Emotions can erupt from the unconscious in such a way that the individual can feel as if they are being dissolved or drowned by their feelings. The issues are likely to revolve around the themes of Cancer, Scorpio and Pisces – feelings about belonging and nurturing, emotional dependence on others, empathy and compassion, and emotional pain.

With a lack of water, we may well try to feel by using one of the other elements with which we are more comfortable. We might try to feel with our fire function, dramatising or acting out our feelings without actually processing them on an emotional level. Or we might use our air function to learn a range of theories about feelings, and talk about their feelings all the time, whereas the water function itself is mute. Or we might use our earth function and work with feelings, by becoming a therapist, for example. A more self-destructive way of trying to access our feelings with the earth function might be to cut our bodies. These are all examples of compensating for a difficulty in feeling and processing emotions on an inner level. A lack of water is often found in the charts of exceptionally talented musicians, such as John Lennon, or Claude Debussy, who wrote the *Sea Symphony*. The same thing is true of many outstanding psychoanalysts, such as Jung, Freud, and Rollo May. It is well recognised that psychotherapists and counsellors often seek to heal themselves by working with their clients' emotional problems.

There can also be a very concrete obsession with water or liquid, as in the case of alcoholics, or people who use drugs to block out their feelings, or swimmers such as Mark Spitz, who won five Olympic gold medals, or even those, like Virginia Woolf or Percy Shelley, who drowned. In one way or another, the missing water function seems to demand outward expression in the lives of those who have a lack of this element in their charts.

Audience: I have certainly heard that people who are afraid of their emotions also have a fear of water.

Audience: Just before we end, can you say something about unaspected planets?

Clare: Yes, although the themes are identical to the ones we have been looking at tonight. A planet is considered to be unaspected if it makes no major aspects – conjunctions, oppositions, trines, squares or sextiles – or perhaps just one aspect. An unaspected planet, by definition, lacks integration with the other planets in a chart, and therefore it is not modified by other chart factors. It is therefore likely to function in a pure, archetypal and autonomous way, unmodified by the influence of other planets in the chart. Unaspected planets are always important, and deserve special consideration in a chart analysis.

Lesson Ten: Whole Chart Interpretation

I want to spend our last lesson this term interpreting a complete birth chart – putting together everything we have learned so far. Inevitably, as we take a chart apart and analyse all the different components separately, we end up with all the pieces of the jigsaw puzzle, but lose the picture on the box. Our task tonight is to integrate everything we have studied in the last two terms, and hopefully we will begin to get a good idea of how the whole chart comes together. As we do this, I am also sure you will realise what an enormous amount you have learned in a very short period of time.

Very many thanks to Kate for offering to be our guinea pig and letting us use her chart. Hopefully, Kate, you will let us know how we are doing as we go along. You also wanted to use the Placidus house system, which is fine. In fact, it is a good opportunity to experience for ourselves how the two different house systems work. Here is Kate's chart. Whenever we first look at a whole chart I think it is normal to feel a moment of sheer panic. Staring back at us from the sheet of paper or from our computer screens is a flat, two-dimensional diagram composed entirely of meaningless hieroglyphics.

Audience: I'm glad you said that, because it is exactly what I am feeling at the moment.

Clare: I think it is very helpful to develop a methodical and fairly ritualistic approach to chart interpretation, for two main reasons. Firstly, a methodical approach helps us to develop our craft. It enables us to stay within the astrological discipline itself, listening for clues and messages. Otherwise – and this is something which almost always happens when a whole chart is put up for discussion – it is too easy to go off on interesting tangents and start having our own opinions and emotions and reactions to the chart, which may well have more to do with us personally than with the information provided by the astrology itself. The second reason is that the whole purpose of ritual is to evoke the gods, and this is in fact what we are doing when we analyse a birth chart. If we can stick faithfully to our ritual, then we develop a kind of trust in the process itself and the chart begins to come to life as we study it. Here is a 'Guide to Chart Interpretation' that you might find helpful to start with, and no doubt you will evolve your own approach as you gain more practice in chart interpretation. There are two sections in this guide – the Overview and the Focus. I want to spend this evening just looking at the overview, which alone will give us a great deal of information.

GUIDE TO CHART INTERPRETATION
Birth Chart Analysis
OVERVIEW

SHAPE	East/west, north/south; lunar phase
EMPHASIS	House emphasis; sign emphasis
ELEMENTS	Element balance; emphasis on particular elements? Lack of particular elements?
MODES	Cardinal/fixed/mutable balance; lack of particular mode?
INTERCEPTED SIGNS	Planetary strengths and weaknesses
RULING PLANET	Ruling planet's house and sign; aspects to ruling planet
ANGULAR PLANETS	Special emphasis
ASPECTS AND ASPECT PATTERNS	
	Planetary strength and weaknesses

Audience: How long does it take you to analyse a chart before you see a client?

Clare: Well, I have been doing charts for about eighteen years now, so it gradually becomes a more fluent process. But over the years I have found that, by developing a ritualistic approach, the process is gradually strengthened, so that it does get quicker and easier. But all the same, I know that every time I sit down to analyse a chart, I will be entering into unknown territory and embarking on a new adventure. Nowadays I spend about an hour or two on the preparation, and then I always sleep on it before seeing my client – although not literally, of course.

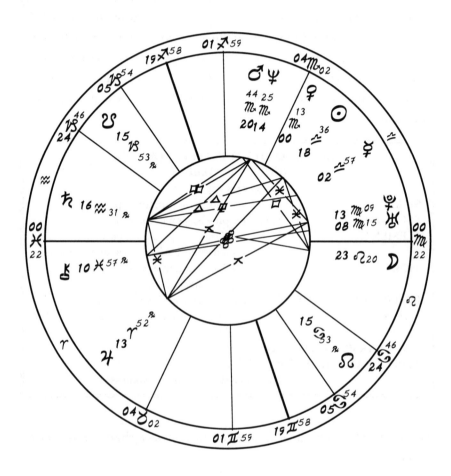

Kate
Chart data omitted for reasons of confidentiality
Placidus house system

Overview

1. Shape

It is a good idea to start by standing back and looking at the whole pattern of the birth chart from a distance. We will then see the general shape of the chart, which immediately tells us which areas of life are going to be significant, obviously in the broadest terms. For example, is there a marked hemisphere emphasis, either east/west or north/south?

Audience: Not really. Most of the planets are in the western hemisphere, but Saturn, Chiron, and Jupiter are in the eastern hemisphere. And most of the planets are in the southern hemisphere, but Chiron, Jupiter, and Moon are in the northern hemisphere.

Clare: There is always so much information in a chart that we don't need to force anything to fit. In this case there doesn't seem to be a clear hemisphere emphasis, so we can simply move on to the next stage.

2. Lunar phase

Audience: As far as the lunar phase is concerned, this is a waning Moon, so it is rather *quiet and mature.*

Clare: That's right. We will be looking at lunar phases next term, but you are right that this is a quiet and mature Moon. We don't yet know if this will be important, so we will just make a note of it.

3. House and sign emphasis

Do you think there is a marked house emphasis?

Audience: Yes, there is a strong 7th house. Three personal planets and two transpersonal planets make five planets altogether in the 7th house. That has got to be important.

Clare: Yes, so we now know that something is happening here which means that *relationships* are going to be an important theme in Kate's life. Do you think there is a marked sign emphasis? Here we will be looking to see if there is a stellium in any one sign, which would be three or more planets.

Audience: Well, there are three planets in Scorpio – Venus, Mars and Neptune.

Clare: What does that tell us?

Audience: That Kate has a passionate nature, and that her relationships will be deep and emotionally complicated.

Clare: Good. Once again, this concerns *relationships*, so it looks as if we may have the beginning of an important theme emerging. But let's see.

4. Elements and modes

The next step is to look at the element balance, counting just the seven traditional planets. You can see that Kate has two planets in fire (Moon in Leo and Jupiter in Aries), no planets in earth, two planets in water (Venus and Mars in Scorpio), and three planets in air (Sun and Mercury in Libra, Saturn in Aquarius). What does that tell us?

Audience: On balance, she is a naturally thinking type. And with nothing in earth, then presumably *issues of personal security, work, money, body and health* could be something of a challenge for her.

Clare: Yes, the lack of earth tells us that Kate will need to find her sense of security and substance outside herself, perhaps in the form of possessions or through her work. Moving on to the modes, Kate has two cardinal planets (Jupiter in Aries and Sun in Libra), four fixed planets (Moon in Leo, Venus and Mars in Scorpio and Saturn in Aquarius), and no mutable planets. So we now have a strong theme, because with no planets in either mutable or earth signs, we are going to start to think about *Virgo issues*, since Virgo is the mutable earth sign. I would therefore imagine that Kate feels a strong need to be *useful and practical* but, on the other hand, her lack of mutability may haunt her, causing *uncertainty about her direction* in life.

Audience: Although there are no planets in mutable signs, the angles are both mutable. How would we make sense of that?

Clare: I think this points to the fact that, although Kate's natural inner orientation is mostly fixed, she feels less certain when it comes to engaging with the outside world, where her approach is more flexible and adaptable. As we begin to find these kinds of inherent conflicts, the chart starts coming to life.

Kate: Structured work is something I've always had a problem with, because I find it hard to commit to regular hours and to other people's expectations. As a result, I've had a series of varied jobs, including teaching English as a foreign language, library assistant, PA, and working in an art shop.

5. Intercepted signs

Clare: The next thing to do, since we are using the Placidus house system here, is to check for intercepted signs and repeated house cusps to see whether any planets are 'floating' because they are not house rulers, and whether any planets are particularly strongly anchored in the chart because they rule more than one house. You can see that the signs of Aries and Libra are intercepted in the 1st and 7th houses. With a chart that seems so far to be primarily relationship-based, that is particularly interesting. However, since Venus and Mars also rule Taurus and Scorpio, they are still house rulers in their own right, ruling the 2nd and 8th houses respectively. Otherwise, we might start wondering if Mars and Venus would have difficulty expressing themselves.

Whenever you have intercepted signs in a quadrant based house system, you are also going to have planets ruling more than one house, so in this chart the Moon rules both the 5th and 6th houses, which have Cancer on the cusp, and Saturn rules both the 11th and 12th houses, which have Capricorn on the cusp. We would therefore expect *Moon and Saturn* to be particularly strongly emphasised in this chart, and in fact they are in opposition, so we need to spend some time teasing that out.

Audience: I have just noticed something rather curious about that, because the Moon and Saturn are also intercepted in the signs of Leo and Aquarius in the 6th and 12th houses. How can we make sense of that?

Clare: Yes, that is a rather unusual phenomenon. I think the way to approach this is to pay special attention to the *Moon-Saturn opposition* in the chart. We know it is going to be particularly significant, and we also know that it will be rather hard to get at and possibly rather hard for Kate herself to understand clearly.

As we have seen, the Moon rules both the 5th house of creative self expression and the 6th house of useful and skilful activity, and yet it is buried in the intercepted sign of Leo. Saturn rules both the 11th house of groups and the 12th house of seclusion and retreat, and yet it is buried in the intercepted sign of Aquarius. So the questions that emerge here hinge around Kate's ability to discover and fulfil the needs of her Moon, and her ability to learn to face her own inner fears and take responsibility for herself. These two questions may well indicate significant life themes for Kate, and it is worth mentioning here that it is not our task to try to make sense of this or to try to find solutions or to make suggestions. Our task is simply to record and to communicate as faithfully as we can the themes that are revealed by the chart. But we can leave this for now, since the Moon-Saturn opposition is part of a T-square, so we will look at it more closely when we get to aspect patterns.

6. Ruling Planet

Now we can move on to the ruling planet, and because the Ascendant is in Pisces, there are two chart rulers, with Jupiter being the personal ruler and Neptune being the transpersonal ruler. Jupiter is in the 1st house in Aries. This placement is subjective, determined and goal-oriented, indicating a great deal of personal faith, courage and focus. The transpersonal ruler of the chart links Kate directly and personally to the dreams and ideals of the Neptune in Scorpio generation to which she belongs. And Neptune is in the 8th house, so she is no doubt something of an emotional sponge, a theme which is supported by the fact that her Ascendant is in Pisces. In the water houses, we are going to be sensitive to hidden emotional issues, so this is doubly sensitive to others. As I am sure you can see, there is another *self-other theme* here, with the personal ruler, Jupiter in Aries, wanting to stand alone and do its own thing, and the transpersonal ruler, Neptune in the 8th house, indicating that she has a tendency to lose herself in close relationships.

Audience: But Mars rules both Aries and Scorpio, so presumably there is some kind of relationship between these two chart rulers.

Clare: Yes, that's a very good point. And Mars, which is the ruler of Aries, is also conjunct Neptune. We are beginning to get a story here which concerns Kate's faith in herself, and her sensitivity to the needs of others or to collective emotional issues. It looks as if she is something of a crusader, and these rulers can come together nicely if Kate dedicates her own personal will and strength and vision to a collective cause. Let's move on to the angular planets to see what else we can find.

7. Angular planets

Audience: There are two angular planets on the Descendant. One is Moon, and the other is Uranus. They are linked together by the Descendant.

Audience: This looks like early disruption and separations.

Clare: We know that the Descendant is the point of contact with significant others, and we know that *relationships* are important in this chart, so what do you think these angular planets are about?

Audience: Sudden changes, sudden meetings and separations. There is something very unpredictable about a Moon-Uranus connection.

Audience: Is this about a detached and distant mother?

Clare: Perhaps. And that might link us back to the *Moon-Saturn opposition* and the theme of early self sufficiency – having to rely on herself.

Audience: But Saturn is in dignity and, in traditional astrology, it is in the house of its joy, so it must be a strong Saturn.

Clare: Yes, these points support what we have already discovered, that both the Moon and Saturn are extremely important in this chart. I think it is likely that Kate needs to spend quite a bit of time on her own, and that this is a way of nurturing herself. Nevertheless, on some level she is bound to feel rather alone and isolated, although this doesn't have to be a bad thing at all. The lunar phase also indicates that this is a mature moon, so Kate is perfectly capable of *providing for herself and standing on her own feet,* and no doubt this is something which makes her feel secure and safe. After all, with Uranus conjunct Pluto in the 7th house, relationships are unlikely to be simple or straightforward. Rather, they are likely to bring unpredictability into her life (Uranus), along with issues of power and control (Pluto). She may well need to retreat from relationships from time to time, in order to nurture and heal herself.

Audience: That is very interesting, because Kate has a Libra Sun, and in the 7th house, too. It looks as if there is a really strong theme around *wanting to find herself through another and needing to be alone.*

Clare: That's absolutely spot on.

8. Aspects and aspect patterns

Before we look at the aspect patterns, it is worth looking through the aspect grid to see if there are any planets which make significant aspects to the angles, or which are unaspected or otherwise rather alone and unsupported by the rest of the chart. Can you identify any?

Audience: Mercury only has one aspect – a sesqui-quadrate to Saturn. That's all it does.

Audience: Venus is completely unaspected, apart from a trine to the Ascendant.

Audience: The Moon is trine the MC.

Audience: Uranus is only conjunct Pluto and opposite Chiron. It doesn't make any personal aspects, apart from being on the Descendant and opposite the Ascendant.

Audience: The same is true of Pluto, although it does square the MC.

Clare: Let's extract some general themes from these observations. Mercury is fairly isolated, so that makes it very important for Kate to find her voice. The sesqui-quadrate to Saturn indicates that she has a structured and disciplined mind, and may not feel particularly confident about speaking up, until she has considered her ideas carefully. The only outlet for Venus in Scorpio is through the Ascendant in Pisces, so there is a quiet, sensitive, and rather magnetic and attractive quality about the way Kate engages with the world.

Audience: Yes, I think that is certainly true from what we can see.

Clare: The Moon in Leo trine MC in Sagittarius indicates that she finds it easy to project her personality in the public arena and in her work. Public attention is food for her, and this might explain why she has offered her chart for us to discuss.

Kate: You may be right. I am really enjoying this opportunity to focus on me!

Clare: There are no personal planets associated with Uranus, which means that Uranus cannot really be incorporated or brought under ego control, or taken down in voltage. She is likely to experience Uranus as a particularly autonomous and possibly disruptive force, appearing to come from nowhere, without warning. This can feel quite shocking. Pluto squaring the MC/IC axis indicates that Kate is likely to find herself confronted by several radical changes of direction in both her public and private life. Now we need to see if we can find some aspect patterns, because they will contain important stories. What can you find?

Audience: Jupiter makes two quincunxes to Neptune and Pluto, so that is a *yod*.

Audience: There is a *fixed T-square*, with the Moon opposite Saturn and both square Neptune-Mars. There is also a *cardinal grand cross*, with the Sun-Jupiter opposition square the nodal axis.

Audience: There is a *grand trine in water* between Chiron, north Node and the Mars-Neptune conjunction.

Audience: Actually, there is a *kite*, because there are sextiles from this grand trine to Uranus and Pluto in Virgo.

Clare: There are lots of really nice aspect patterns here, with four major shapes emerging. Let's have a look at these separately, to see what they might mean.

Yod

With this yod, our attention is drawn once again to Jupiter, which I have just noticed is not only the chart ruler, but also rules the MC. This indicates that significant events are likely to occur in Kate's life that will focus on, and revolve around, her strong sense of self-belief and self-agency. In fact, it is not so unusual to have a yod that involves the Neptune-Pluto sextile, since this is a collective aspect which almost all of us will have in our charts, given that Neptune and Pluto move so slowly. But with Jupiter as the focus of this yod, we could imagine that Kate will give some kind of individual expression to the collective background into which she has been born. On a personal level, with Pluto in the 7th house and Neptune in the 8th, Jupiter will give her the strength and determination to survive the intense and possibly overwhelming issues which arise for her in relationships. The theme once again is *the self and the other.*

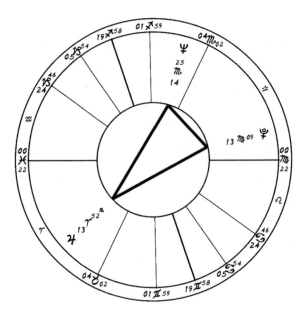

Audience: We can also bring in Mars and Uranus as well, can't we? Mars is conjunct Neptune, and Uranus is conjunct Pluto.

Clare: Yes, that's right, and there is an element of the freedom fighter around Mars and Uranus. This makes the Neptune-Pluto sextile rather more dynamic and active, and supports the self-belief of Jupiter.

Kite

You can see that both the grand trine in water and the kite are collective in their nature, and will be found in the charts of everyone born around this time in 1963, because there are no personal planets involved. However, we can explore how this generational pattern functions in Kate's own life by concentrating on the houses that are involved. Let's tease out the trine first, before adding the Uranus-Pluto conjunction. What kind of story does a Node-Chiron-Neptune trine suggest?

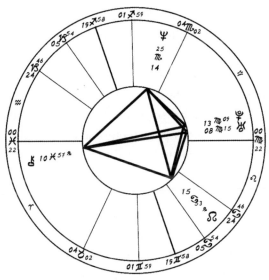

Audience: Is this about healing?

Audience: I would imagine that this is extremely sensitive and rather vulnerable, too. Neptune-Chiron is about devoting yourself to others, and with the Node there, it could indicate that this is your function and destiny.

Clare: What do you think Chiron in Pisces in the 1st house is about?

Audience: Perhaps a wounded sense of self. Some kind of identification with the wound or with healing. Longing to merge and to belong, but always feeling like an outsider.

Clare: The Pisces Ascendant is very exposed, because it has no personal boundaries. It is extremely sensitive and prone to absorbing the feelings and emotional states of others.

Audience: And the Node in Cancer in the 5th house, ruled by the Moon, indicates that Kate needs to care for herself, to learn to put herself first – although, with the Mars-Neptune conjunction in the 8th house, she will always be very sensitive to the needs of others.

Kate: I am certainly interested in the expression of subtle energies, including dowsing, energy healing, and shamanism. After a lifetime of being what others have labelled 'oversensitive', I am now comfortable with the idea that I just pick up energetic and emotional stuff from other people when I'm with them, and I need to find a way to work positively with this. One option is training to become an energy healer or shiatsu practitioner, but I'm held back by my fear of being overwhelmed by other people's energies. Energy-wise, I like to keep myself to myself. I'm interested in the Buddhist world-view and philosophy. It matters a lot to me to be able to fit work into my natural rhythms, as my energy level varies a lot – I can be buzzing one day and completely lethargic the next. And there are times when I just need to escape from all pressure, and I need to go with my own internal flow at those times.

Clare: This is a perfect expression of the Pisces Ascendant and Chiron in Pisces in the 1st house. Now let's put the Uranus-Pluto onto that and make it into a kite. What effect does this have on the grand trine? The emotional reservoir of the grand trine in water is channelled into earth, into Virgo. In this particular case, the connection to the earth function is quite disruptive, and will be constellated through Kate's relationships which, however difficult and personally painful, may well provide the kinds of experiences which eventually compel her to undergo a powerful transformation of her relationship to herself and to her body (Chiron in Pisces in the 1st house). Working with subtle energies in healing work sounds very appropriate and could certainly describe your Chiron path.

Fixed T-square

Turning to the fixed T-square, what are the themes around a Moon-Saturn connection?

Audience: A lonely childhood, and perhaps a lack of nurturing?

Audience: A feeling of being denied what we need?

Audience: A strict family background?

Clare: We are beginning to think along certain lines, which have to do with the Moon and Saturn. This opposition is on the axis of service, because it is across the 6th and 12th houses, so it is about the development of personal will and the surrender of personal will. Let's see if we can think of a story that might make this T-square easier to understand. T-squares often lend themselves to stories in which there are three characters, each of which has a part to play. The Moon in Leo, for example, might describe a princess or a queen. There is a need to be special, a sense of deserving praise and recognition for her talents and skills (6th house). With Saturn in the 12th house, we might imagine that this specialness is somehow hidden away, out of sight. This is almost like the fairy story image of the princess in the tower – of being particularly special and deserving of love and praise, but being trapped, imprisoned, and locked away in isolation. And Mars-Neptune might describe the masculine as rescuer and redeemer – so we might have a fantasy image around the masculine that might take the shape of a knight in shining armour.

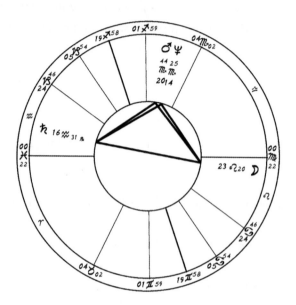

Audience: This sounds like the fairy story about Rapunzel, who was trapped in a tower, waiting to be rescued.

Clare: Yes, that is a beautiful image, and probably very telling, too, since the Mars-Neptune conjunction is in the 8th house.

Audience: But Kate is also quite self-sufficient, so she could be the rescuer as well.

Clare: That's right, and it is likely that she will play all the characters in this fairy story at different times. There seems to be quite a bit of trapped or frozen anger caught up in this T-square, since it includes a Mars-Saturn square, which makes it difficult to act, as well as a Mars-Moon square, which can be very sensitive and defensive. In addition, the Moon-Neptune involvement is appropriate to the theme of romantic longing, sacrifice, and dreams of being rescued. This is a powerful configuration. It is also potentially gifted and talented, and the T-square will provide Kate with both the resistance and the determination to give shape and form to her talents.

Cardinal grand cross

Let's have a look at the cardinal grand cross, composed of the Jupiter-Sun opposition square to the nodal axis. We know that this is a dynamic, determined and self-contained aspect pattern. The Jupiter-Sun opposition emphasises the major relationship theme of *self-other* in this chart, being across the 1st and 7th houses and in the self-other signs of Aries and Libra. With the Sun in Libra in the 7th house, Kate will seek to find peace, harmony, balance and personal fulfilment through her partner. Jupiter in Aries will give Kate the energy and determination to stand up for herself if she finds that her relationship is out of balance in any way, or unjust, or if the balance of power is unequal. However, Mars and Venus, which rule Jupiter and the Sun, are both in Scorpio, so it is not quite as simple as that, and deep emotional struggles are likely to emerge in relationships, which will take her into her the emotional depths and bring any hidden issues to the surface. This is particularly uncomfortable for a Libran Sun, and Kate has Mercury in Libra as well, which is very rational and fair-minded. So she finds it particularly distasteful to find herself having to do battle with the dark and archaic and irrational forces of Scorpio which emerge in her relationships, although these are likely to be the agents of her own personal transformation and eventual empowerment.

Kate: I was twelve or thirteen when my parents separated and divorced and, over time, I have come to realise that this had a huge effect on me. When I eventually separated from my husband in 1988, many powerful feelings emerged which had been deeply buried until then.

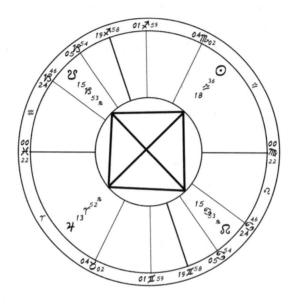

Clare: In Cancer/Capricorn, the message of the nodal axis concerns the collective challenge to find a conscious relationship between neediness and dependency versus self-sufficiency and personal responsibility – between the child and the parent. And once again, this takes us to the *Moon Saturn opposition*, since the Moon and Saturn are the rulers of the Nodes. For Kate, this axis falls across her 5th and 11th houses, so we could say that it is Kate's destiny to discover and believe in her unique creative talents, and to offer them to the world in some way. With the Sun square the nodal axis, her unique purpose is to learn to believe in herself, and to develop her particular artistic talents – a theme which is supported by the Moon in Leo in the 6th house. With Jupiter square the nodal axis, we could say that, in spite of all the difficulties indicated in other parts of this chart, Kate may have a sense of being protected by the gods, since Jupiter often functions as a kind of personal guardian angel when it picks up the nodal axis. There is a strong sense of purpose and destiny in this cardinal grand cross.

We have now completed the general overview of the chart, and several important major themes have emerged. If we are preparing an interpretation for a client, the next stage would be to move on to an analysis of the specific details, which I have outlined in the Guide to Chart Interpretation. We might, for example, start focusing on the parental story, by examining the 10th and 4th houses and their rulers, Jupiter and Mercury, and at the detailed interpretation of the Sun and Moon, the parental significators. And a major focus when we are preparing a chart will be on the current transits, progressions, and so on, which tell us which parts of the chart are being activated at the moment, and therefore why the client is coming to see us. That is what we will be looking at next term. Do you get the sense that we have understood you?

Kate: You have certainly pulled together all the major themes in the chart in an insightful way, and yes, it has all be helpful – on all sorts of different levels.

Clare: Do you feel accurately reflected and mirrored?

Kate: I feel that you have reflected and mirrored my potential, but I feel that the actual reality is not like that yet. I am still in my midlife crisis, and feeling very restless and unsettled. Three years ago I let my house in London and went to live in Cambridge. Since then I have moved house nine times.

Clare: That must have been very difficult for you, because you are quite fixed by nature and, because of the lack of earth, you need to feel safe and secure. It seems as if your mutable angles have been particularly active during the last three years, and this is in fact supported by major transits to your angles.

Kate: I don't do so much on the creative side. I see myself more as a crusader, because I am a charity fundraiser at the moment and I actually go door to door to raise money. That is something I love.

Clare: So you use your courage and crusading energy in the service of and for the benefit of others?

Kate: That's right, and it is important for me that the training and ethos of the company I work for is very ethical, and that everything is done with the right attitude.

Clare: Presumably it is important for you to do something you believe in, with Jupiter ruling both your chart and the MC.

Kate: I certainly think I am moving in that direction now. I used to work in very safe, structured jobs, but I am now finding I can only work in more fluid jobs. There has been a gradual progression from trying and failing to fit myself into structured jobs, to freer work where I can be myself more, and follow my spontaneous inclinations.

Clare: Do you feel that you are beginning to develop more self-confidence?

Kate: That's a really big one. The fixed T-square is quite a difficult pattern, so it is a rather slow process.

Clare: What about the theme of self and other – do you feel that dichotomy?

Kate: Absolutely. Basically, I seem to have a pattern of being taken over by the feelings and moods of others, and by their drive and energy, and then I have to fight to become myself again, and I sometimes think I am too strong.

Clare: So you have had to get quite tough and learn how to fight for yourself?

Kate: Yes. I really feel that.

Clare: And now you know that you have the courage and determination to stand up for yourself when necessary.

Kate: Yes, but it feels like there are two very separate parts of me – the Saturn-Moon T-square part and the Jupiter part, and they can each come out at different times.

Clare: What sort of charities do you fundraise for?

Kate: Overseas development charities.

Clare: That's perfect, with your Jupiter ruler and Sagittarius on the MC. Is that something you are passionate about?

Kate: Yes, particularly the one I am working for at the moment, which is raising money for community projects abroad.

Clare: This is an absolutely beautiful expression of your cardinal grand cross, and of the nodal axis, which is concerned both with your personal contribution to community work. Do you feel you have a special gift for this?

Kate: No, but it is something I just think I can do naturally. There is a kind of conflict. My personal interests are more creative – I sing in a harmony group, and we do concerts and that kind of thing, so I'm not too sure. Sometimes I think I should be developing that more, but my work always seems to be about communities and groups.

Audience: The nodal axis is also about doing creative stuff for yourself as an individual, versus the work you do for others.

Audience: Neptune is also about music, and Mars-Neptune can be the expression of music.

Clare: And the Moon in Leo wants to perform, to sing and to play music – to express itself joyfully. The themes of individual self-expression and service to the community or to the collective do seem to be strong in your chart. And it feels as if these two things are separate at the moment.

Kate: Yes, they feel separate. My creative outlet at the moment is my singing. I don't play an instrument, but I study music theory because I am interested in composition. During my twenties, I did some creative writing and article writing, and I would like to pick this up again at some point. All this has disappeared since the beginning of my mid-life crisis, and I am lacking a direction.

Clare: These are particularly appropriate expressions of the Moon in Leo and the Sun in Libra. But I definitely get the sense that you are not feeling as optimistic as your chart indicates.

Kate: In a way, I do, but I am still struggling, and I feel very vulnerable at the moment. It is a hard journey without any earth in the chart!

Audience: What about the strong emphasis on the 7th house and on relationships?

Kate: It doesn't mean that I have had wonderful intimate relationships. I have been on my own for the last three years, and have found it difficult to enter into any significant relationships since the end of my marriage.

Clare: That could be appropriate for now, because it is an indication that you are looking after yourself at the moment.

Kate: Yes, but I am sorry about it, really. It's just that I can't deal with another relationship at the moment!

Clare: I think this is very understandable, since it is clear from your birth chart that Pluto and Uranus are going to get evoked whenever you are in a relationship, because they are in your 7th house. And that means that your very sensitive grand trine in water will also come to life in relationships. For the time being, there is nothing wrong with taking the emotional pressure off yourself and giving yourself a rest. Perhaps you need to retreat back into your Saturn in the 12th house tower, and give yourself some time and space. The Moon-Saturn opposition is also about learning to care for yourself, and to protect yourself when necessary.

Kate: Thank you, you've been really positive.

Clare: Well, I have been trying to reflect the astrology of your chart as accurately as I can, and although I can understand why you are not feeling particularly positive or optimistic at the moment, no doubt you will look back at this period in your life and see that it represented an important and positive transition. Thanks to everyone for their contributions. That brings us to the end of our class and to the end of our term. Have a good break, and I look forward to seeing you again next term.

GUIDE TO CHART INTERPRETATION
BIRTH CHART ANALYSIS

1. OVERVIEW

GENERAL EMPHASIS

Hemisphere emphasis; lunar phase; house emphasis; sign emphasis

ELEMENTS

Element balance – strengths and weaknesses

MODES

Cardinal/fixed/mutable balance – strengths and weaknesses

INTERCEPTED SIGNS (quadrant house systems)

Planetary strengths and weaknesses

RULING PLANET

Ruling planet's house, sign and aspects

ANGLES AND ANGULAR PLANETS

Special emphasis

ASPECTS AND ASPECT PATTERNS

Planetary strengths and weaknesses

2. BACKGROUND

PARENTS
  MOTHER:
    10th house: planets in 10th; ruler of 10th, its house, sign & aspects
    Moon: house, sign and aspects
  FATHER:
    4th house: planets in 4th; ruler of 4th, its house, sign and aspects
    Sun: house, sign and aspects
  PARENTAL AUTHORITY:
    Aspects of Sun and Moon to Saturn
  PARENTAL EXPECTATIONS:
    Saturn in 4th or 10th house; Saturn aspecting planets in 4th or 10th

EARLY HOME ENVIRONMENT
>   **4th house**: planets in 4th; ruler of 4th, its house, sign and aspects

CHILDHOOD
>   **5th house:** planets in 5th; ruler of 5th, its house, sign and aspects

SIBLINGS AND EARLY EDUCATION
>   **3rd house:** planets in 3rd; ruler of 3rd, its house, sign and aspects
>   **Mercury:** its house, sign and aspects

BASIC PHYSICAL SECURITY
>   **2nd house:** planets in 2nd; ruler of 2nd, its house, sign and aspects

3. THE ADULT

NEEDS
>   **Moon:** sign, house and aspects

CREATIVE SELF-EXPRESSION
>   **Sun:** sign, house and aspects;
>   **5th house:** planets in the 5th; ruler of the 5th and its aspects

MIND, COMMUNICATION STYLE, IDEAS
>   **Mercury:** sign, house and aspects
>   **3rd house:** planets in 3rd house, ruler of 3rd

VALUES AND TALENTS
>   **Venus:** Venus' sign, house and aspects

PERSONAL DIRECTION
>   **Roots:** IC, its ruler, sign and house of ruler; planets conjunct IC
>   **Vocation:** MC, its ruler, sign and house of ruler; planets conjunct MC

RELATIONSHIPS
>   **Partnerships:** 1st & 7th Houses: planets in 1st and 7th, and their aspects; rulers of 1st and 7th by house & sign
>   **Value of self and of other:** 2nd and 8th houses; planets in 2nd and 8th and their aspects; rulers of 2nd and 8th by house and sign
>   **Friends and love affairs:** 11th and 5th houses; planets in 11th and 5th and their aspects; rulers of 11th and 5th by house and sign

SEXUALITY
>**Mars, Venus and Pluto:** their signs, houses and aspects
>**8th house:** ruler and planets in 8th

CHILDREN
>**5th house:** planets in 5th and aspects; ruler of 5th, its house and sign

HEALTH
>**6th house**: planets in the 6th and their aspects; ruler of the 6th by house, sign and aspects

WORK
>**Earth houses:** 2nd, 6th and 10th houses; planets in earth houses; rulers of earth houses by sign, house and aspect

RELATIONSHIP TO AUTHORITY/SOCIETY
>**Saturn:** social expectation, duty, ambition; Saturn's house, sign and aspects
>**10th and 11th houses:** planets in 10 and 11th; rulers of 10th and 11th by sign, house and aspects

MEANING, PHILOSOPHY, FAITH
>**Jupiter:** Jupiter's house, sign and aspects
>**9th house:** planets in 9th and their aspects; ruler of 9th by house, sign and aspects

FAMILY/PSYCHIC INHERITANCE
>**Water houses:** planets in 4th, 8th and 12th; rulers of 4th, 8th and 12th by house, sign and aspects

COLLECTIVE, ARCHETYPAL, GENERATIONAL ISSUES
>**Transpersonal planets:** Uranus, Neptune, Pluto, their houses, signs and aspects to personal planets

Chart Data

Astrological references to a number of well-known figures are mentioned in this book. Unless otherwise stated, all data for the charts below is taken from Astrodatabank, Version 3.0, Ratings A or AA, or from the Astrotheme website at http://astrotheme.fr.

Winston Churchill: 30 November 1874, 1.30 am, Woodstock, England (Astrotheme)

Kurt Cobain: 20 February 1967, 19.20 PST, Aberdeen, WA (Astrodatabank)

Sean Connery: 25 August 1930, 6.05 pm BST, Edinburgh, Scotland (Astrodatabank)

Charles Darwin: 12 February 1809, 3.00 am, Shrewsbury, England (Astrotheme)

Claude Debussy: 22 August 1862, 4.30 am LMT, St. Germain, France (Astrodatabank)

Rene Decartes: 31 March 1596, 2.00 am, Le Harvre, France (Astrotheme)

Diana, Princess of Wales: 1 July 1961, 7.45 pm BST, Sandringham, England (Astrodatabank)

Jacqueline Du Pré: 26 January 1945, 11.30 am BST, Oxford, England (Astrodatabank)

Albert Einstein: 14 March 1879, 11.30 am LMT, Ulm, Germany (Astrodatabank)

Sigmund Freud: 6 May 1856, 6.30 pm, Frieberg, Germany (Astrodatabank)

Bill Gates: 28 October 1955, 10.00 pm PST, Seattle, WA (Astrodatabank)

Bob Geldof: 5 October 1951, 2.20 pm BST, Dublin, Ireland (Astrodatabank)

Johann von Goethe: 28 August 1749, 12.00 pm, Frankfurt-am-Main, Germany (Astrotheme)

Thomas Hardy: 2 June 1840, 8.00 am, Upper Buckhampton, England (Astrotheme)

Carl Gustav Jung: 26 July 1875, 7.32 pm LMT, Kesswil, Switzerland (Astrodatabank)

Johannes Kepler: 27 December 1571, 2.37 pm, Weil Der Stadt, Germany (Astrotheme)

John Lennon: 9 October 1940, 6.30 pm BST, Liverpool, England (Astrodatabank)

Martin Luther: 19 November 1483, 10.46 pm LMT, Eiselben, Germany (Astrodatabank)

Nelson Mandela: 18th July 1918, 2.54 pm, Umtata, South Africa (Astrotheme)

Rollo May: 21 April 1909, 2.20 am CST, Ada, OH (Astrodatabank)

Wolfgang A. Mozart: 27 January 1756, 8.00 am, Salzburg, Austria (Astrotheme)

Dennis Nilsen: 23 November 1945, 4.00 am GMT, Fraserburgh, Scotland (Astrodatabank)

Michel de Nostradamus: 14 December 1503, 12.00 pm, St. Rémy, France (Astrotheme)

Aristotle Onassis: 20 January 1906, 10.00 am, Smyrne, Izmir, Turkey (Astrotheme)

Elvis Presley: 8 January 1935, 4.35 am CST, Tupelo, MS (Astrodatabank)

Auguste Rodin: 12 November 1840, 12.00 pm, Paris, France (Astrotheme)

Dante Gabriel Rossetti: 12 May 1828, 04:30 am LMT, London, England (Astrodatabak)

Bertrand Russell: 18 May 1872, 5.45 pm, Trellek, England (Astrotheme)

Sir Walter Scott: 15 Augsut 1771, 10.00 am, Edinburgh, Scotland (Astrotheme)

Percy Bysshe Shelley: 4 August 1792, 10.00 pm LMT, Horsham, England (Astrodatabank)

Mark Spitz: 10th February 1950, 5.45 pm PST, Modesto, CA (Astrodatabank)

Leo Tolstoy: 9 September 1828, 10.52 pm LMT, Tula, Russia (www.khaldea.com/charts)

Tina Turner: 26th November 1939, 10.10 pm CST, Nutbush, TN (Astrodatabank)

Vincent Van Gogh: 30 March 1853, 11.00 am LMT, Zundert, Netherlands (Astrodatabank)

Bruce Willis: 19 March 1955, 6.32 pm MET, Idar-Oberstein, Germany (Astrodatabank)

Virginia Woolf: 25 January 1882, 12.15 pm GMT, London, England (Astrodatabank)

William Butler Yeats: 13 June 1865, 10.40 pm LMT, Sandymount, Ireland (Astrodatabank)

Bibliography and Recommended Reading

Bibliography

Baring, Anne and Jules Cashford, *The Myth of the Goddess* (London: Penguin/Arkana, 1991)

Bruyere, Rosalyn L., *Wheels of Light: A Study of the Chakras*, Volume 1 (Sierra Madre, CA: Bon Productions, 1989)

Burckhardt, Titus, *Alchemy* (1986), tr. William Stoddart (London: Element Books Ltd., 1986)

Campbell, Joseph, *The Inner Reaches of Outer Space: Metaphor as Myth and as Religion* (Novato, CA: New World Library, 1986)

Dethlefsen, Thorwald, *The Challenge of Fate* (London: Coventure Ltd., 1984)

Ebertin, Reinhold, *The Combination of Stellar Influences*, trans. Alfred G. Roosedale (Aalen: Ebertin Verlag, 1940 [1960])

Edinger, Edward F., *Anatomy of the Psyche: Alchemical Symbolism in Psychotherapy* (La Salle. IL: Open Court Publishing Company, 1985)

Guggenbuhl-Craig, Adolf, *From the Wrong Side: A Paradoxical Approach to Psychology* (Dallas, TX: Spring Publications, 1995)

Harpur, Patrick, *Daimonic Reality: A Field Guide to the Otherworld* (Enumclaw, WA: Pine Winds Press, 1994)

Harpur, Patrick, *The Philosophers' Secret Fire. A History of the Imagination* (Chicago, IL: Ivan R. Dee, 2002)

Hillman, James, *The Soul's Code: In Search of Character and Calling* (London: Bantam Books, 1996)

Jung, C. G., 'The Psychology of the Transference', *in The Practice of Psychotherapy*, CW 16, trans. R. F. C. Hull (London: Routledge & Kegan Paul, 1954)

Lawlor, Robert, *Sacred Geometry* (London: Thames and Hudson Ltd., 1982)

Moore, Thomas, *The Re-Enchantment of Everyday Life* (?? HarperPerennial, 1996)

Narby, Jeremy, *The Cosmic Serpent: DNA and the Origins of Knowledge* (Phoenix, AR: Orion Publishing Group, 1998)

Paracelsus, *Selected Writings*, ed. Jolande Jacobi, trans. Norbert Guterman, Bollingen Series XXVIII (Princeton, NJ: Princeton University Press, 1951)

Plato, *The Republic*, trans. H.D.P. Lee (London: Penguin, 2003)

Von Franz, Marie-Louise, *Projection and Re-Collection in Jungian Psychology: Reflections of the Soul* (London: Open Court Publishing, 1978)

West, John Anthony, *Serpent in the Sky: The High Wisdom of Ancient Egypt* (New York, NY: Julian Press/Crown Publishing Group, 1987)

Recommended Reading

Arroyo, Stephen, *Astrology, Karma & Transformation: The Inner Dimensions of the Birth Chart* (Reno, NE: CRCS Publications, 1978)

Camilleri, Stephanie, *The House Book: The Influence of the Planets in the Houses* (St. Paul, MN: Llewellyn Publications, 1999)

Ebertin, Reinhold, *The Combination of Stellar Influences* (??: American Federation of Astrologers, Inc., 1988)

Greene, Liz, *Barriers and Boundaries: The Horoscope and the Defences of the Personality* (London: CPA Press, 1996)

Greene, Liz, *The Horoscope in Manifestation: Psychology and Prediction* (London: CPA Press, 1997)

Greene, Liz, *The Dark of the Soul. Psychopathology in the Horoscope* (London: CPA Press, 2003)

Hamaker-Zondag, Karen, *Aspects and Personality* (York Beach, ME: Samuel Weiser, Inc., 1990)

Hamaker-Zondag, Karen, *The Yod Book* (York Beach, ME: Samuel Weiser, Inc., 2000)

Hamaker-Zondag, Karen, *The Twelfth House: The Hidden Power in the Horoscope* (York Beach, ME: Samuel Weiser, Inc., 1992)

Houlding, Deborah, *The Houses: Temples of the Sky* (Bournemouth: Wessex Astrologer, 2006)

Idemon, Richard, *The Magic Thread: Astrological Chart Interpretation Using Depth Psychology* (York Beach, ME: Samuel Weiser, Inc., 1996)

Idemon, Richard, *Through the Looking Glass: A Search for Self in the Mirror of Relationships* (York Beach, ME: Samuel Weiser, Inc., 1992)

Pelletier, Robert, *Planets in Aspect* (Gloucester, MA: Para Research Inc., 1974)

Pelletier, Robert, *Planets in Houses* (Gloucester, MA: Para Research Inc., 1978)

Reinhart, Melanie, *Incarnation: The Four Angles and the Moon's Nodes* (London: CPA Press, 1997)

Rudhyar, Dane, *The Astrological Houses: The Spectrum of Individual Experience* (Reno, NE: CRCS Publications, 1972)

Rudhyar, Dane, *New Mansions for New Men* (La Verne, CA: El Camino Press, 1978)

Rudhyar, Dane and Leyla Rael, *Astrological Aspects: A Process-Oriented Approach* (Santa Fe, NM: Aurora Press, 1980)

Sasportas, Howard, *The Twelve Houses: An Introduction to the Houses in Astrological Interpretation* (Wellingborough: Aquarian Press, 1985)

Sasportas, Howard, *Direction and Destiny in the Birth Chart* (London: CPA Press, 1998)

Tierney, Bill, *Dynamics of Aspect Analysis: New Perceptions in Astrology* (CRCS Publications, Reno, NE: CRCS Publications, 1983)

Tompkins, Sue, *Aspects in Astrology* (London: Element Books, 1989)

Von Schlieffen, Alexander, *When Chimpanzees Dream Astrology: An Introduction to the Quadrants of the Horoscope* (London: CPA Press, 2004)

About the Author

Clare Martin has been teaching astrology since 1990 at the Faculty of Astrological Studies and the Centre for Psychological Astrology. She has an MA in Integrative Psychotherapy, and works in London as a counsellor and astrological consultant. Clare is currently President of the Faculty of Astrological Studies and a supervisor and lecturer at the CPA.

About the Faculty of Astrological Studies

Patrons: **Baldur Ebertin**, Ph.D., Hon. D.F.Astrol.S.
Liz Greene, Ph.D., D.F.Astrol.S., Dip.Analyt.Psych.
Robert Hand, B.A., Hon. D.F.Astrol.S.
Julia Parker, D.F.Astrol.S.

Past Patrons: **John M. Addey**, M.A., D.F.Astrol.S.
Dane Rudhyar, Hon. D.F.Astrol.S.

President: **Clare Martin**, M.A., D.F.Astrol.S., Dip.Psych.Astrol.

The Faculty of Astrological Studies was founded in London on 7th June 1948 at 19.50 BST. Its aim, then and now, is to raise the standard of astrological education and to provide a first class professional training for the practising astrologer. Over the years more than 10,000 students from over 90 countries have enrolled on the Faculty's courses. The Faculty is internationally recognised and respected and, as the list of alumni shows, many of the world's leading astrologers have been students of the Faculty. Liz Greene, Mike Harding, Charles Harvey, Julia Parker, Melanie Reinhart and Howard Sasportas are just a few of the Faculty's Diploma holders who went on to become leading lights in the world of modern astrology. The Diploma of the Faculty of

Astrological Studies is a highly regarded professional qualification, and Faculty Diploma holders are entitled to use the letters D.F.Astrol.S. and to be included in the Faculty's Directory of Astrological Consultants.

The Faculty's Courses

The Faculty aims to guide its students through astrology's abundance and complexity, as they gradually build their knowledge, learn to think for themselves, and to use astrology with skill and confidence. The Faculty's courses are designed to provide a comprehensive, thorough and ethically aware professional training for the modern consultant astrologer.

Foundation Course

The Foundation Course is designed for complete newcomers to astrology and for those who wish to consolidate their previous knowledge and reading within a structured course. The Foundation Course provides a basic understanding of the language of astrology and the ability to calculate and interpret a birth chart. It also includes an introduction to the astronomy of the solar system, an overview of the history of western astrology, and students will be encouraged to start exploring their own ideas about some of the philosophical questions that arise from the study and practice of astrology. There are no formal admission requirements, although basic mathematical skills and good written and verbal communication skills are necessary. Students for whom English is a foreign language should have the ability to write in English reasonably well.

Diploma Course

The Diploma Course is designed as a two-year course for students who have completed the Foundation Course. During the first year of the Diploma Course, students are introduced to the major timing techniques used in modern astrology – transits, lunations and eclipses, solar returns, progressions, the progressed lunation cycle, and directions. They continue to develop their chart interpretation skills, integrating the timing techniques, learning to use the graphic ephemeris, and exploring the major house systems in use today. During the second year of the Diploma Course, students are introduced to further techniques – midpoints, harmonics, synastry, and electional astrology – and explore astro-geography and the relationship between the individual and the collective. The Diploma Course culminates with a study of practical astrological consultancy techniques and the development of advanced interpretation skills.

Studying with the Faculty

The Faculty's courses are flexible, enabling students to study by Distance Learning, live classes, or at Summer School. Students are free to choose whichever method of learning most suits their circumstances at the time.

- **Distance Learning**

The advantage of Distance Learning is that students can begin their studies at any time and work through the courses at their own pace, with the one-to-one support of their own personal tutor.

- **Classes and weekend seminars**

Classes and weekend seminars are held in central London. The advantage of studying astrology at live classes is the opportunity to meet like-minded people and to learn from the experience and examples of other students. A Saturday fast track Foundation Course is held each year, beginning in January. Weekend classes are particularly popular with Distance Learning students, providing a balance between home study and live classes.

- **Summer School**

The Faculty's annual Summer School attracts students from all over the world for weekend and week-long programmes suitable for both beginners and experienced astrologers. It is also possible to study complete Diploma subjects at the Faculty's Summer School.

Faculty tutors

All the Faculty's tutors are holders of the Faculty's Diploma. Their aim is to ensure that students have a rewarding and individually supported learning experience. Whichever method of studying is chosen, the tutors provide guidance and feedback to ensure that students work through to the successful completion of their studies.

Qualifying with the Faculty

Students are welcome to enrol on any of the Faculty's courses, whether or not they intend to gain the Faculty's qualifications. For those students who wish to work towards the Faculty's Diploma, examinations are undertaken at home, in their own time.

For further information, contact the Faculty at: The Faculty of Astrological Studies, BM Box 7470, London WC1N 3XX. Tel/Fax: 07000 790143. General enquiries: info@astrology.org.uk. Website: www.astrology.org.uk.

About the CPA

Director: Liz Greene, Ph. D., D. F. Astrol. S., Dip. Analyt. Psych.

The Centre for Psychological Astrology provides a unique workshop and professional training programme, designed to foster the cross fertilisation of the fields of astrology and depth, humanistic, and transpersonal psychology. The main aims and objectives of the CPA professional training course are:

- To provide students with a solid and broad base of knowledge within the realms of both traditional astrological symbolism and psychological theory and technique, so that the astrological chart can be sensitively understood and interpreted in the light of modern psychological thought.

- To make available to students psychologically qualified case supervision, along with background seminars in counselling skills and techniques which would raise the standard and effectiveness of astrological consultation. It should be noted that no formal training as a counsellor or therapist is provided by the course.

- To encourage investigation and research into the links between astrology, psychological models, and therapeutic techniques, thereby contributing to and advancing the existing body of astrological and psychological knowledge.

History

The CPA began unofficially in 1980 as a sporadic series of courses and seminars offered by Liz Greene and Howard Sasportas, covering all aspects of astrology from beginners' courses to more advanced one-day seminars. In 1981 additional courses and seminars by other tutors were interspersed with those of Liz and Howard to increase the variety of material offered to students, and Juliet Sharman-Burke and Warren Kenton began contributing their expertise in Tarot and Kabbalah. It then seemed appropriate to take what was previously a random collection of astrology courses and put them under a single umbrella, so in 1982 the "prototype" of the CPA – the Centre for Transpersonal Astrology – was born.

In 1983 the name was changed to the Centre for Psychological Astrology, because a wide variety of psychological approaches was incorporated into the seminars, ranging from transpersonal psychology to the work of Jung, Freud and Klein. In response to repeated requests from students, the Diploma Course was eventually created, with additional tutors joining the staff. The CPA continued to develop and consolidate its programme despite the unfortunate death of Howard in 1992, when Charles Harvey became co-director with Liz Greene. Finally, in February 2000, Charles Harvey tragically died of cancer, leaving Liz Greene as sole director. In the new Millennium, the CPA continues to develop along both familiar and innovative lines, always maintaining the high standards reflected in the fine work of its former co-directors.

Qualifications

Fulfilment of the seminar and supervision requirements of the In-Depth Professional Training Course entitles the student to a Certificate in Psychological Astrology. Upon successfully presenting a reading-in paper, the student is entitled to the CPA's Diploma in Psychological Astrology, with permission to use the letters, D. Psych. Astrol. The successful graduate will be able to apply the principles and techniques learned during the course to his or her professional activities, either as a consultant astrologer or as a useful adjunct to other forms of counselling or healing. Career prospects are good, as there is an ever-increasing demand for the services of capable psychologically orientated astrologers. The CPA's Diploma is not offered as a replacement for the Diploma of the Faculty of Astrological Studies or any other basic astrological training course. Students are encouraged to learn their basic astrology as thoroughly as possible, through the Faculty or some other reputable source, before undertaking the In-Depth Professional Training Course. The CPA offers introductory and intermediate courses in psychological astrology, which run on weekday evenings.

THE CPA DIPLOMA DOES NOT CONSTITUTE A FORMAL COUNSELLING OR PSYCHOTHERAPEUTIC TRAINING. Students wishing to work as counsellors or therapists should complete a further training course focusing on these skills. There are many excellent courses and schools of various persuasions available in the United Kingdom and abroad.

Individual Therapy

In order to complete the In-Depth Professional Training, the CPA asks that all students, for a minimum of one year of study, be involved in a recognised form of depth psychotherapy with a qualified therapist or analyst of his or her choice. The fee for the CPA training does not include the cost of this therapy, which must be borne by the student himself or herself. The basis for this requirement is that we believe no responsible counsellor of any persuasion can hope to deal sensitively and wisely with another person's psyche, without some experience of his or her own. Although it is the student's responsibility to arrange for this therapy, the CPA can refer students to various psychotherapeutic organisations if required.

Criteria for Admission

The following guidelines for admission to the In-Depth Professional Training Programme are applied:
- A sound basic knowledge of the meaning of the signs, planets, houses, aspects, transits and progressions, equal to Certificate Level of the Faculty of Astrological Studies Course. The CPA's own introductory and intermediate courses will also take the student to the required level of knowledge.
- Being able and willing to work on one's own individual development, as reflected by the requirement of individual therapy during the programme. Although a minimum of one year is required, it is hoped that the student will fully recognise the

purpose and value of such inner work, and choose to continue for a longer period.

- Adequate educational background and communication skills will be looked for in applicants, as well as empathy, integrity, and a sense of responsibility.

Enrolment Procedure

Please write to the Centre for Psychological Astrology, BCM Box 1815, London WC1N 3XX, for fees, further information, and an application form. Please include an SAE and International Postage Coupon if writing from abroad. The CPA may also be contacted on Tel/Fax +44 20 8749 2330, or at www.cpalondon.com.

PLEASE NOTE:

- The CPA does not offer a correspondence course.
- The course does not qualify overseas students for a student visa.
- The course is for EU and Swiss residents only, although exceptions may sometimes be made.

About the CPA Press

The seminars in this volume are two of a series of seminars transcribed and edited for publication by the CPA Press. Although some material has been altered, for purposes of clarity or the protection of the privacy of students who offered personal information during the seminars, the transcriptions are meant to faithfully reproduce not only the astrological and psychological material discussed at the seminars, but also the atmosphere of the group setting.

Since the CPA's inception, many people, including astrology students living abroad, have repeatedly requested transcriptions of the seminars. In the autumn of 1995, Liz Greene, Charles Harvey and Juliet Sharman-Burke decided to launch the CPA Press, in order to make available to the astrological community material which would otherwise be limited solely to seminar participants, and might never be included by the individual tutors in their own future written works. Because of the structure of the CPA programme, most seminars are "one-off" presentations which are not likely to be repeated, and much careful research and important astrological investigation would otherwise be lost. The volumes in the CPA Seminar Series are meant for serious astrological students who wish to develop a greater knowledge of the links between astrology and psychology, in order to understand both the horoscope and the human being at a deeper and more insightful level.

The hardback volumes in the series are not available in many bookshops, but can be ordered directly from The Wessex Astrologer, PO Box 2751, Bournemouth BH6 3ZJ, Tel/Fax +44 1202 424695, www.wessexastrologer.com.

Hardback volumes available in the CPA Seminar Series:

Water and Fire by Darby Costello

Earth and Air by Darby Costello

*Where In the World? Astro*Carto*Graphy and Relocation Charts* by Erin Sullivan

Venus and Jupiter: Bridging the Ideal and the Real by Erin Sullivan

Planetary Threads: Patterns of Relating Among Family and Friends by Lynn Bell

Astrology, History and Apocalypse by Nicholas Campion

Paperback volumes available in the CPA Seminar Series:

The Horoscope in Manifestation: Psychology and Prediction by Liz Greene
Apollo's Chariot: The Meaning of the Astrological Sun by Liz Greene

The Mars Quartet: Four Seminars on the Astrology of the Red Planet by Lynn Bell, Darby Costello, Liz Greene and Melanie Reinhart

Saturn, Chiron and the Centaurs: To the Edge and Beyond by Melanie Reinhart

Anima Mundi: The Astrology of the Individual and the Collective by Charles Harvey

Barriers and Boundaries: The Horoscope and the Defences of the Personality by Liz Greene

Direction and Destiny in the Horoscope by Howard Sasportas

The Astrologer, the Counsellor and the Priest by Liz Greene and Juliet Sharman-Burke

The Astrological Moon by Darby Costello

The Dark of the Soul: Psychopathology in the Horoscope by Liz Greene

Incarnation: The Four Angles and the Moon's Nodes by Melanie Reinhart

The Art of Stealing Fire: Uranus in the Horoscope by Liz Greene

Relationships and How to Survive Them by Liz Greene

When Chimpanzees Dream Astrology: The Four Quadrants of the Horoscope by Alexander Graf von Schlieffen

Mapping the Psyche: An Introduction to Psychological Astrology, Vol. 1: The Planets and the Zodiac Signs by Clare Martin

The Outer Planets and Their Cycles by Liz Greene

Cycles of Light: Exploring the Mysteries of Solar Returns by Lynn Bell

The Family Inheritance by Juliet Sharman-Burke

Mapping the Psyche: An Introduction to Psychological Astrology, Vol. 2: The Planetary Aspects and the Houses of the Horoscope by Clare Martin

The CPA Master Class Studyshop Series

Due to the numerous requests from students for live recordings of CPA seminars, selected seminars given by CPA tutors are now available as Studyshops – classic audio workshops supported with articles, images and background information, all contained on one CD. Each Studyshop contains around four and a half hours of lectures via MP3 files which play in a computer's CD or DVD drive, and are designed to play on Windows (Windows 98 or later) and any Mac or Unix platform. The CPA Master Class Studyshops are published by Astro Logos Ltd. in conjunction with the CPA Press. The following Studyshops are currently available:

The Soul in Mundane Astrology by Charles Harvey
Karmic Astrology by Howard Sasportas
Astrology, Myths and Fairy Tales by Liz Greene
Neptune by Liz Greene
Mercury the Translator by Charles Harvey
The Progressed Horoscope by Howard Sasportas
The Alchemical Sky by James Hillman and Liz Greene
Pluto and the Inner Planets by Liz Greene

The following Studyshops are currently available in the Astro Logos Master Class Series:

Delineation: Unfolding the Story Within a Chart by Darrelyn Gunzburg
The Practice of Relationship Astrology by Bernadette Brady
Predictive Astrology by Bernadette Brady
The Complete Astrolabe Kit for Beginners by Bernadette Brady
Fixed Stars Volume 1: Sky Myths, Star Phases by Bernadette Brady
Fixed Stars Volume 2: Charts and Stars by Bernadette Brady
Eclipses: Their Role in Charts and Prediction by Bernadette Brady
The Zodiac: Urban Tribes by Bernadette Brady

Living with Change: The Astrology of Dealing with Crises by Darrelyn Gunzburg

Information on the purchase of Studyshops can be obtained on line at www.AstroLogos.co.uk or by mail order from Astro Logos Ltd., PO Box 168, Fishponds, Bristol BS16 5ZX, United Kingdom.